A.J. Musgrove,
Michael Thornton, et al.

Windows NT and BackOffice Integration

Windows NT 4 and Web Site Resource Library

SAMS 201 West 103rd Street
PUBLISHING Indianapolis, IN 46290-1097
317-581-3500

Copyright © 1997 by Sams Publishing

FIRST EDITION

All rights reserved. No part of this book shall be repro-
duced, stored in a retrieval system, or transmitted by
any means, electronic, mechanical, photocopying,
recording, or otherwise, without written permission from
the publisher. No patent liability is assumed with
respect to the use of the information contained herein.
Although every precaution has been taken in the
preparation of this book, the publisher and author
assume no responsibility for errors or omissions. Neither
is any liability assumed for damages resulting from the
use of the information contained herein. For information,
address Sams Publishing, 201 W. 103rd St., Indianapolis, IN 46290.

International Standard Book Number: 0-672-30993-9

Library of Congress Catalog Card Number: 96-70404

2000   99   98   97   4   3   2   1

Interpretation of the printing code: The rightmost
double-digit number is the year of the book's printing;
the rightmost single digit, the number of the book's
printing. For example, a printing code of 97-1 shows that
the first printing of the book occurred in 1997.

*Composed in New Century Schoolbook and MCPdigital
by Macmillan Computer Publishing*

Printed in the United States of America

Trademarks

All terms mentioned in this book that are known to be
trademarks or service marks have been appropriately
capitalized. Sams Publishing cannot attest to the
accuracy of this information. Use of a term in this book
should not be regarded as affecting the validity of any
trademark or service mark.

Publisher	*Richard K. Swadley*
Publishing Manager	*Dean Miller*
Director of Editorial Services	*Cindy Morrow*
Managing Editor	*Kitty Wilson Jarrett*
Assistant Marketing Managers	*Kristina Perry*
	Rachel Wolfe

Acquisitions Editor
Grace Buechlein

Development Editor
Brian-Kent Proffitt

Software Development Specialist
Patricia J. Brooks

Production Editor
Colleen Williams

Copy Editor
Kim Hannel

Indexer
Cheryl Dietsch

Technical Reviewer
Vincent Mayfield

Editorial Coordinator
Katie Wise

Technical Edit Coordinator
Lynette Quinn

Editorial Assistants
Carol Ackerman
Andi Richter
Rhonda Tinch-Mize

Cover Designer
Jay Corpus

Book Designer
Alyssa Yesh

Copy Writer
Peter Fuller

Production Team Supervisors
Brad Chinn
Charlotte Clapp

Production
Paula Lowell
Tim Osborn
Gene Redding
M. Anne Sipahimalani

Overview

Contents

About the Authors

A. J. Musgrove is a Novell Certified NetWare Engineer and a Microsoft Certified Professional who has worked both as a programmer and as a network integrator. He is the author of Chapters 1, "The Windows NT Server Environment"; 2, "BackOffice Integration with Windows NT"; 3, "Integration of BackOffice Products"; 4, "Planning for the Implementation of BackOffice"; and 7, "Monitoring the System."

Michael Thornton is a Microsoft Certified Systems Engineer (MCSE) and a former CNE. He has several years of production experience with NT and has been involved with three major NT deployment projects. Michael participates in the Microsoft's Solution provider program, including the Exchange Migration Specialist program. He has consulted at several of the top Fortune 100 companies. Michael is the author of Chapters 8, "Data Access and Integrity"; 9, "Backup and Recovery"; 10, "Product Specifics"; 15, "Auditing"; and Appendix A, "Internet Information Server."

Greg Todd holds a bachelor of science in Computer Engineering from the University of South Florida. He currently works for BMC Software in Houston, TX in the Business Strategy Group. Previously, Greg was a systems engineer at Compaq Computer Corporation for six years. Greg got his start in 1980 when he bought his first computer, a TRS-80 Level II 16K system. Since then, he has spent over 11 years in the industry. During this time he has worked extensively with networks and operating systems, written white papers on performance and systems integration, given technical presentations at industry events, and participated as a contributing author on other technical books. Greg is also the author of the recent *Microsoft Exchange Server Survival Guide* (Sams Publishing), and he is currently at work on the second edition. In his spare time, Greg enjoys spending time with his family and his rottweiler, and experimenting with technology and music in his home studio. He can be reached at gregt@bmc.com. Greg is the author of Chapters 5, "CPU Utilization"; 6, "Memory Utilization"; and 11, "Monitoring File System Usage."

Darren Mar-Elia has over 10 years experience in systems and network design and administration. He was a member of a team that designed a nationwide Windows NT and SMS rollout for a large financial services company. Darren is a graduate of the University of California at Berkeley. He is certified by Novell as a CNE and is currently working on his Microsoft CSE. He was a contributing author of Que's *Upgrading and Repairing Networks* and *Special Edition: Using NT Server 4.0*, and he has written articles for NT-related magazines. You can reach him at dmarelia@earthlink.net. Darren is the author of Chapters 12, "Bandwidth Issues," and 13, "Monitoring Network Utilization."

Terry W. Ogletree is a consultant who divides his time between Atlanta, GA and Raleigh, NC. For over twenty years, he has worked with Digital's VAX/VMS systems and network products and has been involved with Windows NT since it was first released. He has been an active member of Digital Equipment Computer Users Society (DECUS) since 1985. Terry has consulted with Fortune 500 companies such as AT&T and Delta Airlines. He can be reached at togletree@mindspring.com. Terry is the author of Chapter 14, "Product Security."

Tell Us What You Think!

As a reader, you are the most important critic and commentator of our books. We value your opinion and want to know what we're doing right, what we could do better, what areas you'd like to see us publish in, and any other words of wisdom you're willing to pass our way. You can help us make strong books that meet your needs and give you the computer guidance you require.

Do you have access to CompuServe or the World Wide Web? Then check out our CompuServe forum by typing GO SAMS at any prompt. If you prefer the World Wide Web, check out our site at http://www.mcp.com.

> **NOTE**
>
> If you have a technical question about this book, call the technical support line at (800) 571-5840, ext. 3668.

As the publishing manager of the group that created this book, I welcome your comments. You can fax, e-mail, or write me directly to let me know what you did or didn't like about this book—as well as what we can do to make our books stronger. Here's the information:

Fax: 317/581-4669

E-mail: opsys_mgr@sams.mcp.com

Mail: Dean Miller
            Sams Publishing
            201 W. 103rd Street
            Indianapolis, IN 46290

Part I

Implementing
Microsoft BackOffice

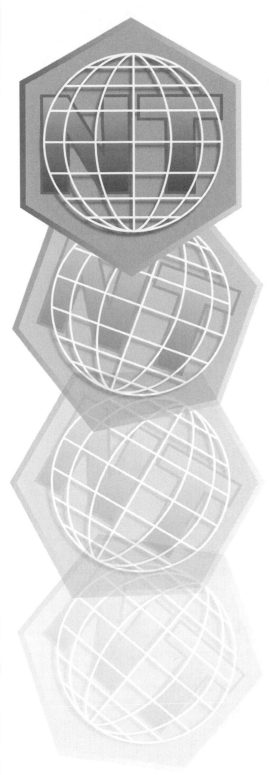

The Windows NT Server Environment

The Microsoft BackOffice family of server products is hosted on Windows NT Advanced Server (NTAS). Unlike other server products, which run not only on NTAS but on other operating systems as well, there are no other platforms that will support any part of BackOffice. Because of this, the developers of BackOffice were able to take full advantage of the special features of the NT operating system that are not available on other operating systems. This dependence of BackOffice on NTAS limits its ability to work in certain environments, but it excels in any organization that is committed to NT.

NT Is Consistent

Consistency is a major part of the philosophy of NT. One of the strengths of BackOffice is this principle. Consistency, however, involves several things, which are not always clear or visible. Complexity makes consistency sometimes difficult to maintain, but, for the most part, the designers of BackOffice succeeded.

User interfaces to BackOffice are consistent with each other and with the operating system. Not only do Windows NT–based applications have a certain look and feel, but the operation and appearance of the BackOffice products are similar. The toolbar in each application looks similar to the others, and a given button will do the same thing in any application. This makes the learning curve and ease of use of BackOffice easy to accept for developers and administrators, and decreases training time for both technical and non-technical users.

Another consistent feature of NT is access to hardware. The *Hardware Abstraction Layer* (HAL) gives a uniform interface to hardware and shields the application and operating system from the gory details of hardware interaction. For instance, when an application plays a sound file, it does not need to concern itself with what type of sound card hardware is installed; and regardless of whether the system is an Intel or PowerPC, the Application Programming Interface (API) calls are the same. These details are handled by operating system services and the HAL.

Not only are users and the operating system presented with uniform interfaces, but developers are given a consistent interface to do their work. APIs are consistent across systems and platforms. This enables developers to write programs that are portable across all platforms that support NT. Through support of existing industry standards, developers also have a limited consistency between NT and other operating systems. An example of this is the WinSock library, which is roughly compatible with the BSD UNIX sockets library. This reduces development and maintenance overhead for a product and increases its support on the platform of the user's choice. Windows NT is supported on several platforms, including Intel, RISC, MIPS, and DEC Alpha. However, after Windows NT version 4.0, the MIPS platform will be dropped.

Robust and Fault-Tolerant Design

Windows NT was designed as a robust and fault-tolerant operating system. The operating system is protected from programs, programs are protected from each other, and, to a certain extent, NT is fault tolerant to outside events (see Figure 1.1). With these mechanisms in place, NT is able to function for weeks or months instead of days or hours.

Figure 1.1.
Applications are protected from each other and can access the operating system only through specific interfaces.

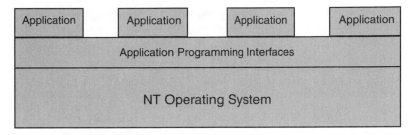

In this respect, NT is more like UNIX than like its Windows predecessors. Users who have become accustomed to Windows crashes and GPFs will be pleasantly surprised by the stability of NT. This has also made NT more acceptable in large enterprises that depend on information technology for their success, and has made NT an alternative to UNIX systems and mainframes.

Without these features, the success of BackOffice would not be possible. Server programs such as SQL Server and Exchange are taking the place of their mainframe and mini counterparts. In an international organization, there is no excuse for downtime, and the designers of Windows NT and BackOffice know this.

Windows NT and Security

A major design goal of Windows NT was security. DOS and Windows were insecure systems, which was acceptable when the systems were designed. As Microsoft makes pushes into larger enterprises, security is becoming a more important issue. NT now incorporates several layers of security and is government C2 security level certified, meaning that the National Security Agency believes that Windows NT is secure enough to hold sensitive government information.

BackOffice security is integrated with Windows NT security. The security subsystem is highly configurable, with the option of several different security models. An administrator is able to secure files, resources, and operating-system services.

Security can be assigned to files, resources, and services on a user, group, or domain level. All user processes must have associated login accounts, which is the base of the security key. By adding users to groups, rights can be assigned to many users at once, which decreases administrative work. For instance, if user John is created and then made a part of group Accounting, he could automatically have access to the directories that contain sample documents for the accounting department.

User administration can take place through a single interface, the User Manager (see Figure 1.2). It presents a list of recognized users and groups, and allows access to various security information concerning the files, system, and security policies. User rights (see Figure 1.3) deal with operating-system services that the user or group of users is allowed to access, and are also configured through the User Manager.

Figure 1.2.
*The User Manager
shows a list of all
users and groups
on the server or in
the domain.*

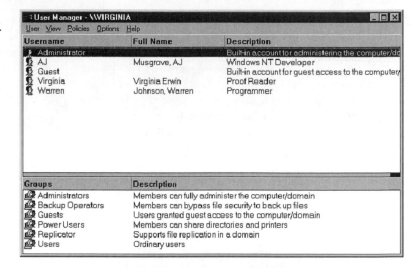

Figure 1.3.
*User access to
system resources
can be changed
through the User
Rights editor.*

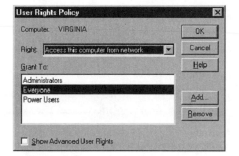

The BackOffice products provide a level of security on top of that provided by the operating system—certain product security features that have no meaning outside that product's environment. For instance, SQL Server has security options for databases, tables, columns, and views. These objects are very important in SQL Server, but have no meaning outside that environment. What is important, however, is that the first line of defense is the operating system, and application security is merely additional protection of data.

NT Scalability

Scalability refers to the capability of Windows NT to grow as its workload demands. There are limits to scalability, and those limits define how scalable the system is. More important than physical limits are practical limits: the points where improvement will become small as resources are added.

Windows NT supports multiple processors, which means there can be several lines of simultaneous execution on one computer. The retail version of NT supports up to four processors, and licenses can be purchased for additional processors. While there is a physical limit of 32 processors, the practical limit is six. This means after the sixth processor is installed, users will experience a smaller performance gain by adding additional processors, as shown in Figure 1.4. All the BackOffice products are written with multiple threads of execution, so they can take advantage of multiple processors. When placing applications on systems and determining workload and number of processors, you must keep the practical scalability limits in mind. This sometimes means that where one server would be preferred, several servers must be installed to handle the workload.

Figure 1.4.
As more processors are added to a system, the realized perfor-mance gain per processor de-creases.

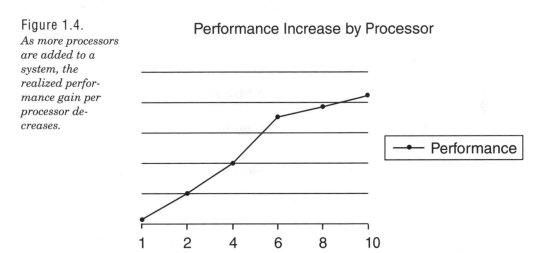

Performance Increase by Processor

The scalability of disk usage is an important part of the BackOffice products. When an application is written for a SQL Server system with a 10MB database, the database size can be increased to much more without application changes (see Figure 1.5). Applications are typically designed on systems that have much smaller capacity than production systems, and are later moved to the higher-capacity systems.

The third primary scalable feature of NT is memory. Windows NT Advanced Server will run on as few as 16MB of memory, but can scale to several gigabytes. When an application outgrows the system, more memory can be added without any applica-tion or operating-system modifications.

Figure 1.5.
No modifications to applications are needed as they are moved to larger systems with more available resources.

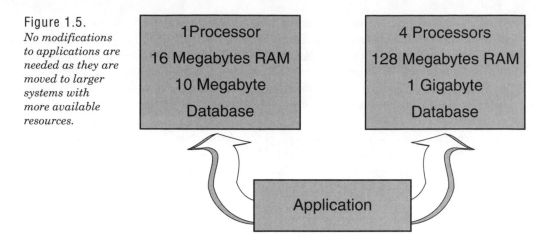

An Open System

Windows NT is referred to as an *open system* by its designers at Microsoft because it supports many different standards through the employment of APIs. Although most of these supported standards were made by Microsoft, the company advertises it as an open system. Whether NT is truly open is not a debate for this book, but you should be aware that the APIs exist.

Table 1.1 lists some of the APIs that are supported by Windows NT. Of course, because all APIs are in a set of library interfaces for developers, new APIs can be added at any time.

Table 1.1. Windows NT–supported APIs.

API	Description
SNA	Systems Network Architecture; a method for applications to communicate with IBM mainframes and AS/400s.
SMTP	Simple Mail Transfer Protocol; Internet mail-transfer mechanism.
MAPI	Messaging Applications Programming Interface; a way for all applications to access mail functions.
ODBC	Open Database Connectivity; provides a vendor-neutral way for applications to access data sources.
ISAPI	Internet Services Applications Programming Interface; a way for applications to communicate with Web servers such as Internet Information Server and Netscape Commerce Server.
Berkeley Sockets	A de facto standard for TCP/IP programming, developed at the University of California at Berkeley.

The BackOffice family is also referred to as open. Unlike NT, however, BackOffice supports many standards that are industry wide and vendor neutral. This has been a major factor in the success of BackOffice. Large corporations have applications and networks that are based on standards, such as TCP/IP and SQL. In order for BackOffice to be considered as a solution to the computing needs of these companies, it had to support those existing systems.

NT Applications' Portability Across Platforms

Applications written for Windows NT are portable across all platforms that support Windows NT. This does not mean that applications are portable to other operating systems on those platforms, or that any Windows NT program will execute on a supported platform.

Windows NT maintains portability across platforms and families of platforms because of its architecture (see Figure 1.6). At the base of the architecture is the HAL, which takes specific hardware on specific platforms and gives a unified, generic view of the hardware to the operating system. For instance, no matter what type of sound hardware is installed on a system, there is a constant set of function calls to make a sound. The abstraction concept is important for stability and portability, and is emphasized in the BackOffice family.

Figure 1.6.
Windows NT uses a layered architecture to increase stability and portability of the operating system and applications.

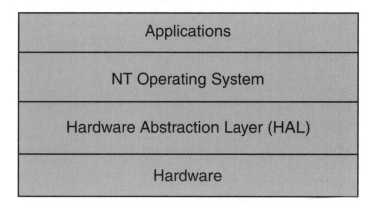

To run on a certain platform, the application must be compiled on that specific platform. The programs are portable in that the source code is compatible between systems. With the standard set of APIs in Windows NT, applications need only be recompiled for the different platforms.

Some of the BackOffice products are available on multiple platforms, but the limited availability of products on different platforms makes the Microsoft roots in the Intel platform apparent. Intel is the only platform that supports all the BackOffice products. Table 1.2 shows which BackOffice products are available on which platforms.

Table 1.2. Availability of the BackOffice products on different platforms supported by Windows NT.

	Intel	PowerPC	MIPS	DEC AXP
Windows NT	X	X	X	X
Exchange	X		X	X
Internet Information Server	X	X	X	X
SQL Server	X	X	X	X
SMS	X		X	X
SNA Gateway	X	X	X	X

In an effort to maintain portability, developers must make an effort not to use any features that are available on only one platform or family. Microsoft attempts this with the BackOffice family, giving it high portability.

BackOffice Integration with Windows NT

The BackOffice products are integrated with the Windows NT operating system. To a large extent, the administrative functions of the products are combined with the administrative functions of the operating system. This integration of the products with the operating system allows the products to utilize operating-system services to work better together.

Because Windows NT serves as the network operating system, the BackOffice products can be accessed by most protocols that are supported by NT. These include NetBEUI, IPX/SPX, TCP/IP, and NetBIOS. Integration with existing networking standards is a key part of the BackOffice strategy and an important part of its success in enterprise-wide networks.

BackOffice is also designed to integrate with existing systems. The SNA Gateway allows clients to access IBM mainframes and AS/400s using Systems Network Architecture. Microsoft provides the Gateway Service to NetWare, which allows integration with existing Novell NetWare networks, as well as Internet Information Server, which allows Windows NT to be a server in a corporate intranet or on the global Internet. Windows NT will also act as a file and print server for existing Windows- and OS/2-based PCs, as well as for other applications and services.

The integration of BackOffice products with the operating system and with each other is not perfect. The development of BackOffice is an ongoing process, and enhancements are added frequently. As BackOffice becomes more integrated with the operating system and with the members of the suite, it will become easier to use and manage.

Summary

The design goals of Windows NT and BackOffice are lofty; however, they are important to Windows NT and BackOffice becoming accepted in the enterprise-computing environment. The core features of NT make it a candidate for things that were once reserved for mainframes and heavy-duty UNIX systems.

As organizations downsize and watch their budgets closely, cost-effective and flexible solutions are needed to remain competitive. BackOffice answers these needs in many ways, with its configurable nature and low entry costs. It also provides many features out of the box that were once either expensive add-on products or unavailable through commercial channels.

These features are useful only if they are implemented properly. The intent of this book is to show you how to make BackOffice work in the enterprise-network environment. It is not intended as a replacement for the guides that come with BackOffice, but rather as an addition that will assist the administrator with a successful implementation and continued usefulness as time passes.

BackOffice Integration with Windows NT

The BackOffice family of products relies heavily on services provided by the Windows NT operating system. This was a design goal of BackOffice, and the level of integration should increase as development continues. This integration has many implications that must be understood to properly implement NT. Indeed, this book is dedicated to implementing BackOffice in the NT environment, and this chapter is an overview of the different ways that BackOffice is integrated with its host operating system.

Integration with Windows NT relieves some of the management burden of the system. In many ways, this gives BackOffice a distinctive advantage over other solutions for NT that serve some of the same functions as BackOffice.

Whether or not this is an unfair advantage is irrelevant to this book, but what is relevant is that the services are shared between the operating system and BackOffice, and BackOffice is tightly integrated with the operating system. By taking advantage of this integration, an administrator can increase the usefulness of the products and lower his burden.

Leveraging Existing Services

BackOffice makes extensive use of existing operating-system services and facilities. There are services provided by the Windows NT operating system that are not provided by other operating systems, so portable server products do not take advantage of them. Because BackOffice is tightly tied to NT, it uses these special services to accomplish tasks as efficiently as possible.

When evaluating the operations of a particular BackOffice product, its apparent simplicity or lack of particular features may be deceiving. Instead of evaluating a product on its own merit, its worth when combined with the operating system must be taken into account. Indeed, once combined with the operating system, the real power of most of the BackOffice products becomes fully realized.

Integration with existing operating-system services also centralizes software upgrades. If certain functionality is added to the operating system, such as a new method of disk handling or network communication, it automatically carries over to the various BackOffice products. This becomes more apparent as operating systems evolve and features are added. Being able to add features in a central place instead of adding them to separate products reduces the development cycle and lowers the time to market for upgrades (see Figure 2.1).

Figure 2.1.
*All applications
on the system
share the same
operating-system
interfaces.*

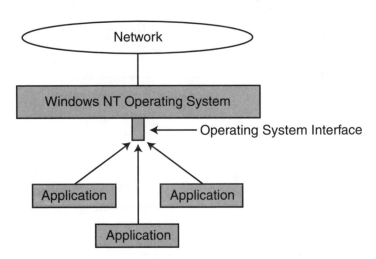

Not so obvious, but equally important in a Microsoft environment, is the centralization of bug fixes and patches. The centralization of patch distribution is part of the overall integration of BackOffice with the operating system. Because services are centralized wherever possible, when a bug is discovered in a particular service, it can be corrected, thus correcting the behavior of all applications that use that service. Microsoft frequently distributes releases called *service packs* that contain a large number of bug fixes. All service packs should be obtained and applied as soon as possible to fix any known problems in either the operating system or BackOffice. It is a good preventive administrative practice to constantly check for new fixes, and install them if available, instead of waiting for a problem to occur that requires the fix.

A simple, yet effective example of integrated services is the *remote access service* (RAS). In the past, applications had their own means of remote access, which usually meant their own set of modems and own communication software and protocols. This leads to high maintenance and resource requirements, as well as an increased amount of training for the administrators. With the RAS in Windows NT, a user can connect to the remote access server and access all resources on the server as if the user were on the local area network (see Figure 2.2). The administration of the RAS is also integrated with the administration of Windows NT, so no additional training or knowledge other than NT is necessary. This also means that remote access does not need to be a technical consideration when designing a server for Windows NT because it is handled on the operating-system level.

Figure 2.2.
The Windows NT operating system abstracts the location of clients so that applications do not need to worry if clients are attached to a network or to incoming phone lines.

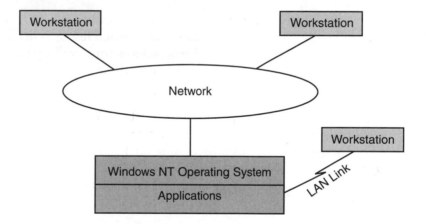

The idea of remote, uniform access through a standard networking protocol originated in the UNIX environment, through a protocol called *Serial Line Internet Protocol* (SLIP). This protocol allowed IP communication through serial ports. Later, *Point to Point Protocol* (PPP) was introduced. Incidentally, PPP is also now a protocol option for RAS.

Integrated Disk Handling

All BackOffice products rely on the operating system's handling of the disk subsystem. This is in contrast to some systems on other platforms that access the disk devices directly. Indeed, Windows NT does not provide facilities for applications to access disk devices directly, so operating-system services are the required method of disk handling. Using high-level OS services abstracts the underlying disk hardware, which is a principle of the NT system as a whole.

Abstraction of underlying disk hardware is an integral part of the design philosophy of the disk subsystem. Applications are not aware of the type of hardware that is being used to store data (see Figure 2.3). Applications are also not aware of the location of the drives or their access method. When an application is running on NT, it doesn't even know if the drive it is accessing is on the local machine. In fact, an application can be run from a rewritable CD-ROM without any application changes. All these things are possible because of operating-system–level disk abstraction.

Figure 2.3.
The operating system abstracts the location of files, so applications can access files from many media using the same techniques.

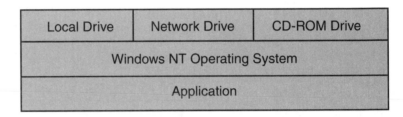

Another major feature of Windows NT is the built-in data protection and integrity features of the disk subsystem. Using these features with the BackOffice server products greatly increases their reliability, and sometimes their performance as well. The actual implementation of these features is covered in Chapter 8, "Data Access and Integrity," but the various options and their possible effects are covered in the following sections for purposes of introduction and continuity.

Volume Sets

The simplest feature of Windows NT disk handling that BackOffice can take advantage of is *disk spanning*. Disk spanning is the spreading of data across disks for the purpose of making the disks appear to be a single unit. If an Exchange post office, for instance, grows to a size that cannot fit comfortably on a single disk, there will be a storage issue, and Exchange itself cannot be told to spread the post office across multiple devices.

Why can Exchange not be told to do this? Because it is a feature of the Windows NT operating system, and, wherever possible, features are not duplicated between the operating system and the BackOffice products.

> A principal design philosophy of BackOffice is that any feature imple-
> mented in the operating system should not be reimplemented in the server
> software.

The Windows NT feature that implements disk spanning is called a *volume set*. The operating system can be instructed to map several physical drives, or volumes, to the same logical drive letter, or volume set. This will, in the view of the application, result in one large, single drive (see Figure 2.4). This is frequently used to solve space problems and to add space without replacing existing drives or reconfiguring applications.

Figure 2.4.

A volume set combines several physical drives into one logical drive, allowing applications to access several drives as one.

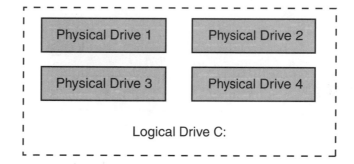

Disk Striping

The speed of data access has a significant impact on the performance of the server. Of course, large amounts of cache RAM and high-speed disk hardware will increase the data access speed, but there are physical limits to hardware access speed. One method of increasing data access speed is by treating many disks as one disk so that they can be read from or written to simultaneously. For instance, if 1,000 bytes of data are requested, and the data are spread across four drives equally, only 250 bytes have to be read from each drive. Because all drives are read concurrently, reading 1,000 bytes from the four drives will take the same time as reading 250 bytes from one drive. The impact this has on performance can be tremendous.

This sequential spanning of data across disks to improve performance is imple-mented in Redundant Array of Inexpensive Disks (RAID) and the disk subsystem hardware. This is called *disk striping*. Windows NT also provides this service in software as part of the operating system. When writing data to a disk or reading data from a disk, the operating system will do all the calculations necessary to spread the data evenly among available drives.

Because of the processing required on the part of the operating system, disk striping is slower in software implementations than in hardware implementations, but it is still much faster either way than accessing only one disk at a time. The network administrator must construct a *stripe set* from equally sized partitions, which are then viewed and accessed as a single drive. As seen in Figure 2.5, all these partitions must be on separate drives. When writing data to the drive, the operating system spreads the data across all the drives equally, thus improving performance.

Figure 2.5.
A stripe set takes several physical disks, presents them as one logical disk, and spreads data evenly across the disks.

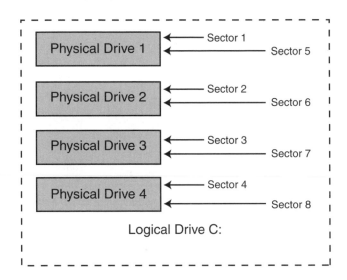

Disk Mirroring

For mission-critical applications, any downtime in operations is unacceptable. In some situations, restoring from a backup that is only a few hours old is also unacceptable because data added in those few hours may be critical to the business. With this type of mission-critical application, there must be an up-to-the-minute backup that is ready to assume control on a moment's notice. The Windows NT solution to these types of situations is mirroring.

With mirroring, two drives are maintained as one. Unlike spanning, which spreads data across drives, *mirroring* writes duplicate copies of data to each drive. The result is one drive that is identical to another (see Figure 2.6). The advantage is that the second drive can then serve as a backup in the event of failure of the first drive. For Online Transaction Processing (OLTP) applications such as SQL Server, this is sometimes a necessity. To lose database changes even over the past few hours is sometimes unacceptable.

Figure 2.6.
Disk mirroring takes two physical drives and keeps them identical so that one can serve as a backup to the other.

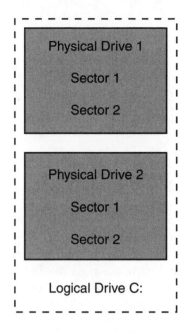

The cost of mirroring is one drive for every drive that is to be mirrored. This is the price of insuring against any downtime or data loss. If your primary concern is protection against data loss, and some downtime is acceptable, there is another method of disk protection—disk striping with parity.

Disk Striping with Parity

Disk striping with parity is a version of disk striping with built-in data protection. As with regular disk striping, disk striping with parity works with an array of partitions on different drives that are roughly the same size. Unlike regular disk striping, the space of one of the allocated drives is used for parity information (see Figure 2.7). Three drives are required for the use of two data drives.

The functionality of disk striping with parity is also implemented in RAID hardware. RAID subsystems can be programmed to place data on disks in a variety of ways for the benefit of both speed and redundancy. RAID hardware is usually faster and more reliable than implementing the same functionality in software. The operating-system services that provide this functionality do so in case of unavailability of proper hardware implementations.

The disk access model of the BackOffice applications is completely integrated with the Windows NT operating system. The operating system must be relied on for data integrity, redundancy, and performance. This section has provided a good introduction to the services made available by the operating system. Chapter 8 details the implementation of these services.

Figure 2.7.
Disk striping with parity spreads information across multiple physical disks, taking a third of the space to store parity information.

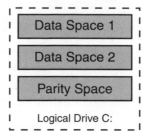

Integrated Security

The security model of the BackOffice applications is integrated with the security model of the Windows NT operating system. This security model includes object access, resource access, and sometimes simply knowing about the existence of a user. Before the integration of interapplication security, it was necessary to set up each user in each application he needed to access. The centralized security of the BackOffice products is a great advantage when administering a server, because any duplicate effort is usually avoided.

The centralization of user account–management allows rules to be enforced about how users can access the system. Users are known to choose insecure or easily guessed passwords, so the operating system can be configured to require certain things of passwords. Because of the centralization of this information, these requirements carry on to application security. When repeated login attempts are detected, users' accounts can be locked out from a central location. When this is done, even if the correct password is guessed by the would-be hacker, the account will not be allowed to use applications on the system.

The first line of security on data and configuration files is the operating system. The configuration files for an application are essential to its proper execution, and therefore require intense security. Windows NT provides that security. Being able to read configuration files can also aid a potential intruder in cracking a system, so being able to deny read access to configuration files is sometimes just as important as being able to deny write or delete access.

There are also some data files that contain sensitive data, such as e-mail messages and passwords. Security on these files must be absolute, and it is up to the operating system to maintain the appropriate security on them. It is up to the administrator to tell Windows NT exactly how to secure the files. They must be accessible to the server application, but should not be accessed by normal users.

When doing this, keep in mind that security holes exist. They have been demonstrated in products like Internet Information Server (IIS). The Windows NT operating system is still young, and problems are still being resolved. Do not think that a one-pass security setup will necessarily secure the entire system. For instance, consider placing vital configuration files on a separate drive from the HTML files and CGI programs for IIS. Also, consider having user data files on a separate drive. Little steps like this can be the difference between a little bug that never really affects the system and a bug that causes a major security breach.

Table 2.1. Example of placing files on the file system.

Drive	Data
C:	Windows NT operating system
D:	BackOffice and other server applications
E:	Internet Information Server data files
F:	Shared directories

One vital component that is important enough to be mentioned here specifically is SQL Server devices. Unlike UNIX systems, where database devices are placed directly on hardware devices that are restricted from users, SQL Server devices are merely files on the hard disk. These files should have extreme security, because SQL Server data is usually of a sensitive nature. The security should be more than merely not sharing the directory they are in, because users can still log in interactively. Figure 2.8 shows the Directory Permissions dialog box that is used to set permissions on the directory and the files contained in the directory.

Figure 2.8.
An example of file-access permissions that might be set on the SQL Server directory tree.

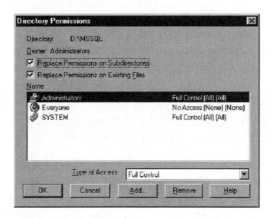

The integration of security features between BackOffice and the Windows NT operating system is indeed a powerful feature. Many of the security functions that have traditionally been in separate places have been centralized to the operating-system level. When functions are centralized, the likelihood of something slipping through the cracks is diminished, and better security usually results.

Integrated Event Tracking

Windows NT has an extensive built-in logging facility that is exploited by both the operating-system services and the BackOffice products. Applications can send messages to the event logs to allow an administrator to monitor the condition of the application. Events can also be generated by certain operating conditions, thresholds, or other user-defined events.

Windows NT has a program called the Event Viewer, which can be used to view log events on the system. The operating system logs events in three categories (see Figure 2.9):

- Application
- Security
- System

FIGURE 2.9.
Application, security, and system events are all logged in the event log for viewing with the Event Viewer.

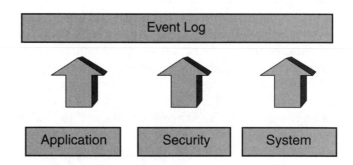

The System log stores messages that relate to the operating system and its services. An example would be that if a service, such as RAS, fails to start, an event is placed in the System log. Events in this section are generally not application specific; they are usually operating system issues. Hardware problems are also logged here, so this is the first place to check if a hardware failure is suspected to be the cause of a problem. See Figure 2.10 for an example of the Event Viewer window.

Events that concern security on the system are placed in the Security log. There are several different things that qualify as security events and are, therefore, placed in this log, including logon, logoff, file access, rejected resource attempts, and auditing information (see Figure 2.11). Auditing integration is covered in the next section, but for now, just remember that the auditing events are placed in the Security log.

Application-specific events, such as server backup and virus scanning notifications, are placed in the Application log (see Figure 2.12). Because of its nature, the Application log is frequently the largest of the three logs. For example, messages resulting from the operations of the BackOffice products go into the Application log. You should probably check this log regularly to watch for any application problems.

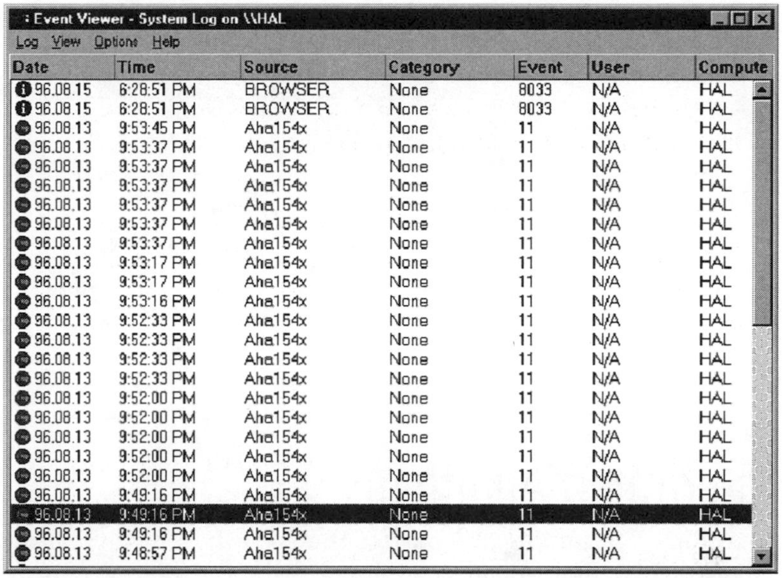

Figure 2.10.
*This is the System
log as seen in the
Event Viewer.*

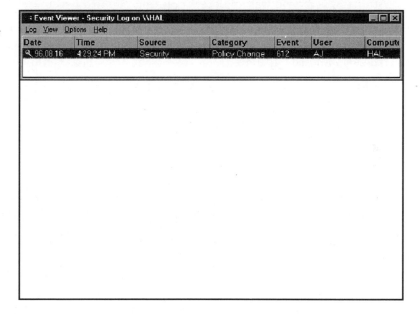

Figure 2.11.
*The Security log as
seen in the Event
Viewer.*

Performance and resource threshold events generated by Performance Monitor can
go into the Application log. It is generally recommended that you use this Performance Monitor option. If you set Performance Monitor to send alerts to the
Application log, you can also check this log for any system resource events that may
have been triggered, giving you a uniform place to view logged system events rather
than several locations.

Figure 2.12.
The Application log as seen in the Event Viewer.

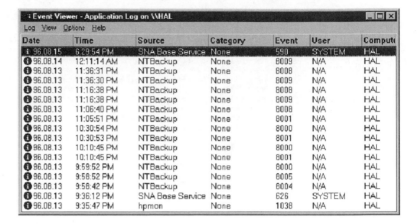

Integrated Auditing

Auditing is an integral part of the security and control model of any enterprise system. No matter how good the security, there can still be problems and breaches. Auditing is a good way to detect real and potential security risks.

Auditing is integrated with the NT operating system. Audit events are placed in the system's Security Log for viewing with the Event Viewer. When auditing is enabled, this log can grow to monstrous sizes, so it probably should be cleared periodically.

In Figure 2.13, you can see the Audit Policy window. This window can be opened through the User Manager for Domains application. From User Manager for Domains, select the Policies pull-down menu and then select Audit. Along with configuring auditing, User Manager for Domains allows you to create and manage user accounts for the NT network.

Figure 2.13.
This is a sample setup in the audit configuration from the User Manager for Domains.

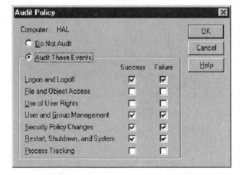

There are many events that can be selected for auditing. Which of these are useful usually depends on the type of activity that is being checked for. Events that can be audited include file access, shutdown and restart of the system, logon, and use of user rights. An important thing that should probably be monitored on most systems is security policy changes. Changes to the security policy will have an effect on the security of the entire system, so they should be monitored and recorded as they happen.

Built-In Multiprocessing

Multiprocessing is a major issue in the industry. It is a complex thing to implement properly; there are underlying issues of re-entry and resource protection that do not exist in the uniprocessor environment. Because of this, many systems don't handle these issues well.

Most modern PC operating systems were designed in uniprocessor environments. Very few of them will even run in multiprocessor environments, which limits the choice of operating systems that can be selected for a multiprocessor system. Of these, most support multiple processors through a set of multiprocessor extensions. This is evident because operating systems that do not fully support multiprocessing capabilities usually require some kind of multiprocessor license to use the extensions. The method of resource protection is usually exclusive locks on the operating system while an application is using it, or a similar solution. Windows NT was designed with multiprocessing in mind; it comes with the capability to support four processors with the option of buying licenses to support up to 32. Because of the original design, NT handles multiprocessing better than operating systems that have multiprocessor extensions.

Because Windows NT has built-in support for multiprocessing, much of this complexity is taken out of the applications. If an application is written to use multiple threads, when the operating system has the capability to run that application on multiple processors, it will do so. The issues of resource sharing are also handled on the operating-system level, which prevents some of the race conditions that have plagued multiprocessing applications in the past.

All BackOffice applications are written with multiple threads. When run on a multiprocessor system, the operating system dispatches these threads to different processors, so there are different parts of the application running concurrently (see Figure 2.14). This has the effect of making the overall performance of BackOffice on a multiprocessor system very good. It also means that, in cases that used to require the addition of more computers, the less expensive route of additional processors can sometimes be taken.

Two issues that should be mentioned about multiple processors are overhead and contention. Adding a processor will not double the speed of a uniprocessor system. If one thread has a resource the other thread needs, it will go into a wait state. Also, when dealing with multiple processors, some overhead is introduced, slowing down the whole system. These things result in a reduction in the overall scalability of the operating system to about six processors. For more information, refer to the discussion of the scalability of Windows NT in Chapter 1, "The Windows NT Server Environment."

Figure 2.14.
When a system is equipped with multiple processors, it can do several different things at exactly the same time.

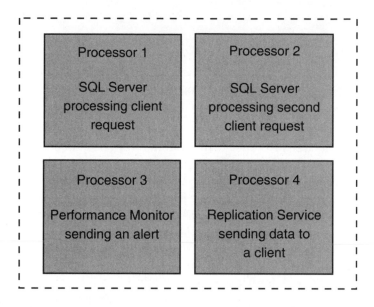

Process Protection

Protecting processes in memory is essential to the stability of the system. All modern processors provide the operating system with the capability to limit access to memory areas and callable routines. With the Intel processor line, this support began in the 80286 processor and was refined in the 80386 processor. On both processors, it is referred to as the *protected* mode of operation. Older operating systems, such as DOS, did not have built-in process memory space protection and were therefore unstable.

As seen in Figure 2.15, when processes are not protected from each other, they can read and write from each other's memory space. On a multiuser system, this is a security problem because that memory could contain sensitive data. This is the reason that Windows NT clears out a memory area before issuing it to an application. If the memory area was in use by one application that placed sensitive data in it and then released it to the operating system, or if it was reallocated to another process without first being cleared, that process would be able to access the sensitive data.

Windows NT is not a true multiuser system, because it does not support multiple interactive users at any one time. The only support for multiple-user access that comes with Windows NT is for network and application connects.

Figure 2.15.
*In systems that do
not employ
memory protection,
one application
may write to the
memory of another
application.*

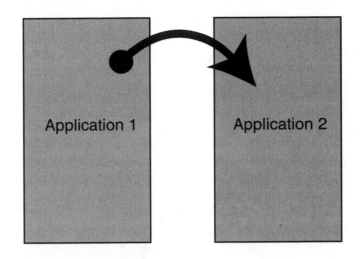

Certain third-party products make Windows NT a multiuser system. Some of them provide command-line access through Telnet or another terminal emulator; some provide full graphical access to the operating system.

In an ideal world, applications write and read from their assigned address space and never anywhere else. All their work is done in memory properly requested and allocated from the operating system. The application will also never try to execute random code inside of the operating system, application programming interfaces, or other applications.

Unfortunately, we do not live in an ideal world. Applications have bugs that cause them to write to the memory of another application. Sometimes an application decides to start executing instructions in another application or on the operating system. When this happens, one application corrupts the data or code of another running application—or worse, that of the operating system—and unpredictable things happen. Problems such as these plagued the DOS and Windows operating systems. With Windows NT, applications must execute operating system procedures through the use of call gates (see Figure 2.16).

Memory protection does not prevent an application from attempting to access memory that does not belong to it. It also will not prevent an application from attempting to execute instructions in memory spaces that it should not be using. Instead, the operating system detects this attempted access through a processor-generated exception and stops the offending process (see Figure 2.17). This process is usually not allowed to continue unless it has set up some special facility for handling such an exception. This results in the application errors normally known as *General Protection Faults* (GPF). The word *protection* in this case means memory protection.

Figure 2.16.
Applications are not allowed to execute operating system procedures directly; instead, they must be accessed through call gates.

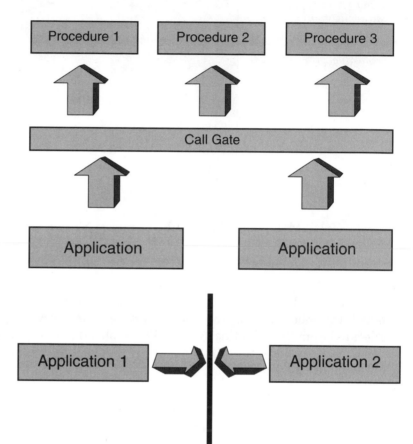

Figure 2.17.
Applications in an operating system that uses protected address space are not allowed to access each other's memory.

NOTE

For UNIX aficionados, this condition is known as a *segmentation violation* and usually results in a "core dump." When the application generates this condition, it is sent the SIGSEGV signal by the operating system, and can either handle the signal, which would allow the application to continue, or allow the operating system to terminate it.

Summary

The BackOffice products run exclusively on the Windows NT operating system, using the services of the operating system to provide much of the functionality. Wherever possible, functionality is not duplicated between the operating system and the BackOffice applications.

The BackOffice applications leverage the existing operating-system service to increase the usability and portability of the products, as well as to reduce the development time for an application. This integration with operating-system services also serves to centralize product updates and bug fixes. When these become available, they should be applied as soon as possible.

The disk services that are provided by the operating system are used for disk management by the BackOffice applications. The operating system takes care of details such as disk hardware and access methods. The operating system is also relied on for data access and integrity, as well as for placing data on multiple disks for space reasons.

The security and event-logging facilities of Windows NT are used by the BackOffice applications. The auditing facilities provide an excellent way of monitoring resource access and system security issues. Application events can be placed in the Application Log by BackOffice for viewing by an administrator.

The architecture of modern processors is exploited by Windows NT to protect the operating system from applications and applications from each other. This protection allows one faulty application to be shut down without affecting the rest of the system.

CHAPTER 3

Integration of BackOffice Products

Not only do the BackOffice products integrate with the Windows NT operating system, but they also utilize services provided by each other.

Shared Resources

The BackOffice products are written to coexist on the same computer; they share resources such as memory, disk space, and network access. Although the operating system is relied on to manage the resource sharing to some extent, the applications are written to share resources with each other in cases where the operating system is not adequate.

There are some products on the market that are designed to run on a machine with no other applications. The vendors of these applications suggest dedicating a computer to just their application and allowing all resources of that computer to be used by that application. BackOffice was designed specifically to have multiple applications running on the same computer.

Because BackOffice is a server family, the sharing of network resources is very important. As is shown in Figure 3.1, one network interface can support a variety of protocols and can be accessed by many products at once.

Figure 3.1.
Multiple applica-
tions can use the
same network
interface for
communication
with clients.

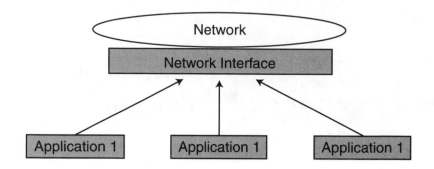

The applications are also expected to share the same disk system with each other. When installed, each application runs in its own directory structure, voluntarily isolating its configuration and operations data from the others. (See Figure 3.2.)

Figure 3.2.
The BackOffice
applications
install themselves
in separate
directory struc-
tures so they can
all share the same
machine and drive
space.

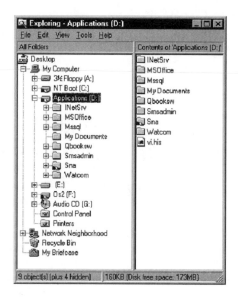

An important set of shared resources is operating-system services. Readers familiar with Novell's NetWare software know that NetWare takes over the DOS operating system while it is loaded, and no other DOS applications can execute until the server is exited (which is rare). The BackOffice applications are written to share the server resources with other applications on the system. Sometimes utilization of the application will dictate how well it shares the system resources, but the capability is there.

Shared Services

Not only do the BackOffice applications share the operating system with other applications, but they also utilize services provided by each other. In some instances, one application can build functionality from another, increasing the capabilities of the suite as a whole.

The Systems Management Server (SMS) is an example of this principle. SMS keeps an inventory of the various computers attached to the network for purposes of administration, management, and reporting. It stores this data in SQL Server tables, thus using the services provided by SQL Server to its advantage. (See Figure 3.3.)

Figure 3.3.
SMS stores its configuration and inventory data in a SQL Server database.

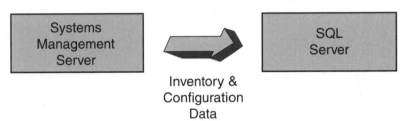

Inventory &
Configuration
Data

Another example of this is using Internet Information Server (IIS) to publish information on the Web. Through various third-party products or Common Gateway Interface (CGI) scripts, IIS can take data from SQL Server and place that data on the Web (see Figure 3.4). IIS can also take data entered by users on HTML forms and insert it into SQL Server or perform various other activities with it.

Figure 3.4.
Through third-party programs or CGI scripts, IIS can publish data from SQL Server.

SQL Server
Data

Summary

The BackOffice products are designed to be fully integrated on the Windows NT server platform. They share operating-system resources such as the operating system itself, disk space, processors, and memory. Some of the applications also make use of services provided by each other. Doing this enables the applications to utilize services provided by other applications to increase their own functionality and usefulness.

CHAPTER 4

Planning for the Implementation of BackOffice

BackOffice implementation involves a lot of planning and careful consideration. Many aspects of the server, network, and personnel should be examined. These aspects are examined in detail, and suggestions and tips are provided in this chapter. Understanding this chapter will place you at an advantage when you begin to tackle BackOffice implementation.

Sizing the Machine

The type of machine purchased to host the operating system and applications depends greatly on the applications and workload that the machine will be expected to handle. It is sometimes hard to determine how big the machine needs to be, but the golden rule of purchasing hardware is: When in doubt, buy a lot. While there are practical limits to the amount of hardware that should be purchased for a single system, there is nothing more miserable than having to ask for more hardware from senior management during the middle of an implementation. Starting out with the proper hardware from the beginning is usually the best plan.

> It is better to buy too much hardware than too little. Extra hardware can always be used, but asking for more hardware is sometimes difficult.

In some cases, workload should be broken down over multiple machines instead of overloading one machine with too many users and applications. Not only does using multiple machines decrease the workload on any single machine, it helps with the dreaded single point of network failure. It also makes upgrades and software changes easier, because installing a new version of SQL Server will have no effect on the Exchange mail servers if they are on separate machines. Isolation of the effects of a change usually makes the entire production environment more stable.

In a multiple-machine environment, it is wise to use some machines as backups for others. For instance, the Systems Network Architecture (SNA) gateway could be installed on the dedicated machine it is intended for, and could also be installed on the Systems Management Server (SMS) machine that is used to centrally manage computers on a network, thus giving redundancy of the server software between machines (see Table 4.1). When the installation is complete, replication should be set up between the machines to maintain the configuration information. If anything should happen to the SNA gateway, the Internet Information Server (IIS) machine could pull double duty as the SNA gateway by simply starting the service on the machine.

Table 4.1. Configuration of machines to act as backups to each other.

Machine	Running	Configured
Machine 1	SQL Server	IIS
Machine 2	SMS	SNA gateway
Machine 3	SNA	SQL Server
Machine 4	IIS	SMS

The possibility of a machine also serving as backup must be considered when the machine is sized. Although it is better to have a dedicated backup machine, in today's world of shrinking budgets that is not always possible. Buy a machine that is big enough to serve as a backup for others and do a little planning to make this a reality. Doing this reduces problems down the road.

> Always have a backup machine for a production machine, even if the machine chosen for backup serves another purpose.

The type of hardware selected should depend not only on the horsepower needed, but also on the expertise of the IS staff that must support it. If the IS department is staffed by experts on the Intel platform, it does not make sense to purchase MIPS-based systems; likewise, it would not make sense to purchase Intel-based systems if the Information Systems' expertise were in DEC Alpha–based systems.

Keep in mind that business needs override using available expertise. If an organization requires the performance of Alpha AXP processors and the only knowledge in the IS department is on the Intel platforms, training is in order. This goes back to the principle that hardware must be selected based on prevailing needs.

> Hardware should be selected first on the basis of prevailing needs, and second on the basis of current expertise within the organization.

Processors and Scalability

To solve performance problems on a single machine that has fewer than six processors, an administrator could add more processors. Indeed, a multiprocessor server is much more cost-effective than several servers performing the same amount of work. Of course, as noted in Chapter 1, "The Windows NT Server Environment," there are limits to the scalability of a machine. After six processors have been added, it is no longer cost-effective to add more processors to gain performance, and the purchase of a new machine is in order.

The ability to add more processors is an important part of the buying decision for BackOffice server machines. It is better to buy a dual-processor machine with only one processor than a single processor machine that cannot be upgraded. It seems that users are always able to fill a machine to capacity, no matter how few the users or how great the machine, so having a viable upgrade path is important.

There are motherboards available that not only support different speed processors of the same family, but processors of different families. This is advantageous in that when the performance of the Intel line of processors is no longer adequate, high-performance Alpha AXP RISC processors could be added in place of the Intel processors on the motherboard. This would require the reinstallation of all applications so that they supported the new processor, so this is not an option for every situation but is an important consideration when selecting a hardware platform.

The ability to add more or different processors to a machine should be part of the buying decision for a machine.

Memory and Performance

Adequate memory is essential to the performance of the server. Starting with more than enough RAM now will save headaches in the future. For small RAM-limitation issues, Windows NT supports the concept of virtual RAM, in which the operating system can take disk space and emulate real memory. Although this may seem to be better than purchasing additional RAM, keep in mind that disk space is much slower than RAM, and there is a limit to how much virtual memory can be allocated. As a rule, one should avoid excessive usage of virtual memory and should, instead, purchase as much as is needed and then purchase additional RAM as workload demands. Remember, the speed of disk drives is measured in milliseconds, but the speed of memory is measured in nanoseconds.

Although virtual RAM provides a quick way to increase the available memory in a system, it should not be overused. Using disk space as memory will have a large impact on the performance of a system.

The speed of memory should also be considered during the purchase. I recommend at least 60ns RAM, if not faster. The BIOS on most systems will add an artificial wait state for anything slower, which degrades the performance of the server. As RAM is added, remember that all RAM in the system will operate at the speed of the slowest RAM. The principle of a chain being only as strong as its weakest link holds very true in memory speed (see Figure 4.1).

The memory requirements of BackOffice are high. SQL Server recommends at least 40MB of memory just for its operations on a normal workload installation, plus whatever is required for the operating system and other applications. The other components will require more and more RAM as workload increases. Also, monitoring and administrative tools sometimes require a great deal of memory. The memory requirements of the system as a whole increase as workload increases, so constant monitoring is essential for continued performance and to keep memory usage in check.

Figure 4.1.
The amount of memory available to programs is a combination of the real memory in the machine and the memory emulated from disk space.

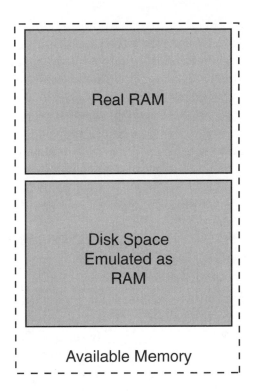

Computer Architecture and Performance

The architecture of the machine will have a significant effect on the realized performance. Technologies such as Peripheral Component Interconnect (PCI) will yield higher performance than older technologies such as Industry Standard Architecture (ISA). PCI is quickly becoming the preferred architecture, and most types of adapters are available in that format. PCI devices will automatically assign themselves hardware resources such as memory and interrupt request numbers as needed, so installation is much simpler and less problematic than that of older ISA hardware.

Not only is PCI a high-performance, industry-standard architecture, but it works hand in hand with the up-and-coming Plug-and-Play standards. These standards allow operating systems to quick-configure themselves to work with new hardware. As of the time of this writing, Plug and Play is supported only by Windows 95, but Microsoft has announced plans to support the standard in future versions of Windows NT. Other PC operating-system vendors have also expressed an interest in supporting the Plug-and-Play technology. This will make additional hardware, such as network cards and disk controllers, much easier to add to the computer. One of the hardest problems to deal with and track down is hardware conflicts, and these new standards promise to alleviate most of those headaches.

NOTE

The PCI architecture is probably the best architecture available today for a server. It is much faster than the popular ISA architecture and promises to reduce the headaches associated with hardware configuration.

The major problem with PCI is that it is not backward-compatible with ISA cards. If backward compatibility is important in your implementation, Extended Industry Standard Architecture (EISA) should be considered. It provides high performance while maintaining backward compatibility with ISA cards. The problem with EISA is that all cards must be configured manually with a configuration program and a set of driver programs provided by the hardware vendor. If there is a loss of internal battery power, this configuration will be lost and must either be set up again or reloaded from some sort of backup. Problems such as these have left EISA as a dying standard.

For companies with high investment in IBM equipment, Micro Channel Architecture (MCA) provides very high performance, but is only available in IBM systems. MCA, like EISA, must be configured by hand with drivers provided by the hardware vendor. Also, the proprietary nature of MCA has hampered its usage in the industry. IBM has made moves to phase out MCA in favor of PCI, such as fitting all new servers, both Intel- and PowerPC-based, with PCI and ISA buses. Unless you already have a high investment in IBM hardware, it is not wise to purchase MCA-based systems or MCA adapter cards.

When you have decided on the system bus, you must address cache memory. Cache memory works in the same way as disk cache, keeping the most recently used memory segments in high-speed cache memory near the CPU. The addition of cache memory has greatly increased the performance of processors, and having insufficient or improper cache memory will hurt the performance of the server.

The operation of the memory cache is not complex and is very similar to disk caching. If a page of memory is requested, which is 4KB in size on an Intel Pentium system, the cache is checked for the presence of that page. If the page is present, which is referred to as a *cache hit*, it is used to satisfy the request. If it is not, which is referred to as a *cache miss*, main memory must be accessed. Before this can be done, the oldest page in cache is removed. If that page has been written to but main memory has not been updated, it is referred to as a *dirty page*, and main memory is updated before the disposal of the contents. When a free cache page is available, the requested page is loaded into the cache, and then the memory request by the processor is satisfied.

For multiprocessor systems, it is a little bit more complex. When a cached page becomes dirty, it must be cleaned as soon as possible. To *clean* a page is to make the contents of main memory match the contents of the cache. After this is done, the other processors are notified that if they have that page in their cache, it is no longer valid. This is referred to as *page invalidation*. This communication of memory change is one reason why the performance gain realized by adding more processors is less and less as more processors are added.

There are two kinds of cache memory: internal and external. The internal cache of the Intel Pentium chip is only 16KB, but systems typically have at least 256KB of external cache. The external cache is configurable and resides on an external chip, as the name implies.

On single-processor systems, the relationship of internal to external cache is simple. It becomes more complex in systems with multiple processors. Incidentally, the main difference between a dual-processor and a multiprocessor (even one configured with two processors) system is the external cache. In a dual-processor system, CPUs have separate internal caches, but share external caches. In a multiprocessor system, CPUs have separate internal and external caches (see Figures 4.2 and 4.3).

The general recommendation of external cache memory is 16KB of cache for every 4MB of main memory. Most single-processor systems today are shipping with 1MB of standard pipeline burst cache, which should be enough for most implementations.

Figure 4.2.
Cache placement in a dual-processor system.

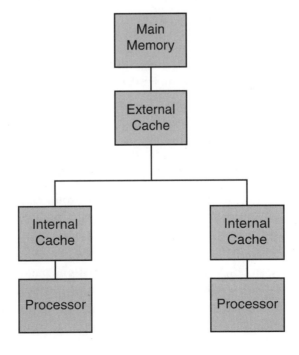

Figure 4.3.
*Cache placement
in a multiproces-
sor system.*

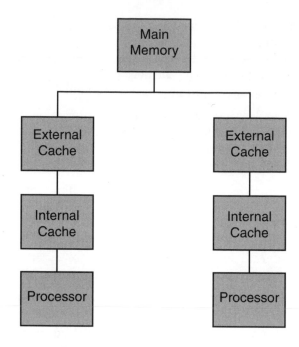

Disk Subsystems

Although ordinary drives and controllers will suffice on a small installation, a good drive array should be considered. A quality disk subsystem will be well worth the investment. The initial investment is expensive, but the increased performance and stability make anyone who has ever used one always demand a disk subsystem.

Windows NT has several built-in features that emulate disk subsystem hardware, which should be adequate in smaller installations. Data protection such as mirroring and RAID are vital in any situation where downtime must be avoided. RAID hardware is more effective, but the Windows NT disk striping with parity option emulates this fairly well.

When disk performance is a serious issue, understand that several small drives will give better performance than one or two large drives. If a stripe set is set up across the small drives, Windows NT can read several drives simultaneously. This can dramatically increase performance of the system.

In spite of the features provided by NT, the server environment will perform better if these things are implemented in hardware. The payoff down the road will be well worth the investment in both performance and stability.

Video and Performance

Video is often neglected as a performance issue. Even if the computer is a dedicated server, it is wise to buy a quality-accelerated video card. With a standard video card, most processing takes place on the computer's CPU for graphical displays and is slow to transfer to and from video memory.

Although on the surface this may not seem to affect a dedicated server, it does. The idea of loading a Performance Monitor and having its drawing of line charts practically shut down the server is unacceptable. In the past, high-speed video hardware was cost prohibitive, but as prices continue to fall on that type of hardware, there is no reason to buy second-rate equipment.

Constructing the Network

Because BackOffice is server-based technology, network performance is critical to the success of the implementation. A network is more than a bunch of cables that connect workstations. It is an integral part of the operations of the entire applications system, and its proper initial design is essential.

There are many tools available to aid in network design. There is no replacement for a quality network engineer, but someone in charge of implementation must understand what he or she is dealing with before even considering seeking someone else's help.

Network Limitations

There are two major limiting factors in the performance of the network: bandwidth and contention. To determine the realizable throughput of a network, both of these factors must be considered.

Bandwidth refers to the amount of data that can be sent across the network at one time. The bandwidth of standard Ethernet is said to have a 10Mbps, or 10 megabits per second, data transfer rate. That does not mean that an application can send 10Mb of data down the network in one second; overhead on the network can reduce that amount. When there is no network contention, users can reasonably expect to send between 7Mb and 8Mb per second down the network.

Network contention exists because several nodes attempt to transmit data down the network at one time. On a large, single-segment network, contention will cause more network performance problems than a lack of available bandwidth. When contention becomes a serious problem, collisions and retransmissions happen. A *collision* is when multiple nodes attempt to transmit a packet of information at the same time. This results in the data from all the transmissions becoming scrambled.

When a collision happens, the data from both nodes must be transmitted again—a *retransmission*.

NOTE

It is interesting that the minimum transmission size of an Ethernet packet was chosen to be the minimum amount of data that could be transmitted and result in the entire length of the Ethernet segment being used by one node. This allows for the detection of collisions.

Devices such as Ethernet switches and bridges attempt to solve problems with contention. Switches and bridges break up the network into multiple segments, which prevents data between two nodes on the same segment from appearing on other segments (see Figure 4.4). In order for segmentation to be effective, servers must be placed properly on the network.

Figure 4.4.
This is a conceptual drawing of a network with multiple segments joined with a bridge.

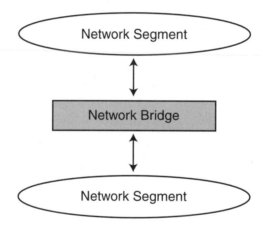

Placement of Servers

As a rule, servers should be placed close to the users who use them. By placing users and the servers they use on the same segment, network traffic across an organization is minimized. It sometimes becomes necessary to use multiple servers where one server is desired, to maintain proper network segmentation. These kinds of decisions are usually judgment calls on the part of the network administrator and are best made by people experienced with network engineering.

Traffic crossing wide area network (WAN) links should be kept at a minimum. The speed of WAN links is usually a fraction of that of local networks. Even if high-speed WAN links are used, there is *propagation delay*, which is the amount of time it takes data to cross a network segment. Although this time is minute on an Ethernet network, it can be measured in seconds on slow links such as satellite communication links.

NOTE

Propagation delay also applies to dial-up services such as e-mail. If a computer delivers mail to its destination only once a day, the maximum propagation delay of that mail system can be said to be 24 hours.

If users must access a central set of servers, replication of the information on those servers across the WAN links should be considered. Directories of files can be replicated, as can SQL Server databases.

By maintaining multiple duplicate copies of the database near the users who use it, WAN traffic and users' response time are reduced. Replication also helps reduce the single point of failure problems. A single point of failure can occur when all data is maintained on one server and not replicated to other servers. If that server goes down, no one can access the data. If the central servers or the network goes down, users at remote sites using replicated copies continue to work, and changes are made to the central database at a later time.

Shared servers, such as those routing corporate e-mail and central database servers, should be placed as close to the middle of the network as possible (see Figure 4.5). This does not always correspond to a corporate headquarters. The idea of placing critical computing resources for the entire enterprise away from the corporate headquarters will not be acceptable in some organizations, so there are trade-offs to be made.

Special servers, such as public Web servers, should be placed as close to the point of service as possible. For instance, if a company's headquarters is in Omaha but the Internet gateway is in San Jose, the public Web server should be placed in San Jose, not Omaha. This, again, may be hard to implement, but it will provide the best performance and stability of service.

Figure 4.5.
This is a conceptual drawing of several local networks with a central mail hub.

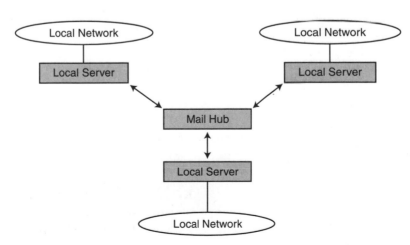

Network Access

User access to resources is essential and requires careful planning. The days when users all worked on one local area network (LAN) are gone. Now users work from local nodes, remote sites, customer sites, and their homes. Wherever a user is, he will need access to his data.

One of the biggest issues in network computing today is remote access. Traveling sales representatives are among the most frequent users of remote access, but all users in an organization can take advantage of it.

Providing remote access raises several issues, one of the most important being security (see Figure 4.6). There are lines into the inside of a company's database exposed to the world. The idea of not giving phone numbers out is hopeless, because phone scanners are freely available to people seeking illegal access to computer systems. Securing the outside lines involves things like requiring long passwords and having the system verify the identity of the caller through a callback system, which identifies the caller and then the system calls the original caller and initiates the connection.

Windows NT provides remote access service (RAS) to allow users to connect remotely. Once connected with RAS, users can access resources inside the company's network via IPX/SPX, TCP/IP, and NetBEUI. For most organizations, RAS provides an effective and inexpensive way to access resources from remote locations.

In cases where RAS is not adequate, there are many third-party products that allow users to dial into the network and work remotely. Many of these are hardware devices that work very much like network hubs and are compatible with existing dial-in software such as the remote access client.

Figure 4.6.
Because of network transport abstraction, server applications do not need to worry about the source of a client connection, whether it be on a local network or over a phone line.

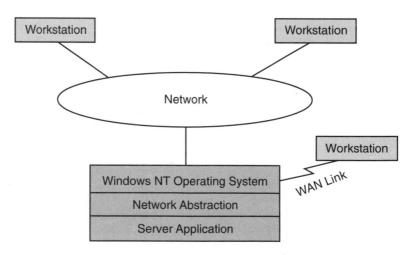

Designing the Servers

Before Windows NT and BackOffice are installed on any machine, there are several design decisions that should be made. These involve administration, fault tolerance, deciding where applications should reside, and many other issues.

Distributed Processing

The move in computing is away from centralized or client-based processing and toward distributed processing. In the past, in a networked environment, data resided on the server, and client applications worked with that data. This produced data-integrity and network-performance problems.

It is interesting to see the move away from client-based processing and back toward server-based processing, a methodology that was all but abandoned with the decline of the mainframe.

The move today is toward *distributed processing*, or having several machines work on the same problem at once. Although multiple-tiered client/server design is not a discussion for this book, as the person implementing BackOffice you must understand the concepts of distributing workload across many systems, because these concepts are very much a part of BackOffice.

For instance, with e-mail, instead of one central mail server, regional mail servers that route mail to each other provide greater performance and fault tolerance (see Figure 4.7). As stated before, having a single point of failure should be avoided, and distributed processing reduces that problem.

Figure 4.7.
Several regional mail hubs with one central mail hub to route messages among them.

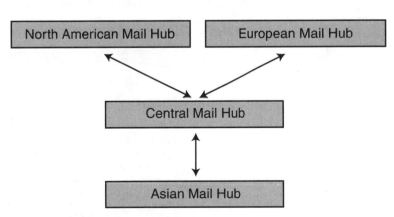

With SQL Server supporting multiple applications with multiple databases, consider having each database reside on a different server, if possible. Not only will that reduce the workload on the servers, but it will decrease the amount of damage if one server fails.

Having multiple regional servers instead of one centralized server eliminates the chance of single point of failure for that service.

Shared Information

There is some information that must be shared among all servers on the network or in a domain. An example of this is user accounts. All servers must know about the existence of a user to be able to allow that user to work and have access to resources.

There are some directory structures that should be shared among machines. This can easily be accomplished on the client by mapping drives to multiple servers. The problem is, again, performance. If the maps must cross WAN links, access will be slow. Windows NT provides a directory replication service to solve this problem (see Figure 4.8).

Identical copies of a directory can be maintained on multiple systems, which improves local performance and minimizes WAN traffic. On a periodic schedule, the replication client and server synchronize the information in the replicated directory.

This feature is also valuable for remote users because systems that are not permanently connected to the network can maintain copies of important file systems. This is similar to the Briefcase folder in Windows 95 and Windows NT 4.0; it allows shared files to be maintained without the necessity of having a permanent connection.

Figure 4.8.
The Directory Replication dialog box accessed through the Server Properties window from within the Control Panel.

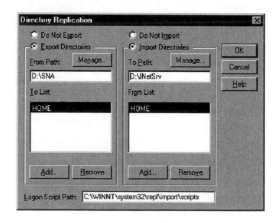

User security information must be shared through the domain. Although it may simplify administration to have one domain across the enterprise, it will increase the performance and robustness of the network to use a separate domain for each geographical location.

Domains

The domain concept is important to the configuration of the network. A *domain* is a collection of Windows NT servers that share login and security information.

Domains are controlled by a Windows NT server that is designated as a *domain controller*, which is the authority for security validation for the domain. In addition, there may be multiple backup domain controllers that can assume the duties of the domain controller if it becomes inaccessible.

Multiple domains can maintain trust relationships. If domain A trusts domain B, domain A will allow users from domain B to access resources in the domain (see Figure 4.9). Groups of users can contain members of other domains, which simplifies interdomain security considerations.

The master domain model is helpful in large organizations. This allows the organization to set up a centralized administration with control over all domains, while giving local administrators control over the resources of their domains (see Figure 4.10).

When designing the domain structure of the network, it is best to keep flexibility, stability, and performance in mind. The final domain model should reflect the needs of the organization and the usage of the network. An experienced network engineer should be consulted during the development of the domain relationship model to ensure that it is optimal.

Figure 4.9.
This is a domain situation where domain A and domain B trust each other. Trust relationships are represented by the arrows.

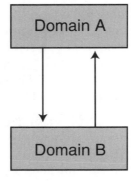

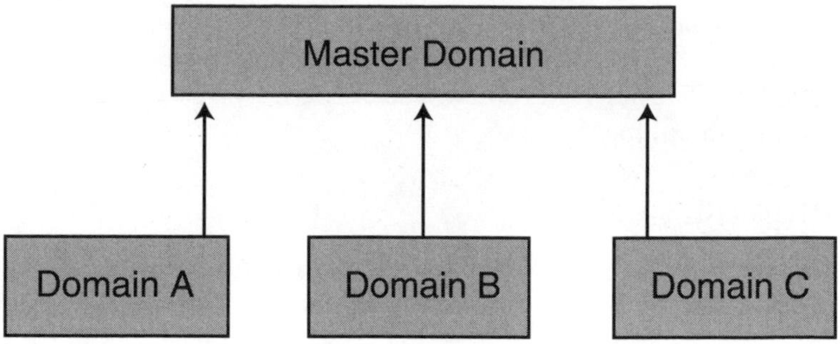

Figure 4.10.
*A set of domains
using the master
domain model.
Trust relationships
are represented by
arrows.*

Organizing Implementation Teams

The BackOffice implementation team should be a group of well-trained and experienced administrators. One of the biggest mistakes that can be made during the implementation is understaffing the team. Each member should be knowledgeable about the product or products he is responsible for and must be able to help other members of the team.

A functional area of the team should never be one level deep. A single point of failure with people is just as damaging as a single point of failure with computing resources. Should a member of the team become unavailable, there should be at least one other member of the team who understands the responsibilities of the missing member and is able to take them over on a temporary basis.

Windows NT Advanced Server

Windows NT is a complex operating system and requires the expertise of someone familiar with it. The person charged with this responsibility is usually referred to as the *server administrator*, and should be well trained and experienced with Windows NT.

The server administrator must be familiar with the installation and configuration of Windows NT. He will be in charge of all new installations and upgrades of existing systems, and he must know enough to make sure these installations and upgrades go smoothly. Bad installations are the cause of more problems than any other single element, because problems in installations sometimes become evident only after the server has been in use for some time.

After the server is installed, the server administrator must maintain it. This involves managing users and groups, as well as security permissions on the files and directories in the servers. This is an ongoing responsibility that requires not only technical knowledge of Windows NT, but the ability to interact with the users of the system.

The server administrator must also make sure the servers are backed up frequently and effectively. Computers are machines, and they do break. An administrator must be sure that when this breakdown occurs, he is prepared to handle it and get the system back in operation as soon as possible. Downtime is costly, so minimizing it is essential. An administrator who does not take backups seriously is not only obviously inexperienced, but a danger to the company.

WARNING

It is estimated that 50 percent of all companies that do not recover from a mission-critical computer system crash within one week will never recover.

Because the job of a server administrator is so complex, multiple operators are usually employed to help. Operators take some of the workload from the administrator, distribute responsibility, and ensure that network operations will continue when the primary administrator is unavailable. Also, in an organization that is operating 24 hours a day, 7 days a week, there will need to be operators for night and weekend operations.

There are several types of operator positions that will be useful with a typical Windows NT and BackOffice installation. These need not be handled each by a separate person. These responsibilities should be handed out based on the size of the organization and the user support base.

The following are possible operator positions:

- Print
- Backup
- Security
- Server
- Network

Print Operators

Printers are a source of never-ending problems on the average network; users seem to need printer support on a constant basis. The person charged with the job of *print operator* should be knowledgeable of all types of printers used on the network, as well as the applications printing on those networks.

Sometimes, a print job will stall at the top of the queue, for one reason or another, and must be dealt with. The print operator would probably stop the queue, remove the print job, and then call the users responsible for the print job to let them know that it was canceled and why. Also, while talking to the user, the print operator should be able to discuss with the user what caused this problem and how to prevent it from happening again.

Users are very sensitive about their printed output. If a job must be re-moved from the queue, tact must be used when letting the user know this was done. Care must also be taken to help the user prevent this situation from arising again.

A typical print operator will usually find himself serving as a hardware support person, either over the phone or in person, depending on the organization and the situation. This can include things like replacing laser printer toner cartridges or fixing paper jams. Experience in hardware work is a favorable feature for this position.

Backup Operators

Backup operators are the people in charge of backing up the system. They are typically night-shift and weekend operators who do not have to deal with end users. For this position, a knowledge of SQL Server is helpful, because the same person who backs up the Windows NT operating system will probably also be charged with backing up SQL Server.

This person is critical to the operation of the network. Backups must be regular and correct, or there will be a problem when a restore is needed. These people must also be trustworthy, because they will be placing all critical information about a company on a set of tapes that should be kept secure.

Security Operators

It is inevitable that users will forget their passwords. *Security operators* will be called on by users to change the users' passwords so they can log in again. Sometimes, users may ask for disk quota increases, access to certain information, and other security-related things. Security operators must use judgment and, in some cases, obtain the proper authorization before taking action related to security.

Users will request that they be told their old password, but this is not possible. Passwords can be changed to new values by authorized adminis-trators, but there is no way to determine the old password.

Security operators must not be careless with their jobs. When a user calls in to have his account password changed, or a locked-out account reinstated, the identity of that person must be verified. Methods of verification must be put into place. The methods chosen will depend a lot on the size of the organization. In a smaller organization, the security operator will most likely know everyone and can verify identities by sight. Larger organizations have a more complicated situation and will have to determine the best method for identification that suits their needs. Security breaches are damaging to companies, and security operators must help ensure against them.

Server Operators

Server operators reboot servers and work with services. When a server starts having a problem, they must be able to respond quickly and effectively. Server operators must know about all the services that run on a server and the operations of those services.

A basic knowledge of each of the products that a server supports is a necessity. Server operators will be the generic troubleshooters on server problems, such as an inaccessible database server. They must be patient with users to help them work through server problems and careful that they do not cause another problem while fixing the first.

Network Operators

Network operators help troubleshoot network problems. With the increasing complexity and reach of corporate networks, problems are more common and require an increasing skill level to solve.

The network operator should have knowledge of both LAN and WAN technology and know how to use network-management tools to troubleshoot both connectivity and performance problems.

They should also have an understanding of network hardware. Like the print operator, they will find themselves doing hardware troubleshooting over the phone or in person, including duties such as replacing patch cable or installing a new network card.

The network operator must also have the ability to interact with users. Users will be irritable when they are not able to connect to the network to do their jobs. The network operator must be patient with them and slowly work through the problem, always maintaining a level of professionalism and not getting angry with hard-to-deal-with users.

Microsoft Exchange Administrator

The person in charge of implementing Microsoft Exchange is sometimes referred to as the *Exchange administrator* or the *mail administrator*. This individual should not only be knowledgeable in the technical aspects of Exchange, but also the corporate e-mail structure.

A major issue with e-mail implementation will be conversion from the old e-mail system. Companies come to depend on electronic mail as their primary means of communication, and any point when mail is unavailable is unacceptable.

> There must never be a time during the implementation of Exchange when electronic mail is unavailable to users.

If the company is currently using Microsoft Mail, the upgrade will be fairly easy. Exchange clients will connect to Microsoft Mail post offices, so clients can be installed and configured before the Exchange server is implemented. With a competent set of key users at each location implementing Exchange, a changeover to Exchange can take place at one time, over a weekend or at night, and users will be using a new e-mail server with their familiar clients.

> A *key user* is a technically competent user who is able and willing to assist the IS department in working with other users in the key user's local work group.

If electronic mail is currently being handled by a UNIX-based mail handler, conversion can be handled in phases. Exchange can route mail through UNIX-based mail systems so that members of both Exchange mail servers and the UNIX mail system can communicate. Because of this, users can be converted one group at a time, and, if appropriate, only certain sets of users need be converted. This can be a great help in organizations with a large base of UNIX users in certain departments that are not converting to the Windows NT-based system.

During the implementation of Exchange, it is usually helpful to have a meeting with key users in each geographic location of an organization. These are the users who are going to help make the implementation a success, so they should be well informed of what is going on and made to feel like a part of the entire process.

Internet Information Server

The person in charge of the implementation and operation of the Internet Information Server is usually referred to as the *Webmaster*. A Webmaster in a typical organization is usually expected to wear many hats, including administration, content providing, network troubleshooting, and technical support to the users of the server. Webmastering is a new field, so there is no formal training and no certifications that can be looked for by a manager. Instead, experience must be considered, as well as checking out projects that a prospective Webmaster has completed.

On UNIX-based electronic mail systems, the person in charge of e-mail is referred to as the *postmaster*. The Web is a UNIX-born technology, and it inherited many traits from its UNIX host computers. One of these was the term *Webmaster,* which became accepted as representing the person in charge of Web publishing and operations on a Web server.

When interactive Web content is desired, and it is in most modern Web implementations, the Webmaster will require some of the same skills as the DBA (discussed in the next section). He needs a knowledge of the SQL language and connecting to the SQL Server. He also needs to know the architecture of the company databases in order to effectively access that information for publishing on the Web.

Whatever the Web server is going to do, a Webmaster must have an in-depth knowledge of *Hypertext Markup Language* (HTML). This is the language that Web pages are written in, and is an extension of the Standard Generalized Markup Language (SGML). It did not used to be a necessary requirement for a prospective Webmaster to know HTML, because it was an easy language and could be picked up quickly. At the time of this writing, however, the current version of HTML is 3.0, and it is a complex and feature-rich document-formatting language. To effectively use it requires experience and patience. Web publishing is becoming so complex that it is not uncommon for an organization to employ someone whose only job is HTML design, and for that person to have apprentices. The Web page is how the world will see a company, and it should not be taken lightly.

Depending on the future uses of the Web page, there are some other skills that may be required of a Webmaster. For instance, the Perl programming language is popular when writing Common Gateway Interface (CGI) applications.

CGI allows Web pages to be dynamic instead of static, or unchanging. Using it, Web browsers can enter information forms and then submit those forms to CGI programs for processing, which then display the results of the program.

Perl is the preferred language for scripting on the Web and is available for almost any operating system, including UNIX, DOS, and Windows NT. It simplifies the processing of text forms and, as an interpreted language, the code is portable between systems.

Java is a hot topic on the Web today. As opposed to CGI applications, in which the servers process the information, Java programs execute on the client. They can display enhanced graphics, access sound hardware, and do other eye-catching things. Java programs can also access database servers via the Java Database

Connection (JDBC), which is the Java equivalent of ODBC. Java programming is a complex topic that might not be a skill required of the Webmaster at an organization, but he should at least be familiar with the concepts and be able to install Java applets on Web pages.

An often overlooked skill of a potential Webmaster is the understanding of WAN bandwidth issues. Web documents will usually be published over WAN links that are slow compared to the speed of the LAN on which the Web page is designed. It is not uncommon for new Webmasters to create pages full of high-resolution graphics that cause the pages to take literally minutes to load over the Internet. When selecting a Webmaster, make sure to question him about his experience publishing over WANs, such as the Internet.

SQL Server

The person in charge of the installation, implementation, and operating of SQL Server is usually referred to as the *database administrator* (DBA). The responsibilities of a DBA include installing and configuring SQL Server, maintaining backups of data, optimizing database structure with indexes and views, troubleshooting database connectivity, and providing technical support for users.

NOTE   The code base for Microsoft SQL Server originally came from Sybase SQL Server version 4.2, so a DBA with experience with either Sybase or Microsoft SQL Server will be adequate for administration of SQL Server.

The Microsoft SQL Server adds extensions on top of the American National Standards Institute (ANSI) standard (which does not support flow control), such as if statements and while loops. Any potential DBA should not only be familiar with the ANSI-standard SQL, but with the extensions on the language by Microsoft SQL Server.

NOTE   Structured Query Language (SQL) was originally designed by IBM in the late 1970s as a convenient way of accessing its DB2 database system. At the time, the popular database-access method was COBOL programs. It is ironic that the main competition to IBM's mainframes and minicomputers are database servers based on the SQL language.

A DBA's responsibilities sometimes, but not always, include database design. If these will be among the responsibilities of a potential DBA, an in-depth knowledge of database normalization is desirable. Experience with database design is also necessary because what works in theory does not always work in practice, and there is no replacement for experience.

Regardless of whether a DBA will be doing database design, a knowledge of database optimization is essential. No matter how well designed a system is, performance problems must be dealt with; they *will* creep into the system over time. Creating indexes and views on tables is not a simple thing, and the implications require experience to understand.

> Do not turn an inexperienced DBA loose on a mission-critical database.
> This can result in downtime and unexpected problems.

The selection of a DBA is complex and often difficult. The person chosen must be patient with users and technically knowledgeable. A qualified DBA is essential to the well-being of an organization's data.

Systems Management Server

The person in charge of SMS is usually referred to as the *SMS administrator*, *systems management administrator*, or *system administrator*. This job is widespread and complex, and usually time-consuming.

Because SMS stores its information in SQL Server databases, knowledge of the operations and use of SQL Server and the SQL language is useful for the system administrator. Sometimes, in a large organization, it is useful to have SMS use a SQL Server that is dedicated to it, because maintaining such a large database of information can be taxing on a system.

One thing that SMS can keep track of is computer inventory. As users use the network, SMS *agents* record information about the computers on the network. This information can be used for querying computers eligible for software installation, software upgrades, and hardware upgrades.

The more common use for SMS is software distribution. In a large enterprise, it is often impossible for an administrator to go to each and every computer and install a new piece of software or an upgrade to existing software.

> Allowing users to install software off the server, even when software
> licenses are not available, can cause licensing problems. Ensure that
> licenses are purchased for all users installing programs from SMS.

A system administrator must be familiar with hardware configurations and the installation of software. In addition, the system administrator will undoubtedly be contacted for technical support for products that are installed via SMS, so he should be familiar with those products.

A system administrator should also be patient with users. He will probably become the person whom users deal with the most, because most problems will occur during software installation. Experience in dealing with people is a necessity, as well as a demonstrated ability to communicate without overusing technical jargon.

SNA Gateway

The SNA administrator will be vital to the ability of the users in an organization to access data residing on IBM mainframes and minicomputers. This person should usually come from a mainframe or minicomputer background, and will require training on the use of Windows NT.

Although client/server computing and PCs are gaining popularity, it is a fact of life that most large organizations depend on their mainframe or minicomputer for their mission-critical applications such as accounting. A network and a set of applications, no matter how good and useful, will be useless if they do not provide a way for users to access the legacy data and applications residing on the mainframe.

WARNING

Do not underestimate an organization's reliance on the mainframe. Although client/server applications may be friendlier and look nicer, most large organizations depend on the mainframe for day-to-day, mission-critical applications.

The person selected for this job should have experience on the host computer or computers that must be accessed via the gateway. Although someone with experience on both Windows NT and the host computer is desirable, someone with experience on just the host computer will be more useful than someone with experience on just Windows NT. As stated before, the ease of use of BackOffice makes training an administrator on the SNA gateway a far easier task than training someone on the network aspects of the mainframe.

NOTE

SNA was developed by IBM as a way for mainframes to communicate. SNA shares many similarities with TCP/IP, and they were developed in parallel around the same time. IBM kept SNA as a proprietary protocol; consequently, TCP/IP is much more popular and is now being offered as an alternative protocol on IBM mainframes and minicomputers.

The TCP/IP alternative to SNA should be considered. IBM's modern mainframes support access via TCP/IP, which usually simplifies connectivity issues and allows routing of mainframe traffic across corporate TCP/IP networks. Although this solution is not effective in all organizations because the TCP/IP approximation of IBM terminal access is not nearly exact, it may be appropriate and can help with support issues of users who access the system less frequently.

End Users

The most likely members of the implementation team to be forgotten are the end users, but user involvement with the implementation is essential, because many technical users will overlook basic needs and desires of the common users.

> For each group that needs to be represented, seek out a user who is willing to help, is computer literate, and is respected in the group he will be representing.

The ideal set of users needs to represent a cross section of all the departments and divisions in a company, as well as the geographical regions in which the company has offices. The users should be computer literate, but not necessarily technically inclined. Avoid users who are pessimistic or who fear change. They will only slow the project down and have very little useful input.

Senior Management

Although they are not active members of the installation team, senior management's support for the implementation is vital for its success. A project leader should find a member of senior management to champion the project with the executives of the company, and to get proper budgeting and policies in place.

The senior management should be kept well informed and made to feel like an active part of the project. The greater support they have for the implementation, the better the momentum will build throughout the course of the project.

Supporting End Users

Supporting the end users of a system is part of any successful implementation. Users will be unfamiliar with and doubtful of the software and procedures, and IS must be ready to give them help and support as needed. If the organization already has a help desk in place, the members of the help desk should be trained on the system. If it does not, a help desk should be set up.

A proactive approach needs to be taken. This includes training classes and getting users involved during all the phases of implementation, not just when it is time for them to use the system. By training the users, you will help them feel more confident in the system, and they will be more supportive during the implementation.

A drop in productivity will also accompany any new software implementation. Users will need time to learn the software and become comfortable with its use. Proper support will minimize this loss in productivity and will breed more support from management for the implementation. If an implementation results in a significant drop in productivity that affects the company's bottom line, maintaining support will be difficult.

Building User Confidence

In my experience, users always complain about existing systems. Then, when the new system is installed, no matter how wonderful it is, users will say the old system was much better. The implementation team should not let this discourage them and should not lose patience with the users, but should instead try to gain user acceptance.

The key to overcoming this is building user confidence in the system. Most of the time when users believe that the new software will not do something the old software did, it is not because of lack of functionality of the software, but lack of training of the users.

Another key to user confidence is making sure that IS appears responsive to the needs of the users, which includes keeping users updated as problems are being solved. Even if it is not possible to work on a problem immediately, it usually helps to just give users a call and let them know that their problems have not been forgotten. Gestures such as these go a long way in increasing user acceptance.

Hardware Support

Hardware support is one of the most difficult support issues. Unlike supporting software problems, hardware support usually requires someone to be present at the point of the problem.

There usually needs to be at least one qualified hardware support person at each geographical location of a company to assist with user problems. There are certifications available for hardware technicians, but there is no replacement for real experience. Make sure the people chosen to support hardware are able to do the job.

Hardware support not only requires a technical knowledge of hardware, but also the ability to purchase replacement hardware if needed. If there is bad hardware in a machine, the support person needs to order new hardware quickly. Delays through approval chains are usually unacceptable, especially on inexpensive parts such as network cards. A company needs to ensure that the hardware support people have appropriate buying power or their ability to support the hardware will be diminished.

Product Support

Product support involves technical support of the software that users use as well as the operating systems on the computers. Most product support will take place from remote locations over a phone line, so product support people must be effective voice communicators who can instruct users on how to fix problems or accomplish a task.

Because there is a great deal of software to support and that software is constantly changing, product support people must be well trained. Training must be continued as new products and upgraded versions of existing products are installed.

A major aid to product support is remote console access software. SMS provides a means for support people to look at and interact with a user's computer from across a network. The ability to do this makes supporting users much easier, because the support person can watch what users are doing, quickly determine the problem, and then show users the proper way to accomplish something, without the need to ever leave the computer operations offices.

Help-Desk Strategies

Constructing the computer help desk for an enterprise depends greatly on the size and type of organization. The help desk interacts with the end users on a day-to-day basis, so it must be functional, knowledgeable, and efficient.

For any large organization, the help desk should be staffed by a dedicated person or group of people. Help-desk people should know how to use the software they are supporting and be able to work with the system operators to ensure that user problems are resolved.

In a smaller organization, the help-desk people may also be members of the administration or development teams. However, care must be taken not to overload these people; help must be brought in if their workload becomes too great for them.

There are several responsibilities that are typically the domain of the help desk:

● Providing software support
● Providing hardware support
● Taking applications for new accounts
● Retrieving user-acceptance feedback
● Informing users of upcoming system changes
● Helping users recover from system errors and downtime

The people working at a help desk must be able to work on several problems at once, and must not lose patience with users they believe are demanding too much of the help desk.

Double Duty Help Desk

The double duty help desk is most common in smaller organizations. The duty of the help desk is rotated between the operators and administrators of the system. Because they are the ones who designed and operate the network, they are most effective in this job. However, problems happen in this approach when too much is expected of people and they become overloaded.

Another situation is where developers are used for user support. This is usually not desirable because these people are usually busy anyway. Also, programmer types do not interact well with users and tend to lose their patience.

When using this approach, care must be taken not to overload one person. It is tempting to avoid hiring additional people for the purpose of user support; while this may be good for the budget, it may not be good for the larger issue—implementation and operation success.

Dedicated Person

A dedicated person being used as the help desk is most common in medium-sized organizations or implementations. One person, usually a former operator or light developer, is assigned the job of handling the help desk. This person may call for help from the administrators and operators of the system, but should be knowledgeable enough to handle all routine problems without help.

A typical mistake in using this approach is choosing a person simply because he or she is viewed as having no other job after the implementation. Although it is noble to try to retain people through software and system changes, the larger goal of implementation success must be the highest priority.

The person dedicated to user support must have extensive and ongoing training on the software being used, and must be kept informed of all changes to software and the network as they are made. He should be the one the users view as their contact, and he should send out notices about system changes and upgrades.

This approach sometimes leads to problems with end users not trusting the help-desk person and attempting to bypass him and go directly to the operators or developers, who are busy with their tasks. This should be discouraged. Help-desk personnel usually have a database configured to log all users' requests and solutions. If end users bypass the help desk, many calls will not be logged and solutions for problems will not be available for future reference. It is usually enough to have operators and developers merely route those types of contacts back to the help desk, saying that they are not able to do support and that the users should contact the help desk.

Help Desk Department

Most large enterprises will find it best to have a department to serve as a dedicated help desk. The people in this department should be well trained and patient. The advantage of this approach is that there is no need for each person to know each product.

If someone in the department gets a call about a product he doesn't know, he can transfer the call to someone who knows more about it and is more capable of helping. In a large corporation with many software packages, this case is common, and help desk personnel are trained to do this.

Users also seem to be more trusting of the dedicated department. If they feel they are not getting help from one person, they can try someone else in the department. Care must be taken to make sure users do not feel as if they are being transferred from person to person, which will breed distrust and frustration from the user community.

Help Desk Summary

Whatever the approach is, users must be supported and kept informed. The actual approach will depend on many factors, must be carefully considered, and may be modified as experience with the help desk grows.

Licensing BackOffice

Licensing is a complex issue, and care must be taken to ensure license compliance. Licensing is especially complex with BackOffice, as opposed to products like Microsoft Word, where there must simply be one license per executing copy of the application.

When purchasing licenses for BackOffice applications, it is sometimes better to purchase a license for the entire BackOffice suite instead of buying a license for each product. Even if some products are not used on the server the suite was purchased for, it is probably still cheaper to purchase the entire suite instead of only two or three components. An example of the licensing applet provided with Windows NT is shown in Figure 4.11.

Figure 4.11.
For simple licensing on one server, Microsoft provides a convenient licensing applet that can be run from the Control Panel.

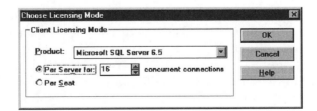

It is also helpful to check for packages and promotions when purchasing BackOffice. There are times when the suite may be offered with several client licenses, or it may be advantageous to purchase multiple suites at the same time. There are also cases where there may be price incentives to switch between the similar packages of competing vendors, sometimes called a competitive upgrade.

> I try to avoid using the term *competitive upgrade*, because referring to a switch from, say, Oracle or Sybase SQL Server to Microsoft SQL Server as an upgrade tends to cause heated debates in the computing world. The term *competitive switch* tends to avoid most of those debates.

Server licenses and client licenses must be purchased when licensing BackOffice. This is in contrast to some packages that allow purchasing of licenses for just the number of used client connections or purchasing a server license for an unlimited number of client connections.

Server Licenses

For each server running an instance of a server application, a license must be purchased. There are no exceptions to this rule. It is sometimes tempting to install a copy of a server product on a developer's personal computer or a development server, and it may seem harmless to do so, but that is illegal.

> License compliance has become a major issue with Microsoft. In the past, software was freely copied from PC to PC without proper licensing, and software companies such as Microsoft looked away. Microsoft is now seeking to put a stop to that practice, and has strict license compliance requirements for mainframes and minicomputers.

As stated before, it is usually best to buy a license for the entire BackOffice suite instead of for just the particular products that will be used. There is an obvious push by Microsoft to sell BackOffice as a complete package, and the pricing reflects this.

Also, as BackOffice components become integrated with each other, it will be necessary to have several licenses to run one component. An example is SMS, which requires a Microsoft SQL Server to store its database. A license must be purchased for not only SMS, but also SQL Server. Microsoft provides a convenient program that can be used to administer licenses across all servers. In Figure 4.12 you can see the Enterprise-License Manager, which allows you to see all BackOffice applications and the number of licenses purchased across the enterprise-wide network.

Figure 4.12.

For enterprise-wide license management, Microsoft provides a program to administer licenses across all servers.

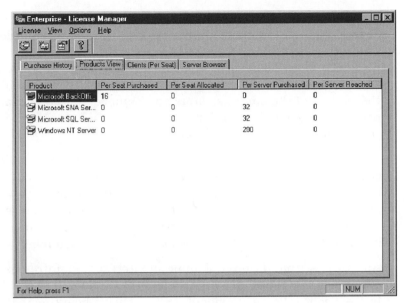

SMS is also a special server in that it can have satellite servers that feed information to the main server. This is typical in a large installation. Licenses must be purchased not only for the main server, but also for all satellite servers, to ensure proper license compliance.

Client Licenses

Not only do licenses have to be purchased for each instance of server software running, but separate licenses must be purchased for each client that accesses the server. There are different ways to license clients, as explained in the next section, but whatever the license method, a license must be purchased for each client.

The client software differs in distribution from the server software. The server software is generally distributed with a license, so having the CD-ROM containing the license implies purchase of the license, unless that CD-ROM is installed on multiple machines. The client software (but not the licenses) is distributed with the server software.

For instance, Windows NT File and Print Services client software is distributed with Windows 95, Windows NT Workstation, and Windows for Workgroups. In addition, client software for Windows and MS-DOS–based systems is distributed on the Windows NT Server CD-ROM. Even though the client software is easily made available, licenses must still be purchased before clients access the server services.

An exception to the rule, and there always has to be one, is Internet Information Server. Hypertext Transfer Protocol, on which the World Wide Web is based, is a connectionless protocol and therefore cannot be tracked on a license basis. Also, it does not make sense to have to purchase a license for each user who will be accessing Web content via the Web server, because the number of people doing so is outside the control of the administrators and managers of an organization. Indeed, it is usually the goal to have as many users as possible, and not to limit users based on something like client connection licenses.

When SQL Server data is published via the Web, licensing of SQL Server becomes complex. Generally, very few licenses will be sufficient for all Web access, because generating content from a database usually involves connecting to the server, gathering the data, sending the data to the Web browser, and disconnecting from the server. Per-server licensing (discussed in the next section) must be used, because the number of viewers on the Web cannot be determined in advance or controlled.

An old trick from the days of minicomputers and mainframes is to set the number of licenses recognized to a number less than the number purchased. Then, when a lack of licenses becomes evident through clients being denied access, the number of server licenses can be increased legally, giving a time buffer in which to purchase new licenses. Using this technique, there is never a time when a client is using an invalid connection license.

Licensing Options

As stated before, there are different types of client licensing techniques available. What an organization chooses to use will depend on the size of the organization and the frequency of access to server applications by clients.

There are two primary types of licensing available:

- Per-server
- Per-seat

Per-Server Licensing

The traditional type of licensing on networks and host computers is licensing based on concurrency of use. In other words, a license is obtained for each user who will be using an application at any given time, as opposed to each user who could use the application. This licensing is very simple and straightforward, and the number of connections can be monitored and controlled from a central point. As licensing options are explored, this is usually the best one to start with, because it is probably the one that is most understood by the administrative team.

NOTE

> Administrators coming from a traditional LAN or host computer back-ground will be familiar with the per-server type of licensing. It is probably better to start with this type, because of its simplicity, and look at the per-seat option after the usage patterns of the organization have stabilized and are known.

BackOffice offers this type of licensing as the *per-server* option. The number of users who will be using an application at any one time is generally much lower than the number of users who access an application at any time during the lifetime of a system. Because of this, per-server licensing is cost-effective for a user base that will be accessing server applications infrequently. This option is also the easier to enforce, because licenses are handed out from the point of view of the server, and the server can refuse a connection if there are no licenses available.

An exception to the rule of starting out with per-server licensing is Systems Management Server, which is only licensed on a per-seat basis because SMS client software does not maintain a constant connection to the server. When initially purchasing licenses for SMS, buy enough licenses for all clients on the network, and probably a few extra, to be available as clients are added.

Per-Seat Licensing

Sometimes it is more effective to purchase a license that allows the client to access a particular type of application, no matter how many servers or connections to the servers the client requires. For instance, a client may want to access four SQL Servers with 10 connections, which would be fairly expensive on a per-server license basis. Microsoft provides the per-seat licensing option for this type of situation.

A per-seat license is purchased for a single client to access a specific type of server, such as Exchange, no matter how many servers the client wants to access with any number of connections. Although users tend to open only one connection to a product like Exchange, applications typically open several connections to things such as SQL Server, making purchasing a per-seat license cost-prohibitive.

Per-seat licenses are the only option for Systems Management Server, because there is not a constant, monitorable connection between an SMS client and the SMS Server. Per-seat licenses, although not required, are usually advantageous for SQL Server.

When an organization first implements BackOffice, it is usually wise to purchase per-server licenses. Later, as usage patterns increase and users start doing more and starting more applications at once, per-seat licenses are a better option.

Microsoft allows a one-time conversion between per-server and per-seat licenses for just that situation. Because of this, it is usually better to start with per-server licenses that could be converted later than to start with per-seat licenses.

License Configuration Examples

For a company that is just starting out in BackOffice implementation, it is usually best to purchase per-server licenses. This is especially true for a development department or testing lab. When the systems are first installed, a set of per-server licenses can be installed as developers work or testers try out different systems. If a company is starting its first installation of BackOffice, it is also usually better to start by buying a batch of BackOffice licenses.

After the usage patterns become more pronounced, licenses can be converted on a one-time-only basis to per-seat licenses. Per-seat licenses are especially useful for heavy and critical users. Because the license is dedicated to just that one user, that user is guaranteed the ability to logon to the system. The per-seat license is also useful in a SQL Server environment with an application that opens up several connections to the SQL Server to do its work. I have seen applications that open as many as 10 connections to the server, and users of these applications are therefore good candidates for per-seat licensing.

As more servers are added, you can either purchase licenses for each product, or for the entire BackOffice product. If a server is added to support only one application, such as a central Exchange mail router, it is usually more cost-effective to purchase a license for just that product. If a server will be a server for multiple BackOffice applications, it is usually better to purchase the BackOffice products as a suite, even if one or two applications will not be used. Sometimes there are also incentives, such as free client licenses, for purchasing the entire suite.

License counts can be set lower than the actual purchased number, to ensure license compliance. There will be a time when the number of licenses available is not enough to serve the number of users requesting services. When this happens, the number of allowed connections can be immediately increased to serve the user load without going out of the bounds of license compliance. Notice that this technique can only be used with per-server licensing, because per-seat licensing does not apply to server connections and cannot be monitored for client compliance on the server.

When managing many servers, the *Enterprise-License Manager* (ELM) should be used to simplify license management. The ELM gives a view of all the servers and applications in an organization. As licenses are purchased, they can be added to servers from one console, removing the need to be at specific servers to change licensing parameters.

ELM makes it easy to remove licenses from one server and add them to another. When this is done, the servers immediately recognize and enforce the changed licensing parameters. This also simplifies license management, because licenses can be moved from servers that are not using them to servers that need them, all from one control.

Licensing Summary

Licensing is a complex issue that requires careful thought and planning. An organization should strive to make sure it is compliant with licenses and license agreements, and should constantly monitor its networks for usage patterns that violate the license agreements.

When purchasing licenses, consider per-server licenses for initial investment, then switch to per-seat licenses later, as usage patterns dictate. Microsoft allows a one-time conversion from per-server to per-seat licenses, which makes the risk of buying per-server licenses low.

Summary

For a successful implementation of BackOffice, careful planning is a necessity. Without planning, the efforts to start using BackOffice will be uncoordinated, and the chances for success and user acceptance will be greatly reduced.

The implementation team needs to consist of well-trained, experienced people. They are the ones who will make the project a success. Do not pick the team based on personal preference for people, but pick for history of success and demonstrated skill in the area for which each will be in charge.

Be sure to involve users during the implementation. End users are frequently left out during development, and then asked to sign off on the system in the end. The level of user confidence and acceptance will be much higher if they are involved earlier in the process.

When the implementation is complete, support and maintenance must continue. An operator for the servers should look after day-to-day operations, and there should be provisions for user support such as a help desk or an assigned support person.

A complex and flexible product such as BackOffice requires careful planning to implement and a diligent staff to maintain. If these are planned for ahead of time, there will be fewer problems down the road.

Part II

Operating System Resources

CPU Utilization

The utilization of your server's CPU is arguably the most discussed aspect of any production server installation, and rightly so. Choose the right CPU and your system will perform fine, providing your users with quick response time and efficient processing. Choose the wrong CPU and you'll encounter the frustration of trying to cope with slow response times and sluggish overall performance, and the rest of your server investment will be sitting around waiting for something to do while the CPU catches up.

I consider a computer system to be composed of four main categories, or subsystems: CPU, disk, memory, and network. The disk subsystem is covered in Part III of this book, "File System Resources." The memory subsystem is covered in Chapter 6, "Memory Utilization." The network subsystem is covered in Part IV of this volume, "Network Resources."

In this chapter, you are going to take a closer look at the CPU, a key subsystem of any server. From architectures to recommendations, this chapter covers a breadth of topics related to the CPU resource. So, while I cannot tell you exactly which processor to purchase, hopefully this chapter can provide insights into understanding the CPU on Windows NT Server and BackOffice. You can then make intelligent decisions for yourself.

Here is a quick glance at the topics covered in this chapter:

- Multiprocessor technology
- Scalability of Windows NT
- Performance Monitor and the CPU
- BackOffice product requirements

Multiprocessor Technology

Multiprocessor technology, MP for short, is nothing new to the computer industry. Although it is relatively new to the PC and PC-server industry—for years PCs only had single processor, or uniprocessor (UP), designs—the issue has been dealt with for years in the minicomputer and mainframe industries. Fortunately for us in the PC industry, there is a lot of experience to draw on.

The basic idea is quite simple: If one processor is good, two processors must be twice as good, and three must be three times as good. Extrapolating the idea further conjures up thoughts of hundreds of processors, all working in parallel to solve complex problems at lightning fast speeds. And, in fact, there are some computer systems out there that fit the description. Problem is, today they are highly customized, very costly, and not suited for general purposes. Besides, today you don't need a hundred-processor computer just to run your e-mail system. What you do need, however, is a computer that can easily work with your operating system, is flexible enough to run on varying hardware, and can grow to meet increasing demands.

Multiprocessor Operating Systems

One major challenge has been that MP computers have traditionally required an operating system specifically engineered for that MP implementation. If you wanted to upgrade the MP hardware underneath the operating system (OS), you were stuck, because the OS was designed specifically for that kind of hardware.

The solution is to create an operating system that will work across hardware types, a hardware-independent operating system, if you will. With the development of operating systems such as UNIX and Windows NT, that has largely been accomplished. NT is designed with an architecture that allows it to function with both UP and MP hardware, and with Intel-based hardware and non-Intel hardware alike. If you want to add more processing power, just drop in another CPU. Simple, right?

As with most things in the technology world, it's not quite *that* simple, but it's getting there. Today Windows NT supports Intel, Alpha, MIPS, and PowerPC chips in both UP and MP configurations. It accomplishes this by the use of a *Hardware Abstraction Layer* (HAL). The HAL does exactly what its name implies: It is a layer of NT that abstracts, or disassociates, the hardware from the operating system. That way, you can change the hardware beneath the HAL, and all you have to do is replace the HAL, rather than the entire operating system. Figure 5.1 shows the architecture of NT with the HAL.

Figure 5.1.
The HAL is in place to isolate the rest of Windows NT from specific hardware.

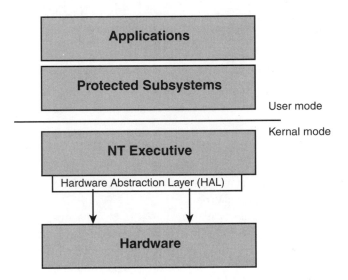

The design of Windows NT is really outside the scope of this chapter. Fortunately, there are many resources available on the architecture and design approach of Windows NT. However, I wanted to introduce you to the concepts in case you were not familiar with them. Having said that, let's focus on what's inside the hardware box in Figure 5.1. It could be a desktop PC or a multiprocessor high-end server. It could even be a laptop. Regardless, you need to have an understanding of the architecture of MP systems and how the CPU resource is used by NT, to better understand how these concepts apply to your BackOffice implementation.

Multiprocessor Computer Architecture

As I alluded earlier, there is a lot more to a multiprocessor computer than just making it work with more than one CPU chip. Thought has to be given to every aspect of how the computer functions, including I/O, bus architectures, memory access, and cache design.

This section provides an overview of some basic MP architecture concepts. Understanding them will provide better insight into how Windows NT does its job.

Before we continue, it's important to make a distinction in terminology. When I refer to processor subsystem or CPU subsystem, I'm talking about the aspect of the computer that performs the central processing for the computer. It could be thought of as *CPU resource*, whether comprised of a single CPU chip or many CPU chips.

When I refer to CPU or processor alone, I'm referring to the individual CPU chip, such as Intel Pentium Pro or DEC Alpha, and so on. While the discussion in the following sections centers around Intel Pentium and Pentium Pro processors, most of the concepts apply to non-Intel processors as well.

With that in mind, let's jump into some MP tech talk. There are two main design approaches to understand in MP systems: loosely coupled and tightly coupled.

Loosely Coupled Design

You may have heard of Microsoft's forthcoming clustering product, code-named *Wolfpack*. This product is the foundation of a loosely coupled multiprocessor system.

There is nothing new about a loosely coupled design, commonly referred to as a *cluster*. In fact, it has been around the mainframe and minicomputer industries for years. But over the past few years it has started to make headway into the PC industry, with recent advancements that include Wolfpack and another Microsoft product code-named *Viper*.

In a loosely coupled design, each processor in the cluster has its own local system memory, processor cache, system bus, and peripheral-support components. It runs its own copy of the operating system and has its own I/O. It is, in essence, a standalone computer.

The approach is what I would classify as a multicomputer approach to multiprocessing. However, strictly speaking, a loosely coupled architecture could be contained in one physical box. The current trend is that you add an entire computer to the cluster to add its processing power to the collective.

It is the sort of add-as-you-go approach that fits perfectly with high-power commodity computers that are so prevalent these days. The idea of just purchasing another computer and adding it to the cluster is rapidly becoming a reality, and it's a good option for the bottom line. Figure 5.2 provides a look at the cluster architecture.

There are a few things to consider about a cluster. First, the technology isn't all here yet for the PC industry. As of this writing, the software infrastructure is still being built, so you probably won't be rolling out many clusters of PCs during 1997. Even so, the first version of Wolfpack only supports two computers in the cluster, but you have to start somewhere.

Second, note that in Figure 5.2, there has to be an interconnect between the computers. This interconnect is a key design element, because it can be a point of breakdown in the design. For example, if different hardware vendors adopt different interconnect designs, you'll be unable to connect one brand of computer with another brand in a cluster. Also, the interconnect has to have a high bandwidth or else it can become a bottleneck to system performance. The interconnect is really the bus that connects each system to the others, so high bandwidth is critical, especially as more computers are added to the cluster.

Figure 5.2.
The loosely coupled architecture combines standalone computers in a cluster.

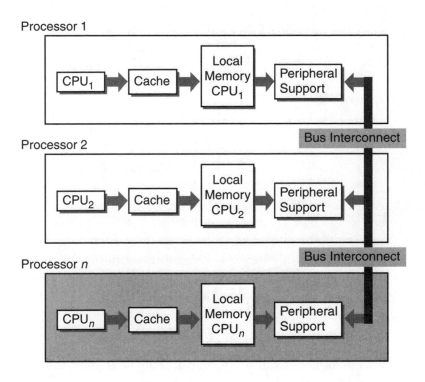

Third, there must be a way to bundle operations the computers in the cluster work on so that the data is guaranteed to remain viable between computers. This implies the need for a transaction and for software to manage those transactions, which is where Microsoft Viper comes into the picture. Viper's responsibility is to manage the operations that occur in the form of transactions, so that data is not corrupted as it travels among the computers in the cluster to be processed.

Clustering is an interesting approach to multiprocessing, and it holds promise for the future. However, if you want multiprocessor PC-based computers today, you will have to look at another approach—the tightly coupled design.

Tightly Coupled Design

Most MP computers available today for commercial applications employ a tightly coupled design. When most people refer to MP computers, they are, by default, referring to multiprocessor computers with a tightly coupled architecture. Figure 5.3 shows the design of a tightly coupled MP computer.

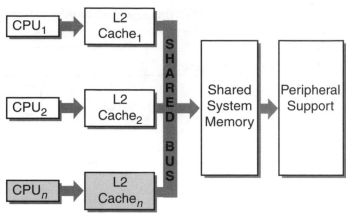

Figure 5.3.
*The tightly
coupled design
approach is
common in today's
commercial
multiprocessor
computers.*

In contrast to the loosely coupled design, these systems are almost always contained in a single box, because they share system memory, system bus, and peripheral support components. They sometimes have a dedicated processor cache, but sometimes they may even share that. Cache design is discussed in detail later in this chapter.

The advantage of a tightly coupled design is that you need only to add CPU chips to the system in order to increase its processing resource. Another advantage is that a powerful computer can be contained in a fairly small space. There are MP servers and workstation computers on the market today that have huge processing resources, but they can sit on your desktop or at your desk's side.

The disadvantage is that, to date, the PC industry has only gotten decent wide-ranging scalability out of about four CPUs. Beyond four CPUs, the systems don't tend to scale well, and the performance does not justify the cost. There are definite exceptions to this rule that do perform well beyond four CPUs, but they tend to be costly.

There are two basic types of tightly coupled architectures that provide quite different performance models: symmetric multiprocessing (SMP) and asymmetric multiprocessing (ASMP). What are these? I'm glad you asked.

Symmetric Multiprocessing

When most people refer to a multiprocessor computer in the commercial PC server market, they are referring to a tightly coupled SMP computer.

The SMP design employs an approach that places all the CPUs in the computer on an equal playing field. In other words, all CPUs have the capability and privilege to run the operating system's kernel, to process I/O and interrupts, to run device drivers, and to access system memory. In short, each CPU has no special features or restrictions, and each has equal access to system resources. That sets the stage for a group effort to get the processing done as quickly as possible. The problem of load balancing is simplified, and you can add additional processors to increase the amount of CPU resource.

Windows NT is designed to work effectively with SMP computers and to provide a foundation for applications to leverage the power of multiple processors. It has a scheduler that manages all the tasks and distributes them among the available CPUs for completion. Figure 5.4 shows a diagram of an SMP system.

Figure 5.4.
SMP multiprocessing systems distribute the load among the available CPUs.

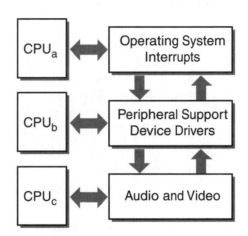

SMP systems have at least one requirement for application software: They must be designed properly. That is, application software needs to be designed with the possibility that it will run on a computer with more than one CPU. That is not to say the software has to be customized; it just has to have the proper architecture that will facilitate efficient execution in SMP environments.

For example, if you design an application that is a single-threaded single-process application, it will not gain any benefit running on an SMP system. In fact, it will probably run slower because the processors are wasting their time passing around a single thread of execution. Therefore, a fast, single CPU is best for a single-threaded application.

On the other hand, if you design an application properly with multiple threads of execution, threads can be executed simultaneously on multiple processors. That's where the performance benefit becomes apparent. Certainly it's not as simple as spawning a bunch of threads in your application to solve all your worries. But if careful consideration is given during the design phase, it will pay big dividends when your application runs on an SMP system.

As for BackOffice applications, they are designed with precisely this goal in mind. SQL Server and Exchange Server are prime examples. They run well on single-processor systems, but if you run them on SMP systems, their performance definitely benefits.

There are many considerations to designing a good SMP computer, including shared bus bandwidth, bus arbitration, good processor cache design, and operating system efficiency. In fact, the design and refinement of Windows NT itself has benefited from a large amount of work by hardware and software engineers who bang on Windows NT in their labs in an effort to make things run as quickly and efficiently as possible.

Asymmetric Multiprocessing

ASMP has been around for a while. Compared to SMP, it's a pretty simplistic way to implement MP technology. Depending on the implementation, ASMP can definitely yield performance improvements in the system.

As the name implies, the various processors in the computer are not the same, or they do not have the same access to all system resources, such as interrupts and I/O addresses. Figure 5.5 shows a typical asymmetric design.

Figure 5.5.
In asymmetric designs, CPUs are dedicated for specific tasks.

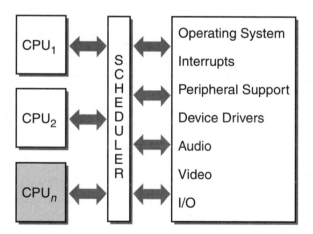

If you think about it, this approach makes sense for some applications. You may remember the Amiga computer. It had several processors in it that performed various functions. There were dedicated video chips, audio chips, I/O chips, and so on, and they were all tied together with an operating system to function as a coherent whole. For its time, the computer had phenomenal performance and unmatched capabilities, and you could do some neat things with it. This was largely due to its ASMP design. Each processor had a dedicated job to do, whether it was audio, video, I/O, central processing, or whatever. No one chip in the system was required to do all the work for the entire computer. That was how the Amiga was able to do such marvelous stuff. The ASMP approach can apply to the commercial server market to a degree, but the approach is not as well suited to general applications as the SMP design. Certainly Windows NT is built for the SMP design, so you should focus your attention on SMP computers.

The Processor Cache

In a computer, there can be several caches, each performing a specific function. There are three for a BackOffice server: application/database cache, Windows NT system Cache, and processor cache. This section focuses on the processor cache, which is crucial to good CPU performance.

There are four main types of processor caches you should be aware of. You may already be familiar with some of these:

- Level 1 cache
- Shared Level 2 cache
- Dedicated Level 2 cache
- Level 3 cache

These four types of caches work together to produce varying degrees of performance when employed in any computer system, not just MP systems.

The purpose of these processor caches is all the same. First, they keep the system from having to fetch an instruction or data from main memory. Because accessing main memory is at least an order of magnitude slower than accessing a cache, frequent cache hits will benefit overall system performance in both UP and MP computers.

Second, in MP computers, processor caches are there to offload traffic from the shared bus. All the processors sit on a bus that connects them to each other and to the rest of the system. When a CPU needs something from memory, for example, the request goes onto the shared bus. In UP computers, bus contention is usually not a problem, but in MP computers, it can quickly become a problem as more processors are added. If a request can be satisfied from a processor cache, that request need not show up on the shared bus, and that keeps the bus from getting congested and performing slowly.

Naturally, caches cost money, so there's always a tradeoff between performance and cost. The best performing designs, such as large dedicated Level 2 caches and Level 3 caches, usually come at a price. Whether it is worth the price depends upon how important it is to you to have absolute top performance.

Many of the system's hardware vendors and CPU manufacturers supply white papers that provide comparative performance results for their different designs. I encourage you to check these out for yourself to see how much difference the extra money is buying.

Level 1 Cache

The Level 1 (L1) cache is the most rudimentary of all. In Intel Pentium and Pentium Pro chips, the L1 cache is 16KB in size, extremely fast, and located within the chip itself. Now 16KB may not seem like much, but the L1 cache makes a significant difference when it is present.

As with all caches, the L1 cache's purpose is to hold a small amount of the most recently used instructions and data close to the CPU. If no cache were present on the CPU, the CPU would have to go off-chip to access all instructions or data. L1 caches are always dedicated to a specific CPU.

Level 2 Cache

Let's say the L1 cache misses. Without a Level 2 (L2) cache, the CPU would have to go to main memory for the data. However, most modern computers have some amount of L2 cache present to improve performance.

L2 cache sizes vary. Some are as small as 256KB; others are up to 2MB. Although not as fast as the L1 cache, accessing an L2 cache is still much faster than accessing main memory. The performance benefit derived from using one can be significant.

There are two types of L2 cache—shared and dedicated. Figures 5.6 and 5.7 depict shared and dedicated L2 caches, respectively.

Figure 5.6.
This architecture is the one Intel uses for their two processor–shared cache design.

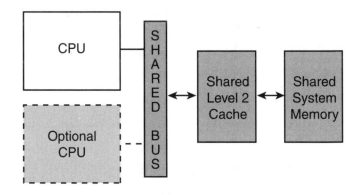

The shared L2 cache architecture by design lessens performance potential in two ways. First, all L1 cache misses appear on the shared bus ahead of the L2 cache. Secondly, there is a greater chance of a cache miss if two CPUs are vying for the same cache space than if only one CPU is vying for that space. The goal for this design is to provide some performance boost at a modest cost. However, you sacrifice scalability.

Figure 5.7.
A dedicated Level 2 cache provides added performance in multiprocessor computers.

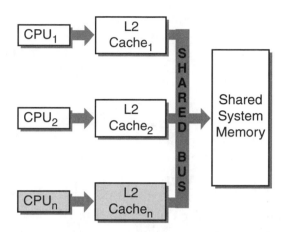

The dedicated L2 cache design is not as cost effective as the shared cache design. The tradeoff, naturally, is performance. Technically speaking, an L2 cache in any UP computer is, by definition, a dedicated L2 cache, because there are no other CPUs to share it with, so you would expect maximum performance benefit from the cache. However, the notion of a dedicated L2 cache really becomes desirable when there are multiple CPUs in the computer. Each CPU gets its own cache to pull from before it must send a request over the shared bus to main memory. This fact, combined with large L2 cache sizes of 2MB or more, provides excellent CPU performance and scalability.

Level 3 Cache

Use of Level 3 (L3) caches is generally reserved for specific applications that will take advantage of them. They usually only help performance in multiprocessor systems of three or more CPUs. Typically, an L3 cache is only available as an option. Moreover, recently advanced L2 designs appear to provide better performance than using an L3 cache. Again, it is a matter of design. Figure 5.8 shows a basic L3 cache design.

It doesn't take a rocket scientist, or a computer engineer for that matter, to figure out that the L3 cache looks just like an extension of the L2 cache. Actually, an L3 cache may or may not help performance, because L3 cache memory access is not faster than main memory access. However, after examining the figure, it is apparent that the benefit the L3 cache provides is keeping requests for data off the system's shared bus. In large multiprocessor computers where shared bus contention is a problem, minimizing bus traffic is a real advantage.

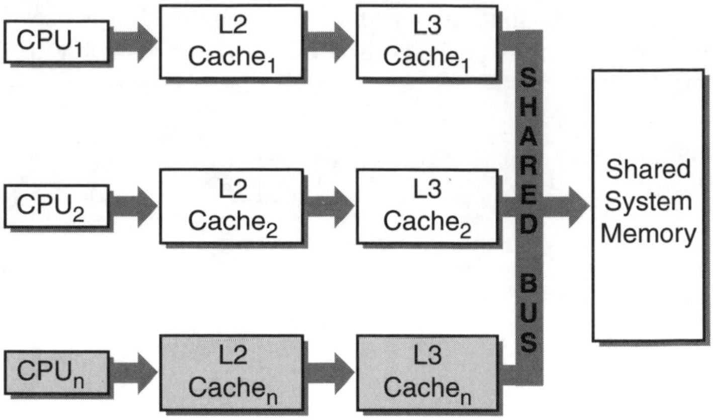

Figure 5.8.
*Dedicated L3
caches can provide
a performance
benefit in multi-
processor comput-
ers with three or
more processors.*

Scalability of Windows NT

After all this talk about MP designs and caches, it's time to come up for air. While I'm certain you are marveling at this great knowledge you now have, you may want to know how it relates to Windows NT.

You have likely heard or read the term *scalability*. In general terms, scalability refers to the ability of a computer system to maintain or increase performance as more resources are added. In the context of Windows NT, it can be applied a couple of different ways, such as user scalability or processor scalability.

The term *user scalability* implies that the computer system should be able to maintain response time as the number of users increases, provided the system is not encountering a bottleneck anywhere. For example, if you are running Exchange Server, it should be able to handle a jump from, say, 100 users to 500 users without problems or severe performance impact. In fact, this is precisely the case with Exchange Server; it is scalable as you add users.

The term *processor scalability* implies that the computer should increase in performance as more CPUs are added to the system. If the computer provides 2× performance after adding a second processor, 3× performance with a third processor, and so on, you would say the system is 100 percent scalable. It has a one to one scalability ratio.

Unfortunately, the ideal of 100 percent scalability is not attainable with real-world computers. Figure 5.9 shows an example of processor scalability that might be encountered with current commercial MP servers running Windows NT.

Figure 5.9.
Under Windows NT today, you might see scalability that looks something like this.

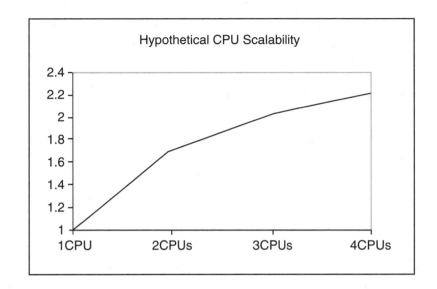

Today, a 70 to 80 percent scalability factor is considered quite good. Why? Well, hopefully now you can see why I spent the time going over multiprocessor architectures in the first part of this chapter. You should also know that there is always overhead associated with running multiple CPUs in a computer. So no matter whether you are running a tightly coupled SMP computer or a loosely coupled configuration of several computers, the scalability will be less than ideal. In fact, as you add CPUs, the scalability will tend to go down, as shown in Figure 5.10.

Figure 5.10.
As you add CPUs to a multiprocessor system, the scalability tends to go down.

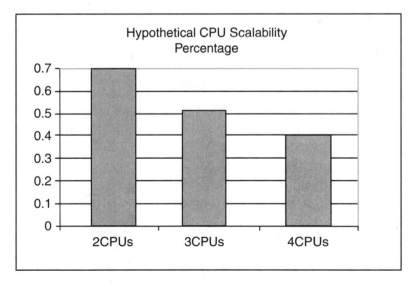

The scalability of multiprocessor computers and Windows NT keeps improving. Some day even the 100 percent ideal may be reached, but for now we have to live with less than ideal.

Performance Monitor and the CPU

You can monitor precisely what is going on with your CPU resource, using Performance Monitor (PerfMon). If you've ever used PerfMon, you know there are a multitude of objects and counters in there. I'd like to introduce the counters that are most useful in monitoring CPU resource utilization.

Many times you want to monitor the overall system CPU utilization. But have you ever needed to monitor the utilization of a single CPU? How about of a specific process, or even a thread within a process? How do you know if your multiprocessor server is using all CPUs efficiently, or if it is spending too much time context switching? All this information is available via PerfMon. Table 5.1 provides a list of the ones to use.

Table 5.1. CPU-related objects in Performance Monitor.

Object Name	Description
Process	Contains counters pertaining to all the processes running in NT
Processor	Contains counters pertaining to the system processor(s)
System	Contains general counters pertaining to the overall state of NT
Thread	Contains counters pertaining to all the threads running in the NT

There are dozens of counters included in these objects. Table 5.2 contains some useful ones and a brief description of what each one is.

Table 5.2. Useful generic counters.

Object Name	Counter	Description
Process	% Processor Time	The amount of processor time consumed by the selected process. This is User and Privileged time combined, and it includes all CPUs in a multiprocessor computer.

Object Name	Counter	Description
Process	% User Time	The amount of User Mode processor time consumed by the selected process. This includes all CPUs in a multiprocessor computer.
Process	% Privileged Time	The amount of Privileged Mode processor time consumed by the selected process. This includes all CPUs in a multiprocessor system.
Processor	% Processor Time	The amount of time the selected CPU is busy doing work. This is User and Privileged time combined for the entire system.
Processor	% User Time	The amount of time the selected CPU is busy doing User Mode work for the entire system.
Processor	% Privileged Time	The amount of time the selected CPU is busy doing Privileged Mode work for the entire system.
Server	Context Switches/sec	The rate at which NT is switching from one thread to another. In UP systems, this number should not be very high. But as with System Calls/sec, this number will increase in MP systems. If it is above 10,000, you may be encountering CPU thrashing problems, especially with more than two CPUs and if System Calls/sec is also high.
Server	System Calls/sec	The rate at which calls are being made to NT system service routines. In UP systems, this number should not be very high. But as with Context Switches/sec, this number will increase in MP systems. If it is above 10,000, you may be encountering CPU thrashing problems, especially with more than two CPUs and if Context Switches/sec is also high.

continues

Table 5.2. continued

Object Name	Counter	Description
Thread	% Processor Time	The amount of processor time consumed by the selected thread. This is User and Privileged time combined, and it includes all CPUs in a multiprocessor computer.
Thread	% User Time	The amount of User Mode processor time consumed by the selected thread. This includes all CPUs in a multiprocessor computer.
Thread	% Privileged Time	The amount of Privileged Mode processor time consumed by the selected thread. This includes all CPUs in a multiprocessor system.
System	Processor Queue Length	The number of threads waiting in the processor queue. Values consistently above 2× the number of CPUs in the computer can indicate processor resource congestion. (You must also monitor at least one thread from the Thread object for this counter to be active.)

BackOffice Product Requirements

This may be the section you have been waiting for, or maybe you have already found the gem of knowledge you've been looking for. In the former case, let me set your expectations before reading on, because I cannot choose your server's CPU for you. I can, however, give you some food for thought and hopefully steer your thinking in the right direction so you can make the best choice. Some ideas may be obvious, but if nothing else, it's always a good idea to reinforce what you already know to be true.

General Recommendations

The following are my general recommendations for things to bear in mind when planning CPU resources for your server:

● If you purchase a single CPU computer—one not capable of supporting multiple processors—get the fastest CPU available. This will extend the usability of the server as long as possible by minimizing the chance of the

CPU becoming a bottleneck as demands on the server increase. If you expect to support a smaller, static number of users, this approach will help provide the fastest response time possible.

● If you purchase a multiprocessor-capable system, consider the information discussed in the preceding section on multiprocessor architectures. You might be able to get away with a single, fast CPU in the system for now, but you will have laid a good path for the future, because the server has the capability of supporting more than one CPU. This capability will be crucial as demands on the server increase, because you can extend the life of the server by adding additional processors.

● Look for a large L2 cache, regardless of whether you implement a multiprocessor computer. A large L2 cache provides benefits in multithreaded applications such as those found in BackOffice. In single processor systems, at least 512KB is preferred. In multiprocessor systems, larger L2 caches (2MB, for example) will produce even better performance. Especially look for large L2 caches when you plan to support multiprocessing.

● Understand that all multiprocessor computer systems are not created equal. I refer you back to the section in this chapter titled "Multiprocessor Computer Architecture," if you need a refresher. Some multiprocessor implementations are rather limited for one reason or another. Maybe they have a shared cache architecture, or maybe they just suffer from a poor overall design. Although you might still get some added performance out of multiple processors in these machines, you won't get as much as with other, better (and probably more expensive) solutions. The better implementations usually provide large dedicated L2 caches and superior host bus and memory designs. The result is quite a boost when you add that second processor, or third, or fourth. If you're investing big bucks in those components, remember you usually get what you pay for.

● Finally, remember that if the system is not CPU constrained, adding additional CPUs will probably not help things. Use PerfMon to help figure out whether the CPU is being pegged or not. A common misconception is that you can add more processors and continue to get significant benefits from doing so—not so if the disk, for example, is the bottleneck in the system. If anything, it will just exaggerate the problem where the bottleneck lies. It might help a little, but your efforts—and your money—will be better spent toward finding and removing the real bottleneck first.

BackOffice Applications

Exchange Server and SQL Server are similar in that they employ a large relational database, and they are engineered as multiprocess multithread applications. They are arguably the premier BackOffice applications, and they are able to take advantage of all the high-powered hardware you can throw at them. Both can definitely take advantage of multiple CPUs, with the biggest advantage coming from the addition of the second CPU. Unless the demands on these applications are small, I do not recommend requiring the computer they run on to perform other tasks.

Internet Information Server (IIS) has one main purpose: to serve data via HTML to users connecting with a browser. Based on that premise, IIS's requirements are most naturally like those of a file server. File servers typically do not require much CPU resource—they are disk- and I/O subsystem-intensive. It is very important to have a powerful CPU for the IIS computer, especially with Active Server pages and the like placing more demands on the server's CPU resource. In this scenario, you really have to look at what the requirements are for the system. If the requirements become processor-intensive, consider adding additional CPUs. For starters, begin with a single CPU—I recommend getting the fastest one available. That will give you a foundation to build on, should you need additional CPUs later.

SMS and SNA Server are more passive applications, with completely different goals than any of the other BackOffice members. While they have multiple threads and multiple processes, the nature of their function most likely will not exploit multiple processors. A fast first CPU provides a good starting point for these applications. However, if the computers they run on perform other tasks, by all means consider additional CPUs.

Summary

In this chapter, you learned about several topics related to CPU utilization in your BackOffice system.

First, for a foundation, I discussed the involved topic of multiprocessor technology, covering the main architectures and design approaches to CPU subsystems.

Next, I related what was learned about multiprocessor technology to the scalability of Windows NT. NT has good user and processor scalability, and it's getting better all the time.

Then you discovered some useful PerfMon counters that can aid you in monitoring how much CPU resource is being used by the server. These counters can help pinpoint when to add a CPU, when to upgrade the CPU, which processes or threads are CPU hogs, and how to spot situations where the system is not making efficient use of multiple processors.

Finally, the chapter concludes with an overview of some suggestions to bear in mind when selecting a CPU subsystem for your computer. Following that are my personal views on how to apply what you've learned about CPU utilization to the various BackOffice applications.

Understanding and managing CPU utilization is a bit of art and science combined. You really have to understand the computers you are managing. Hopefully this chapter has provided some guidance on how to manage your server's CPU utilization so you can get the best performance possible out of your server.

CHAPTER 6

Memory Utilization

Chapter 5, "CPU Utilization," covers an important subsystem of your server—the CPU resource. I suggested that it was the most important subsystem in the server, but if I had to choose a second most important system, it would be the memory subsystem.

While nothing can get done very fast in a computer without a powerful CPU resource, the CPU can end up wasting much of its time if there isn't enough memory in the computer. This certainly holds true for Windows NT, so it is important to understand how memory is used in a Windows NT system if you want to prevent the wasting of system resources.

The following is an overview of the topics that are covered:

- Memory technologies—An overview of available RAM architectures found in commercial PC-based servers. These include discussions of designs incorporating Dynamic RAM (DRAM), Static RAM (SRAM), parity memory, Error Checking and Correcting (ECC) memory, Enhanced Data Output (EDO) RAM, Single Inline Memory Modules (SIMMs), and Dual Inline Memory Modules (DIMMs).

● Virtual memory in Windows NT—This topic forms the basis of how memory is used by the operating system.

● Disk caching and memory—A discussion of disk caching requirements and how they relate to memory consumption. General hardware- and software-based caches are covered, as well as dedicated application caches.

● Monitoring memory usage with Performance Monitor—To help you determine how well the memory is being used in your computer, you'll take a look at how Performance Monitor can help keep an eye on memory usage. You'll also find some useful memory-related performance counters.

● BackOffice product requirements—Suggestions of how to choose the right amount of RAM with BackOffice applications, including suggested quantities of memory for each application.

When you finish reading this chapter, you should have a firm grasp on several aspects of memory usage in a Windows NT computer. This knowledge will provide valuable insights into properly managing your Windows NT and BackOffice systems.

Memory Technologies

As with many subjects, it is prudent to lay some groundwork before delving into the heart of it all. This idea applies to understanding memory usage in Windows NT. This section covers some terms and technology that are germane to the discussion of memory.

These include discussions of designs incorporating Dynamic RAM (DRAM), Static RAM, parity memory, Error Checking and Correcting memory (ECC), Enhanced Data Output (EDO), Single Inline Memory Modules (SIMMs), and Dual Inline Memory Modules (DIMMs).

Having an understanding of these terms is important to understanding what is out there in the market. This section is not meant to provide exhaustive coverage of all available memory technologies. In fact, technology changes so fast it's hard to keep up with all the latest, greatest stuff. Rather, this section is here to introduce available technologies you are likely to encounter today.

Types of RAM

The most common types of RAM available today are Dynamic RAM, Static RAM, and Enhanced Data Output RAM. The following sections are here to summarize these technologies.

Dynamic RAM

Probably the most used type of memory in PCs today is DRAM. It earned its name, because it needs to be updated cyclically in order to maintain its contents. This cycle, called a refresh cycle, comes often—on the order of once every several nanoseconds, depending on the DRAM specifications. If a DRAM doesn't get its refresh in time, the contents are lost. In fact, the major disadvantage to DRAM is the design and performance overhead associated with constantly refreshing it. So, the computer's DRAM support circuitry has to be designed to accommodate the refresh cycle.

The big advantage to DRAM is its low cost. It's inexpensive, so that makes the trade-off of having to deal with the refresh cycle worth it in most cases. Plus, the access time—a direct measure of performance in RAM chips—is reasonably good, with the best being about 60 to 70 nanoseconds.

Static RAM

Sometimes there is a need for fast access to RAM, faster than DRAM provides, and the engineer doesn't want to have to deal with refresh cycles in the design. Enter Static RAM (SRAM).

SRAM gets its name because its contents are static. That is, they do not require a refresh cycle like DRAM. A typical use for SRAM would be a processor cache where fast RAM is required with no refresh cycle overhead. It is not unusual for SRAMs to have access times of 20 or 30 nanoseconds—2 to 3 times as fast as DRAMs.

Of course, we all know in the world of computers that we can't have everything. The downside to SRAMs is its high cost. You won't find any commercial computers out there with main memory implemented in SRAM; it would simply be too costly. In fact, it's quite costly to build the large Level 2 processor caches found in most high-end PC servers.

EDO RAM

There is a relatively new type of RAM available that is sort of a compromise between DRAM and SRAM. It is called Enhanced Data Output (EDO) RAM.

EDO RAM has an output buffer that allows the chip to accept the next address while still holding the previous data result on the data bus. It makes the data available to be read for a longer period of time before it has to be refreshed. This gives it an edge over conventional DRAM in performance.

EDO RAM is getting a lot of use in computers currently because of its low cost and increased performance over conventional DRAM.

Error Protection and Correction

As with all computer hardware, something will eventually malfunction. What happens to data that is stored in a RAM chip when that happens? Does it just get used anyway? Or, for that matter, do RAM chips ever make mistakes?

It is possible for a RAM chip to experience problems, which are referred to as a soft or a hard device error. A soft error is often caused by a temporary loss of charge in a DRAM cell, which causes data to be stored incorrectly in that cell. However, subsequent attempts might store data just fine in that cell. A hard error is a physical failure in a RAM chip that prevents data from being stored in one or more locations.

Fortunately, there are error correction schemes in place to help guard against data corruption when something goes wrong, two of which are parity and ECC. When a malfunction occurs, either you don't know about it because the problem was corrected on-the-fly, or the system halts with a memory error message.

Parity

One early method of memory error protection was parity. The simplest technique of all, it is very common and, as you might expect, has some limitations. For example, it can only detect an odd number of bit errors. Furthermore, it cannot isolate and correct the data bit that is in error. However, if a parity error occurs, it causes the system to halt, rather than letting it continue to use bad data.

ECC

ECC memory is a relatively straightforward way to check for data errors and to correct data on-the-fly. Basically, an ECC scheme involves adding some redundancy to the data so the original data can be duplicated if some of it is missing. How much data can be recovered is a direct result of how complex the ECC algorithm is. It is not uncommon for a computer to have an ECC implementation that will detect single- and double-bit errors, and correct single-bit errors with no interruption in operation.

For your Windows NT and BackOffice applications, consider a computer that incorporates ECC or some other approach that will check and correct memory errors on-the-fly.

Memory Packaging

There are a few different ways RAM is packaged for you to use it. In the good old days, RAM consisted of chips you plugged into the motherboard. These days, however, commercial PCs have gotten away from using chips. Two of the most common forms of memory packaging are Single Inline Memory Modules (SIMMs) and Dual Inline Memory Modules (DIMMs).

SIMM

SIMMs are the most commonly available packages for memory. They have been around for years and find their home in many different manufacturers' computers. Just take a look at the memory advertisements in any computer magazine, and you'll get a feel for how many SIMMs there are out there.

One major advantage of SIMMs is their compatibility across multiple systems. In other words, SIMMs are usually sold as the industry standard. Problem is, there are multiple standards in place. So while a particular SIMM may work in computers within a manufacturer's product line, it may not work in another manufacturer's product. However, it does make things a bit easier.

Another advantage of SIMMs (and DIMMs alike) is that they are easy to handle and install. Their convenient packaging makes quick work of upgrading memory or replacing defective modules.

DIMM

Somewhat newer to the market, DIMMs are finding their way into high-end PC-based servers. DIMMs offer a couple of advantages over SIMMs.

DIMMs consume significantly less power. SIMMs operate at 5 volts and DIMMs operate at 3.3 volts. Because of the lower voltage, DIMMs consume approximately 50 percent power, and they generate significantly less heat than SIMMs. Less heat and power translates into an improvement in overall system reliability and availability.

DIMMs also provide larger memory capacities. For example, let's say SIMM technology was used in a server's memory design, and the total system memory capacity was 1GB. The switch to DIMMs might increase total system memory capacity to 2GB and allow for growth to 4GB in the future.

Some might argue that reuse of existing SIMMs for memory upgrades justifies using SIMMs in newer, faster servers based on state-of-the-art CPUs such as the Pentium Pro. For optimal performance, however, these servers often require memory with a minimum access time of 60 nanoseconds. Because the access time of the majority of SIMMs now on the market is 70 nanoseconds or slower, the need for DIMMs is beginning to grow.

Virtual Memory in Windows NT

Virtual memory is a key component of Windows NT. The proper design and implementation of the virtual memory (VM) Manager are important parts of the overall success of Windows NT. Virtual memory is a major portion of the operating system that lies at the very core (no pun intended) of all NT's memory management.

So what, exactly, is virtual memory and the VM Manager? And how does it relate to BackOffice applications?

While an exhaustive discussion of virtual memory and VM concepts is outside the scope of this chapter, it is important to get an overview of the concept, so you understand how it relates to Windows NT. If you care to delve deeper into the subject, there are various additional resources available on the subject.

What Is Virtual Memory?

According to Webster's Dictionary, the word *virtual* means, "being so in effect or essence, although not in actual fact or name." You know what memory is—physical memory, that is. It's those RAM chips you can never seem to get enough of. So virtual memory is a special type of memory in Windows NT that is effectively there, but not physically there.

The idea of virtual memory has been around for a long while. The first machine to use VM was introduced around 1959, although the concept didn't get popular until about 10 years later with the creation of the Multics operating system. Ever since, there has been a need to run programs that were larger than the available physical memory—a capability that virtual memory buys you—so the mainframe and minicomputer worlds have been using and refining the concept. When the engineers at Microsoft embarked upon the design of Windows NT, they drew upon much of this knowledge and included a powerful and flexible VM Manager.

The reason to use virtual memory is so that the operating system can actually address more memory than what physically resides on the computer. Remember the DOS PCs that had only 640KB of RAM? The memory installed in the computer was exactly what DOS saw, and the programs had only 640KB available on which to run. Although there were eventually some products that helped work around this characteristic, there was no real concept of virtual memory in DOS. In stark contrast, there's no way you'll have enough physical RAM to directly support all the memory needs of a complex operating system like Windows NT. In fact, each individual process that runs under NT is allocated a 4GB virtual memory address space, 2GB for the system use and 2GB for the user's use. That's a lot! This allocation occurs regardless of whether your machine is configured with a humble 16MB or a lofty 2GB of RAM, so you can see that the concept of virtual memory is absolutely essential for an operating system like NT.

Virtual memory is also an enabling technology that opens the door for the existence of a multitasking operating system. Why? Because you can handle addressing more memory than you really have, why not go ahead and run a bunch of programs instead of just one program that is larger than physical memory? That is precisely what happens in Windows NT and in dozens of other multitasking operating systems.

Benefits of Using Virtual Memory

Employing virtual memory in the design of Windows NT yields several important benefits, including those mentioned here.

First, memory can be addressed that exceeds the size of available memory. Figure 6.1 illustrates how this is accomplished.

Figure 6.1.
Pages in the virtual memory address space are mapped to page frames in physical memory.

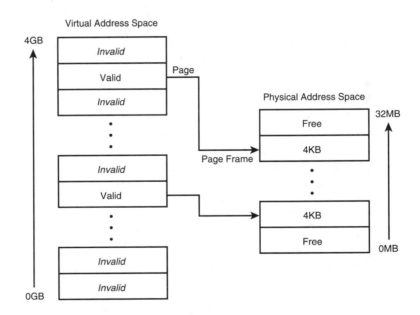

Physical memory is divided into 4KB chunks called *page frames*. Virtual memory is divided into 4KB chunks called *pages*. Basically, the pages fit into the page frames, using sort of a plug-in metaphor. That is, any page from virtual memory can be placed into any available page frame in physical memory.

A second benefit of virtual memory is efficiency of memory use, which yields performance improvements. Figure 6.2 shows an example of this efficiency in the form of memory sharing.

Figure 6.2.
*Physical memory
page frames can be
shared among
multiple processes
in virtual memory.*

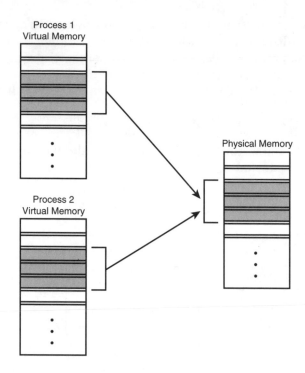

For example, let's say you're running two copies of a program, each in separate processes. For the shareable parts of code, the VM Manager simply maps the proper virtual address space of each process to the same page frame in physical memory, instead of making two copies in physical memory. While in reality you may not actually need to run two entire copies of the same program very often, you often will need to run multiple instances of *components* of a program's code. This capability, in turn, lends itself to code reusability and modularity. Hopefully, you begin to see the benefit.

Paging

In the previous section, I mentioned that any virtual memory page could be placed into any *available* page frame in physical memory. What happens when there are no more page frames available? The situation is bound to occur, because our virtual memory space is much larger than our physical memory space.

What happens is simple. When a page frame is needed in physical memory, and there are none available, the VM Manager steps in to decide which page frame is going to have its contents emptied to make room for the new page. When the contents of physical memory are emptied, they are saved to a *backing store*, usually a disk drive. This emptying and saving to disk is called *paging*. As you might expect, pages can be moved from memory to disk and from disk to memory—paging out and paging in, respectively.

The whole notion of when to page, how much to page, which page frames get paged, and so on is the subject of a much more in-depth discussion. For our purposes, it's sufficient to say that the engineers at Microsoft have spent a lot of time and effort to make the VM Manager do the right thing at the right time.

Disk Caching and Memory

One area where memory use is prevalent in Windows NT is caching. Disk caching is present to improve disk I/O performance, and this section discusses two caching options available on a Windows NT system: the NT system Cache and hardware-based caching controllers.

Windows NT System Cache

Windows NT has a built-in software cache called the *system Cache*. The system Cache is a chunk of memory set aside to buffer data for the disk and, interestingly enough, the LAN subsystems of NT.

The memory used for the cache is memory that is not used by active system processes. Fortunately, you don't have to worry about setting the cache size, because it is dynamically managed by NT. The actual size of the cache fluctuates, depending on how much memory is available in the system, how much disk I/O is being requested, and other variables that NT manages. If you graph the Memory:Cache Bytes counter with NT Performance Monitor, you will see this dynamic sizing as disk activity occurs. Figure 6.3 depicts this behavior.

In Figure 6.3, Windows NT is performing an XCOPY on several files. In this particular system, which has 48MB of RAM, the system Cache has a baseline size of around 10MB.

At the beginning of the copy (toward the left of the graph), the system was idle. Then the copy started, and NT decided it needed to increase the system Cache a bit. At one point during the operation, the cache peaked out at just over 20MB.

The memory allocated to the system Cache is reclaimed toward the right of the graph when the copy operation completes.

Figure 6.3.
*The system Cache
in Windows NT
dynamically
adjusts to varying
demands.*

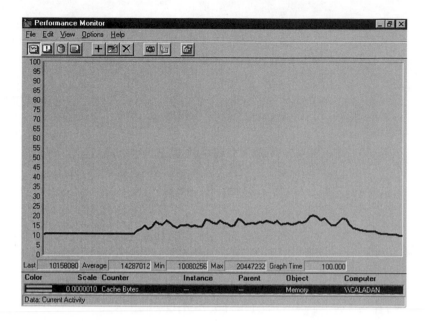

The thing to remember here is that Windows NT is giving all this memory to the cache because it's there to give. In other words, this machine is not experiencing memory pressure from any memory-hungry BackOffice applications. Because NT is configured to optimize the way it handles memory, the extra memory is allocated to the system Cache.

However, if memory was not there to give, NT would not be able to enlarge the cache unless it paged memory out of the working set of other processes. Whether NT will favor the cache over processes, or favor processes over cache, is determined by the setting shown in Figure 6.4.

Figure 6.4.
*You can adjust NT
Server so it will
tend to page the
system Cache
before system
processes.*

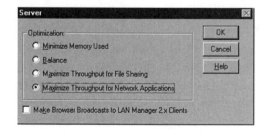

You find the Maximize Throughput for Network Applications setting in the Network applet in the Control Panel, as illustrated in Figure 6.4.

From the Control Panel, start the Network applet. Click the Services tab, highlight the Server icon, and click the Properties button. A dialog box appears that gives you some radio-button options; click Maximize Throughput for Network Applications. Selecting this option helps NT make decisions when choosing what to page to disk when it needs physical memory.

If you choose Maximize Throughput for Network Applications, the VM Manager will tend to page the system Cache before paging system processes. Use this setting for running BackOffice applications on Windows NT Server. You could think of it as the setting that maximizes throughput for client/server applications.

If you choose Maximize Throughput for File Sharing, just the opposite will be in effect. This setting is most useful for using NT as a file server, rather than as an application server.

The Balance option is available for NetBEUI installations, and Minimize Memory Used exists for minimal memory configurations. Assuming you are configuring a server, you probably won't use these two options, because you likely won't be using just NetBEUI, and you should be using more than the minimum amount of memory for your server.

Using Hardware-Based Caching

In high performance servers, an option often available is a caching disk controller, which is a fast disk controller with some amount of fast RAM dedicated specifically for disk caching.

An example of such a controller I have worked with is a PCI RAID controller with 4MB of onboard battery-backed RAM cache. A controller like this can form the foundation of a strong disk subsystem for your server. If you have a lot of disk I/O needs, something like this may be your answer.

The onboard cache in these controllers is a dedicated disk cache, used for any drives connected to the controller. This dedicated cache is in addition to the system Cache that NT is already allocating. Knowing that, some of you may be wondering if it's such a good idea to have double caching like that—one cache on the controller and another cache in Windows NT. The answer is a resounding yes, because each adds its own benefits to overall system performance.

As you might imagine, the cache on the disk controller is quite fast. It has direct access to the data as it passes through the controller and is way more efficient than the NT system Cache. However, being only 4MB (compared with peaks of 20+MB for the system Cache), it definitely will not be able to hold as much cache data as the system Cache. Therefore, the system Cache might be better in some cases, but having both there is still beneficial. Still, with this extra cache, you might want to set the Maximize Throughput for File Sharing option and let Windows NT tend to page that system Cache, so you're not wasting system memory on it when your system processes need the memory more.

Finally, assuming your controller is "intelligent," it can boost performance even more. An intelligent controller is able to apply some logic to improve the efficiency of how data is read from and written to the disk. It can also optimize the order in which I/O commands are executed as they are passed down from the operating system. The bottom line is that all the characteristics of a well-designed caching disk controller combine to form a good synergy with Windows NT.

Monitoring Memory Usage with Performance Monitor

There will be questions about memory that at one time or another will require you to use Performance Monitor. As you have seen, the topic of memory in a Windows NT system is not entirely straightforward. However, if you're interested in the best first counters to look at, see Tables 6.1 and 6.2.

Table 6.1. Memory-related objects in Performance Monitor.

Object Name	Description
Memory	Contains counters pertaining to memory usage in NT
Paging File	Contains two counters pertaining to the size of the page file
Process	Contains counters pertaining to each and every process running in NT

There are dozens of counters included in these objects. Table 6.2 contains some useful counters to get you going.

Table 6.2. Memory-related counters in Performance Monitor.

Object Name	Counter	Description
Memory	Available Bytes	The amount of virtual memory in the system available for use.
Memory	Cache Bytes	Size of the Windows NT system Cache. Note that the system Cache buffers data for both the disk and LAN. This memory is not in use by active processes.
Memory	Pages/sec	Indicates overall paging activity—the rate at which pages are written to or read from the disk. This is the main counter to watch if you are concerned about memory pressure and excessive paging.
Memory	System Cache Resident Bytes	The number of bytes that the system Cache currently has resident in main memory. You can monitor this to see how much memory the system Cache is taking up.
Paging File	% Usage	Shows what percentage of the page file is in use. Could indicate a need to increase your page file if the number is high.
Process	Working Set	Shows the number of bytes in the working set of the selected process (instance). A working set of memory is memory that was recently used by threads in the process—that is, the set of memory with which the process is currently working.

BackOffice Product Requirements

Let me set your expectations before reading on, because I cannot choose for you the correct amount of memory for your server. I can, however, give you some food for thought and hopefully steer your thinking in the right direction so you can make the best choice.

This section provides some general thoughts to bear in mind when choosing memory for your server. I throw out my personal views on memory strategy for each BackOffice application. Some ideas may be obvious, but if nothing else, it's always good to reinforce what you already know to be true.

Choosing the Right Amount of RAM

Microsoft BackOffice applications can use any amount of RAM you throw at them. Anywhere from the generally recommended minimum of 32MB up to 512MB, 1GB, or whatever your server hardware can support, BackOffice will gladly chew up your memory.

It's important to understand how to choose the right amount of RAM for your system. How do you go about it? Here are some suggestions to bear in mind.

Windows NT Server Needs Memory

Windows NT needs a certain minimum amount of RAM for itself—usually in the neighborhood of 16MB for Windows NT Server v4.0. This 16MB is made up of the different Windows NT processes such as CSRSS, LLSSRV, LOCATOR, LSASS, RPCSS, SCM, SERVICES, SMSS, SPOOLSS, SYSTEM, and WINLOGON. Also included in this 16MB minimum will be some memory allocated to the NT system Cache.

Some BackOffice applications, such as SQL Server and Exchange Server, don't actually use the NT system Cache for disk I/O, because they have their own cache, called a database buffer. Even though the network-caching aspect of the system Cache remains useful, it is not nearly as beneficial to the system as the database buffers. Naturally, you want more memory allocated to the buffers, not to the system Cache.

You can minimize the NT system Cache size by selecting Maximize Throughput for Network Applications, as shown in Figure 6.4. With this setting, NT will tend to page memory used by the system Cache before it will page memory used by processes such as your BackOffice applications.

> Windows NT Server automatically chooses Maximize Throughput for File Sharing when it is first installed. However, the Setup program of the different BackOffice applications may automatically change it to Maximize Throughput for Network Applications for you.
>
> **TIP**

The BackOffice Application Needs Memory

Let's look at an example of a typical BackOffice application, Exchange Server, to understand the type of memory requirements you might encounter when configuring a server with BackOffice.

There are four main processes that comprise Microsoft Exchange Server. Depending on the configuration of your Exchange Server software, there may be more, but these four are the basic components that all Exchange Servers will have. They run as Windows NT services. The following list gives the service name, followed by the description:

- MSExchangeIS—The Information Store
- MSExchangeMTA—The Message Transfer Agent
- MSExchangeDS—The Directory Service
- MSExchangeSA—The System Attendant

These all require some amount of memory at start-up time—usually 10–15MB just to start these four services. Furthermore, as the system runs and is put under more stress, these will tend to use more memory, depending on what is happening in the system. This is especially true of the Information Store. If you have adequate memory in your system, it is not uncommon to see the Store's working set jump to 50MB with a couple hundred users.

Fortunately, you can monitor the memory usage for all these processes with the Process object in Windows NT Performance Monitor. That way, you can get an exact picture of how much memory each service has in its working set in your specific installation. For a listing of some useful Performance Monitor counters, including the working set, see the section earlier in this chapter, "Monitoring Memory Usage with Performance Monitor."

There also might be services running for other Exchange Server options you have installed, such as Internet Mail Connector, Key Manager, MS Mail Connector, or Directory Synchronization (DXA). These require memory too—at least 1–5MB each.

Database Buffers Need Memory

Continuing with the example, the Exchange Server buffer cache is comprised of a number of 4KB database buffers. Disk I/O and the amount of memory in your machine are related. Simply put, if you have more memory to allocate as buffer cache, the disk I/O will go down, and vice versa. This is definitely a key aspect of performance, and it will figure into your decision of how much memory to put in the system.

Look at an example of how additional memory might be allocated to the various parts of the system, especially the database buffers. The following two tables illustrate how the Exchange Optimizer—a tool included with Exchange Server to initially configure the many parameters in Exchange—allocates memory as you add memory to the computer.

For example, say you want to support 200 simultaneous users on your server. They will use private and public stores, and there are 800 total users in the organization. Based on recommendations from Microsoft Exchange Optimizer, Table 6.3 gives an idea of how memory might be allocated to the three main consumers of memory in Microsoft Exchange Server: the NT Server and Exchange Server system processes, the Exchange Server database buffers, and the Exchange Server directory buffers.

Table 6.3. An example of Exchange Server memory usage.

Memory	System Processes	Database Buffers	Directory Buffers
32MB	29MB	2.5MB	0.5MB
64MB	47MB	14MB	3MB
128MB	71MB	53MB	4MB
256MB	119MB	133MB	4MB

Although the exact mix changes somewhat, depending on your Exchange Server configuration—the number of users supported, whether you use private and public stores, and so on—Exchange makes good use of the RAM you give it. For example, if you have 256MB of memory for your server, or more, Exchange will put it to work.

To illustrate this, take the example one step further. Say you want to support 600 simultaneous users per server, using public and private stores, and there are 5,000 total users in the organization. Table 6.4 shows how the memory allocation might change to accommodate these changes. Again, this is based on recommendations made by the Microsoft Exchange Optimizer.

Table 6.4. An example of Exchange Server memory usage supporting more users.

Memory	System Processes	Database Buffers	Directory Buffers
32MB	31MB	0.8MB	0.2MB
64MB	56MB	7MB	1MB
128MB	81MB	39MB	8MB
256MB	128MB	106MB	22MB

See how memory is shifted to system processes when there is less system memory? And as you increase system memory, Exchange Server puts it to work in the buffers and in the system processes to prevent paging. Plus, with more total users in the organization, the directory buffers get additional memory. In contrast (shown earlier in Table 6.2), the directory buffers peak at 4MB with fewer users. Perhaps this helps demonstrate the importance of memory to the Exchange buffer cache and to the NT system processes.

Anything Else You Run Needs Memory

We've accounted for NT Server and BackOffice applications. But what about other memory consumers?

Still using Exchange as an example, if your Exchange Server functions as a domain controller—either Backup or Primary—it will have to use a certain amount of memory to support that function. The NT Server SAM and its database take up some memory as well. Also, if you are logged in to the NT Console of your Exchange Server, that takes some extra memory. Each command prompt requires memory. Any console application you might run, such as NT Performance Monitor, also requires memory and imposes CPU overhead.

Bottom line: You want to stay off the server console if possible. Don't even log on; just let Windows NT Server boot and sit at the logon prompt. The Exchange Server processes start automatically and without any intervention on your part. In fact, with servers handling hundreds of users, you should consider dedicating the machine explicitly to Exchange Server. For most functions an Exchange Server performs, there isn't really a need to log on anyway—just let it serve.

CPUs or Memory?

This discussion of memory usage brings us to an interesting question that ties together concepts about CPU utilization and memory utilization.

Do I add CPUs (or get a faster one), or do I add memory? Unfortunately, the answer is, "it depends." You knew I was going to say that, right?

You have to determine where your system is constrained before adding anything—be it memory, CPU, faster disks, or faster network controllers. If you don't know where the bottleneck is, you are probably not getting the most benefit out of investing in new equipment. In other words, if your CPU resource is not the constraining element in the system, adding more CPUs won't help.

Although there are always exceptions, a rule of thumb with Windows NT is that in memory-constrained situations, adding memory helps more than getting a faster CPU or adding additional CPUs. This is especially true of systems with less than 32MB RAM, but it also applies to systems with large amounts of RAM. If there's memory pressure, most often manifested by a lot of paging activity in the Pages/sec counter, chances are you need to add memory to the system. Windows NT needs room to work, and having an inadequate amount of physical memory—no matter how much virtual memory is available —will squeeze the life right out of NT.

Conversely, if there is little memory pressure, there is virtually no paging occurring. If no other system components are presenting a bottleneck, and if other memory indicators look good—% Committed Bytes in Use is less than 70 percent and available memory is above 10MB—you would probably benefit from increasing your CPU resource. This is especially applicable if you are seeing a high value for the % Processor Time counter (for example, 90 percent). At that point, you can either get a faster CPU or add CPUs if your computer supports multiple processors.

BackOffice Applications

Exchange Server and SQL Server are both similar in that they employ a large relational database, and they are engineered as multiprocess, multithread applications. They are arguably the premier BackOffice applications, and they are able to take advantage of all the high-powered hardware you throw at them. Both can definitely take advantage of large amounts of RAM, especially SQL Server, depending upon the number of users they will be required to support; 256MB is not unreasonable. Unless the demands on these applications are small, I do not recommend requiring the computer they run on to perform other tasks. Check to see that Maximize Throughput for Network Applications is enabled with these applications.

Internet Information Server (IIS) has one main purpose: to serve data via HTML to users connecting with a browser. Based on that premise, IIS's requirements are most naturally like that of a file server. File servers typically are, by definition, disk and I/O intensive. Given a powerful CPU for the IIS computer, the disk subsystem is likely to become the bottleneck first. Adding memory to the system will probably alleviate the problem, up to a point anyway. As with SQL Server and Exchange Server, 256MB is not unreasonable for an IIS machine that will be managing tens of thousands of hits and thousands of users per day. Again, much depends on the demands that will be placed on the system. Check to see that Maximize Throughput for File Sharing is enabled.

SMS and SNA Server are more passive applications, with completely different goals than any of the other BackOffice members. While they have multiple threads and multiple processes, the nature of their function most likely will not exploit huge amounts of RAM. The memory requirements are a bit less stringent for these applications than for the other BackOffice applications. Check to see that Maximize Throughput for Network Applications is enabled.

Summary

This chapter covers several topics related to memory usage in Windows NT and BackOffice. It starts with a discussion of memory technologies that forms a foundation for discussion of memory usage. Then you learned about virtual memory and were introduced to some concepts germane to NT memory management. From there, we discussed how disk caching affects memory usage and how you can use Windows NT Performance Monitor to monitor memory usage. Finally, the chapter concludes with some ideas to remember when planning the memory requirements of your server, with a specific example using Exchange Server.

Memory is a key component of any server. Having the correct amount of memory and the right type of memory is crucial to proper performance of BackOffice applications and Windows NT itself. After reading this chapter, you should be able to invest some quality time at your server, understanding just how the memory is being used. And from there, you should be able to decide what needs to be done to make things better.

CHAPTER 7

Monitoring the System

No matter how well configured a server is, vigilant monitoring is vital for continued performance. The system resource usage of the BackOffice products will change as time passes, so an initial acceptable amount of allocation may become unacceptable over time. The only way this condition can be determined is by doing routine checkups of the health of the server.

One common mistake is to assume that because the resources of a particular machine are enormous, they will never be exhausted. The golden rule of software is that it will always expand to fill all available resources. There was a time when 16MB of RAM was considered a luxury, because most systems were being shipped with 2MB of RAM or less.

Performance problems creep up as usage increases. As users are added to the system and their level of use increases with familiarity, the resources required will increase proportionally. An increase in the user base will see an increase in performance demands, and the only way to accurately detect this is proper performance monitoring.

By the time users complain about performance, it is already too late. They are irritated and feel as if the problems should never have happened, which is true.

If the systems were properly monitored, the problems would not have occurred. Any problems or changes in the utilization of a system should be unknown to the users. They should continue to have a responsive system that meets their needs. This is possible with proper monitoring and correction of situations as they occur.

Using Performance Monitor

This section details the use of Performance Monitor, which is essential to monitoring the health of a BackOffice server. It is in your best interest as the system administrator to become an expert with Performance Monitor and use it liberally to monitor BackOffice systems.

Performance Monitor Chart View

The Chart view, selected from the View menu, is the main window for viewing interactive statistics. Chart maintains a time-based graph, updated every polling interval, of the statistics from the selected objects and counters.

Each line in the chart is color coded for ease of recognition. Because there are many different objects that can be monitored at different times, the chart allows the user to save and restore the setting. The setting can include things like remote system settings, so setting up proper graphs to monitor a certain area and then saving them to disk can save a lot of time when viewing the same charts again at a later time. Figure 7.1 shows an example of the Performance Monitor Chart view with several items being viewed.

Figure 7.1.
Viewing several items at once with the Chart view can give a better look at system activity.

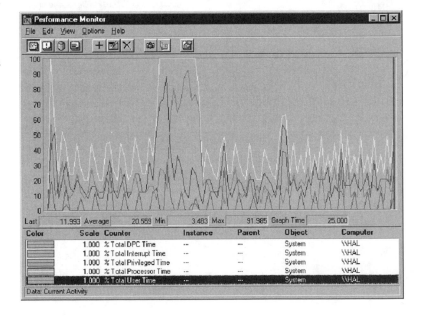

Adding Items to the Chart

To add an item to the chart, either click the Add button or select Add To Chart from the Edit menu. (The Add button is marked with a plus sign.) Choosing Add brings up a dialog box that sets the parameters for the item to add.

When an item is added to the chart, several things can be set. One is the remote system, which determines the origination of the numbers for the chart. Clicking the selection button located beside the Computer field will bring up the Select Computer dialog box, where a remote computer can be selected.

The Objects field lists the general objects for which statistics can be gathered. The objects in the list will depend on the software installed in the system, because any software can report to Performance Monitor. The contents of the object list will also depend on the system selected.

The Counter field identifies the statistic to track. Select the proper statistic for the object that should be tracked. The contents of this list depend on the object selected.

The Instance field also depends on the object selected. For the Processor object, for instance, the instance list will contain one numerical entry for each processor in the system, starting with zero. For the SQL Server Users object, the Instance field will contain a list of current SQL Server users.

Details about the display of the statistic are also selected from this dialog box. The color of the line, as well as its width and style, can be selected. The scale of the graph is also selected here, which greatly affects the display of the statistics. If you select a large scale, some statistics will appear as if the object being monitored is always at a 100 percent level. It is necessary to adjust the scale appropriately.

Chart Options

There are several options that can be configured for the operation of the chart. You do this from the Chart Options dialog box (see Figure 7.2), which you get to either by choosing Chart from the Options menu or by clicking the Options button on the toolbar.

Figure 7.2.
The Chart Options dialog box is used to set viewing properties.

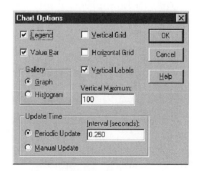

The style of the graph is one of the options that can be selected from this dialog box. The available styles are graph and histogram. Graph is a line graph; histogram is a bar chart of the current level of the statistics. A line graph is usually more useful, because it shows the levels over a short period of time.

The polling interval can also be selected from the Chart Options dialog box. This determines the length of time between polling the operating system for current statistics. Bear in mind that the more often the polling, the higher the load will be on the system. For remote computers, the more often the polling, the higher the network traffic.

The Alert View

The Alert view is one of the most useful features of Performance Monitor for the administrator. Alerts can be triggered on any Performance Monitor statistic. Not only are alerts logged in the Alert log, but they can also trigger programs, such as a pager program that notifies the administrator about a dangerous system condition.

To get to the Alert view, choose Alert from the View menu or press Ctrl+A.

Adding an Alert

To add an alert, choose Add To Alert from the Edit menu, click the Add button, or press Ctrl+I from the Alert window to bring up the Add To Alert dialog box.

When adding an alert, several things can be configured, including computer, object, statistic, and instance. Realize that it makes no sense to place alerts on certain statistics. For example, because the processor time will rise and fall routinely, triggering an alert on processor time for high processor utilization will start triggering alerts whenever the system is doing anything.

The most important part is the Alert If section, which sets the thresholds for the alert. The meaning of the entry depends on the object selected, but for every object, the threshold is set to establish an alert if that object is ever over`or under the administrator-defined threshold. This is most effective with percentages.

If an alert occurs, it will be logged. There is also the option to have a program run and log the alert when it is triggered, such as purge programs and programs designed to notify the administrator. For instance, when the transaction log on a certain SQL Server database fills, a program could be run to dump the transaction log to disk to prevent any application errors.

The final selection in the Add To Alert window is the color of the alert. This is only useful for display; it has no other effect.

Working with Alert Options

Alert options are accessed by choosing Alert from the Options menu while viewing alerts in the Alert window or by clicking the Options button. Alert options can also be accessed by pressing Ctrl+O while in the Alert window.

Performance Monitor can be set to switch to the Alert view whenever an alert occurs. This is generally helpful only if an administrator is constantly monitoring Performance Monitor.

The Log in Application Log option will cause alerts to be sent to the Application log, which can be viewed with the Event Viewer. This provides a uniform interface to view all system events, including alerts.

Performance Monitor can be instructed to send a network alert to any selected workstations when an alert occurs. This can be helpful for setting up each system to be monitored with Performance Monitor running and instructing that system to notify the administrator. To do this, check the Send Network Message check box and then specify the Network Workstation Name to send the message.

The final thing that can be configured in the Alert Options dialog box is the polling interval. This falls under the same rules as the interval on the chart: The more frequent the interval, the more of a drain it will be on system resources. This is especially true for remote servers. The default value is 5 seconds, but a value of 60 seconds is probably adequate.

The Log Function

The Log function of Performance Monitor is used to store historical data. It takes a snapshot of the system status and stores it in the log file at regular intervals.

Unlike the other windows in Performance Monitor, which use a detail level of object, counter, and instance, the Log stores all information about the entire object for each interval. For this reason, log files can become large and consume a lot of disk space quickly if several objects are monitored over a large period of time.

Adding Entries to the Log

Entries are added to the log in much the same way they are added to the Chart and to the alerts. You get to the Add To Log dialog box by either selecting Add from the Edit menu or clicking the Add button.

The only things that need to be selected from this dialog box are the computer to collect from and the object. The computer is selected in the same way it was for the other windows; clicking the button beside the Computer field will display a list of computers.

When the object is selected, all counters and instances from the object are selected for monitoring. Note that selecting many objects will result in a large log file and will cause a significant performance drop during data collection.

Log Options

The log options are very simple; there are only two of them. The file that the log should be written to is the first option. If the file does not exist, it will be created. The second is the update interval. This can be set to manual update, which requires the user to press a button every time the log statistics should be updated. See Figure 7.3 for the Log Options dialog box.

Figure 7.3.
Use the Log Options dialog box to change the settings for the Performance Monitor log.

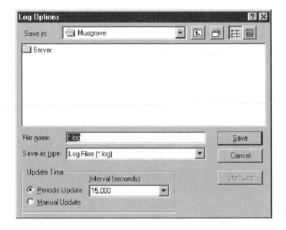

The log will not actually start collecting data until the Start Log button is clicked. Once this has been done, log data is collected until the same button is clicked again. (It should be marked Stop Log at that time.)

The Report View

The Report view provides a convenient way to view current statistics in a report-page format. Sometimes this view is more helpful than a graph, because it shows only current values in a numerical format. The report can also be exported to a text file for import into a Word document or Excel workbook.

Adding Entries to the Report

To add entries to a report, select Add from the Edit menu, click the Add button, or press Ctrl+I to access the Add To Report dialog box.

Once this is displayed, select the object, counter, and instance as you would in the Chart and Alert dialog boxes. The source computer can also be selected, if reporting off a computer other than the current machine.

Report Options

The Report Options dialog box can be displayed by selecting Report from the Options menu or by pressing Ctrl+O from the Report window. The only option that can be configured with the reports is the update interval (see Figure 7.4). The same rules apply to the update interval in the other Performance Monitor windows.

Figure 7.4.
The Report Options dialog box is used to change items in the Performance Monitor report.

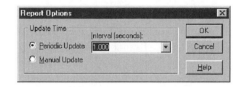

Configuring Options in Performance Monitor

There are several options that affect Performance Monitor on a global level. These options affect all the windows and have a dramatic effect on the format of the data presented.

The Data From Setting

The Data From setting under the Options menu is of particular importance. After data is collected using the Log function, it can be replayed here for analysis with the other tools (see Figure 7.5). Logs can be viewed at a later date or from a machine that is not directly connected to the machine that is going to display the performance data.

Figure 7.5.
Data can come either from the live system or from a log file created with Performance Monitor.

Display Settings

The display settings are accessed from the Options menu. They control the format of the Performance Monitor window, not the operations of Performance Monitor. Table 7.1 lists the available display settings.

Table 7.1. Display settings options.

Option	Explanation
Menu and Title	Determines whether the menu and title are displayed.
Toolbar	Determines whether the toolbar will be displayed.
Status Bar	Determines whether the bottom status bar will be displayed.
Always On Top	If selected, Performance Monitor will remain on top of all the other windows.

Saving and Restoring Formats

The Save Workplace option saves the settings from all four views in Performance Monitor. This is useful for saving an entire set of dependent settings that take a lot of time to set up.

Triggering Events on System Thresholds

The capability to trigger alerts is probably the most powerful aspect of Performance Monitor, at least as far as network management is concerned. There are certain critical system thresholds, such as free disk space, that should not be ignored. If they are, problems can happen, so the ability to monitor them passively is very useful.

Using Alerts to Your Advantage

On a large network, setting too many alerts will lead to not noticing any of them. Instead of setting alerts on everything, make a list of the most critical statistics that affect the network and its applications. This will probably include items from the following list:

- Free drive space
- SQL Server tempdb space
- SQL Server transaction log space
- Logged-on users
- Free memory
- Network utilization

When the most critical system thresholds are determined, set up the Alert log to watch for those items. If *any* alerts occur, they will definitely be serious and require attention. Having too many alerts that are only light warnings leads to not taking alerts seriously.

Monitoring an Entire Network

When monitoring an entire network, attempting to do so from one machine will sometimes overload that machine and the network itself. It is sometimes better to configure each machine to monitor itself and to alert a central machine if a problem occurs. This distributes the workload of monitoring and reduces network traffic.

Monitoring the Local System

System performance is usually monitored with Performance Monitor. There are alternatives, such as using the `dir` command to check disk-space utilization or stored procedures in SQL Server, but Performance Monitor is the preferred method. It also has the advantage of coming with NT, so using it is convenient and fully integrated with the operating system.

There are various third-party commercial tools, as well as some free and shareware tools, that are available from the Internet. These tools are usually targeted at monitoring a specific area of interest, such as disk-space utilization or memory usage. In my experience, with proper setup, Performance Monitor will be adequate for all but the most extreme situations.

Performance Monitor is covered later in this chapter, along with the various methods for viewing and storing information. This section covers the various objects that can be monitored with Performance Monitor and their implications and effects in the BackOffice environment. As you will see later, Performance Monitor can not only show real-time statistics, but also can track trends over time, monitor other systems, and notify an administrator or event log if certain values pass a predefined threshold. Indeed, an administrator usually configures one Windows NT machine to monitor all the servers in his department or domain and routinely checks for conditions that may need attention.

There are literally hundreds of different statistics that can be viewed from within Performance Monitor, certainly more than could be covered here. What will be covered are the statistics most relevant to the BackOffice environment. Some statistics come directly from BackOffice products, while others are operating statistics that could have an effect on the operation of BackOffice products. You should explore the other options in Performance Monitor, because they could be useful in some circumstances.

First, a word on how the statistics are discussed here. In Performance Monitor, statistics are displayed alphabetically. This is not always the most meaningful order in which to discuss them, however, because some statistics are directly affected by others. Therefore, statistics are presented here in their meaningful order for discussion, not in the order they are shown in Performance Monitor. Some of these objects will be present in Performance Monitor only if a specific component is installed. For instance, the SQL Server objects will be present only if SQL Server is installed, and available statistics will differ by SQL Server version.

The three important concepts of Performance Monitor statistics are object, counter, and instance. An *object* is the general area of origin, such as processor, logical disk, or SQL Server. A *counter* is a specific area inside the object, such as free space for the logical disk object. The *instance* is the lowest level and represents a particular occurrence of an object and a counter. Continuing with the example, instance 0 of the Free Space counter for the logical disk object would represent the amount of free logical-disk space for the first disk. Some statistics do not include the instance variable if it has no meaning for the type of measurement.

The Processor Object

The Processor object shows statistics about the usage of the processor. On a multiprocessor system, each processor is viewed individually, by selection of the Processor instance (see Figure 7.6). If viewing a graph in real time, it is usually helpful to add a line to the chart for each processor in the system. The activity of one processor does not give an accurate representation of the system as a whole because work is spread out among all available processors. If the processor activity of all the processors is needed, look at the section about the System object, later in this chapter.

Figure 7.6.
This is the Add to Chart dialog box showing several counters for the Processor object.

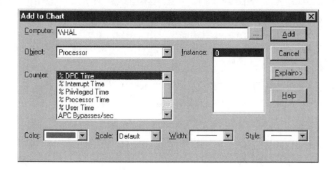

The status of the processor on a uniprocessor system gives a good general view of the system, as does a view of all the processors of a multiprocessor system. Activities such as swapping to disk and network transmission require processor time, as does almost any other activity on the system. Indeed, nearly every activity on the system will affect the processor, making the processor a unique object in that it can give an overview of the performance of a system.

At a glance, the activity of the processor can also be misleading. It is not uncommon for an otherwise lightly taxed system to have the processor usage hit about 90 percent for a few seconds every once in a while. The converse is also true; it is not uncommon for an otherwise unusable system to have periods of processor idle time, although at most times it has an overabundance of processes running. Unlike disk-space usage, a statistic that remains steady and generally will take only a glimpse to determine the status, processor utilization has to be considered over time.

Processor usage will also vary greatly depending on the time of the day. During periods of heavy user logon, such as first thing in the morning, the Primary Domain Controller of the master domain in a master domain model network will probably be very active. If its only responsibility is logon validation for the domain, it will be nearly idle for the next couple of hours. In an operating system that operates only during normal business hours (whatever those are), the servers will not be used very much at night, but could be heavily utilized during the day.

Considering this, even an average over a 24-hour period will not be a good representation of how usable a server is. Instead, computing average statistics for each hour should be considered, because this will show a more accurate represen-tation of how usable a server is at different times of the day. The log in Performance Monitor can be programmed to sample once per hour and can be left running for several days. Once this is done, the Chart view will show an accurate graph of system utilization throughout the time frame, at a granularity of one hour.

An important concept to understanding processor utilization is *idle time*. Idle time does not exist in a pure sense. Windows NT does not ever allow the processor to stop executing instructions at the constant rate determined by the internal CPU clock. What does a processor do when it has nothing useful to do? When Windows NT begins starting processes, it starts an *idle thread* for each processor in the system. The purpose of this thread is to actually waste time—that is, it will waste time until there is some real work to do in the system. Whenever processors are said to be idle, it means the system is executing the idle thread. The computation of *busy time* is actually a measure by the operating system of how much of the time is not spent in the idle thread. Measuring time doing useful activity would put a drain on the system at the time it has real work to do.

Another important concept regarding Performance Monitor and the Processor object is *elapsed time*. Most statistics that are represented by percentages are said to be a percentage of the elapsed time. What is the elapsed time? In Performance Monitor, there is a poll interval that determines how often Performance Monitor requests values from the system. That value will be the elapsed time for each statistic that uses it. In other words, if the poll interval is 5 seconds, Performance Monitor reports the processor to be busy 25 percent of the time—that is, the processor was not executing the idle loop 25 percent of the time over the last 5 seconds.

Percentage of Processor Time

The Percentage of Processor Time statistic represents how busy the processor was during the specific interval. As stated before, peaks and valleys are common, and utilization over time is important. This statistic is the best representation of the overall performance of the system. All the other statistics for the Processor object contribute to this statistic. See Figure 7.7 for a sample graph of the % Processor Time. When attempting to view the overall activity of the system, use this statistic. If a view of the entire system is needed without the detail presented by the Processor object, use the System object.

Figure 7.7.
*A sample
graph from the
% Processor Time
counter.*

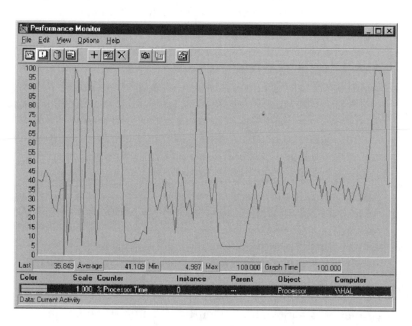

One contributor to the total processor time used is the polling by Performance Monitor to actually gather the statistics. A frequently made mistake is to set Performance Monitor to poll so often that it creates a drain on the system. When this happens, the system is overutilized, but there does not appear to be any one process doing the damage. This situation is easily avoided by setting the polling interval in Performance Monitor at a reasonable time. A reasonable time can be determined by monitoring the system on several occasions and decreasing the polling interval until you can tell a difference in performance.

Keep the polling interval light so as not to overload the system with statistics-gathering.

Percentage of User Time

The Percentage of User Time statistic (which appears onscreen as % User Time) represents the amount of time the system spent during the interval executing user-level application code (see Figure 7.8). This does not completely show how much of a drain an application is placing on the system, however, because an application can spend a great amount of time in system calls, which place a drain on the system but do not affect user time.

Figure 7.8.
A sample chart for % User Time.

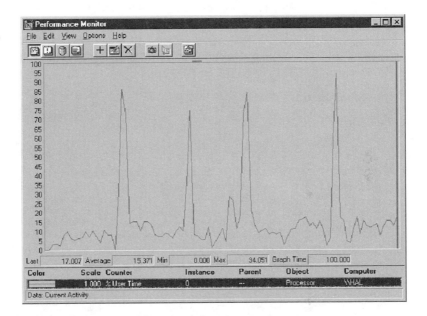

Notice that the % User Time does not have anything to do with logged-in users from the network. During execution of an application on the server, there is a distinction made between the two types of states it will move between, User and Privileged. An application uses Privileged time only when it is using a system service, no matter what user is logged into the system, even if the process is using the system account. Many server applications, such as those with BackOffice, will spend the majority of their time in Privileged time, because disk and network operations require system calls.

When a system switches from User mode to Privileged mode, it is referred to as a *context switch*.

Percentage of Privileged Time

Privileged Time is accumulated while an application is using a system resource. If an application requests data from a file, it must do so through a system call. During the request, the application is paused, and the operating system gathers the data on the application's behalf. Even though the operating system is performing the work, it is because of the application request, so the system credits the amount of time spent to the application. The distinction is kept between User and Privileged Time to aid in determining where performance bottlenecks are in a system. See Figure 7.9 for a sample chart of % Privileged Time.

Figure 7.9.
This is a
sample chart for
% Privileged
Time.

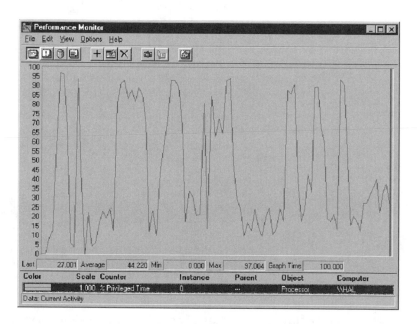

When a system is spending too much time performing system services on behalf of an application, instead of executing application code, there could be a problem on the system. Although it is not always the case, if a system is poorly tuned, it will spend a great deal of time in system services and not much in executing applications, which are generally unaffected by performance tuning.

NOTE

The distinction between User and Privileged Time began in the UNIX environment, where process statistics are tracked based on User, System, and Idle time. In the days of sharing mainframes, users and companies where actually billed based on the amount of CPU time used!

Why are applications unaffected by performance tuning? Actually, this statement is not entirely accurate. The amount of time spent by applications in the User mode is not usually affected by performance tuning. What are affected by performance tuning are things that would have been credited to system time, such as file access, network access, and memory swapping to disk. As a general rule, the less time an application spends executing system calls, the better, so most performance tuning can emphasize reducing time delivering system services.

Percentage of Interrupt Time

Interrupts are signals generated by hardware that tell the operating system that some action needs to be taken. For instance, when data is received on a communications port, a hardware interrupt is generated to let the operating system know that some action should be taken on the port. More commonly, when a disk request is sent to a disk controller, it will generate an interrupt when the request has been fulfilled. When the hardware interrupt is generated, the processor activates a predefined *interrupt service routine* (ISR). The Percentage Interrupt Time statistic (shown onscreen as % Interrupt Time) tracks the amount of time that a system spends in ISRs (see Figure 7.10).

Figure 7.10.
A sample chart showing % Interrupt Time. *As you can see, the system spends very little time in ISRs, compared to processor usage as a whole.*

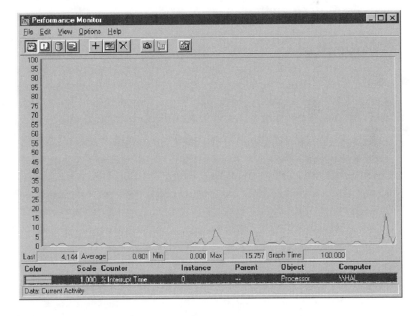

Interrupts are expensive events. When an interrupt occurs, the system goes through a context switch and has to set the process parameters for the ISR. The interrupt routines also execute at high priority, blocking other processes until they are finished servicing the interrupt. When an interrupt occurs, other interrupts are disabled until the servicing of that interrupt is complete. If there is an excessive number of hardware interrupts, system performance can be seriously degraded. This situation usually happens with older software that was not written with multitasking operating systems in mind, when constantly calling ISRs was the best way to accomplish tasks at hand.

> Disabling interrupts when an ISR is activated has been a long-standing part of the Intel processor line. There are debates about whether this is a good idea, but that technique has been used since the original 8086 processor, and remains to ensure backward application compatibility.

The semantics of ISRs can obviously cause serious performance problems in the system. Because of the ISR executing at high priority, some device drivers elect to use a *deferred procedure call* (DPC). Instead of doing all the processing necessary to complete the servicing of the hardware, such as retrieving data from a communications port, processing is set to occur later, after the initial ISR has completed. The DPC runs at a normal priority level and allows other interrupts and system processes to be continued.

Percentage of DPC Time

Deferred procedure calls are generated by interrupt service routines that elect to do the bulk of their processing apart from the ISR (see Figure 7.11). Doing this generally increases system performance, because ISRs run at high priority, and DPCs run at normal priority and fall under the domain of the process scheduler.

Because of extensive use of the DPC concept in Windows NT, the % DPC Time statistic can sometimes be more useful than the % Interrupt Time in determining how many hardware service requests are being responded to and generated. Like processor time, this statistic must be monitored over time because peaks are common. Disk-intensive applications like SQL Server are particularly affected by this, so this should be one of the first things checked to resolve performance issues in that application.

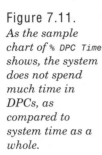

Figure 7.11.
*As the sample
chart of % DPC Time
shows, the system
does not spend
much time in
DPCs, as
compared to
system time as a
whole.*

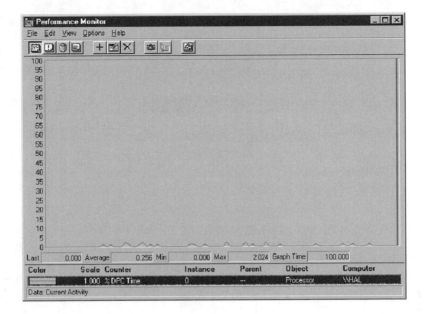

Interrupts/Sec

Sometimes when monitoring hardware interrupts, the percentage of time spent servicing hardware requests is not always adequate. This statistic shows the actual number of hardware interrupts that are occurring every second. Because this is not a percentage, each machine will have a different acceptable level, depending on hardware configuration and system usage. The best way to use this statistic is not only to monitor it over time (see Figure 7.12), but to make sure that there are notes about where the acceptable levels are, because a raw number is going to be meaningless.

There are several other processor statistics that can be monitored. Because they are part of the Processor object, they share the characteristic of normal peaks and valleys during operation. Monitoring over time will be the best way to determine average utilization.

The Memory Object

Other than the processor, memory has the single largest effect on the overall performance of a system. In the case of low memory, adding memory can sometimes increase realized performance more than adding a faster processor or more processors.

Figure 7.12.
*A sample chart
from* Interrupts/
sec. *Because this
number represents
system-specific
information, it
may be necessary
to watch a system
over a period of
time to determine
acceptable norms
for that system.*

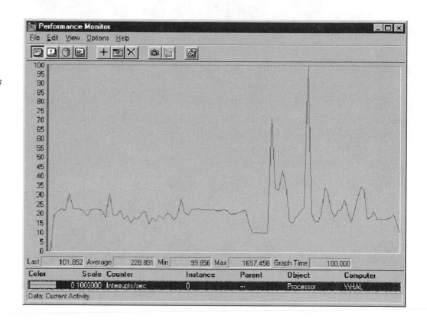

Unlike processor statistics, memory statistics are generally the exact value at the time of the sample, not an average over the poll interval. This is true even for percentage values in the Memory object. The exact memory usage at any given time is a helpful statistic, unlike the processor statistic that must be analyzed over time. Figure 7.13 shows some of the counters for the Memory object.

Figure 7.13.
*This Add to Chart
dialog box shows
the counters for the*
Memory *object.*

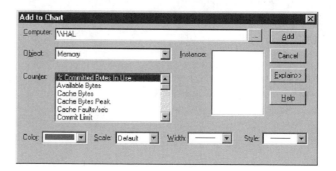

If memory has a spike in its usage, there is a problem. There should not be points in the system operating when the amount of memory being used reaches a critical value. If this situation occurs, either more memory is needed or there is an application or configuration problem.

An important concept when dealing with memory is committed versus uncommitted memory. When an application allocates memory, it can allocate that memory as *uncommitted,* which means that there is no physical memory, either in RAM or on disk, to back up the allocation. At a later time, the application can commit the memory. When the memory is *committed*, space must be allocated to help data in that memory.

Any amount of memory can be allocated as uncommitted, no matter how much real system memory is available. When the memory is committed, however, there must be real memory available to back up the allocation.

Available Bytes

`Available Bytes` is the amount of free memory available in the system (see Figure 7.14). There are several states of memory that can be considered free:

- ● Zeroed
- ● Free
- ● Standby

Figure 7.14.
A chart from the
`Available Bytes`
counter that was
taken as several
applications were
being loaded and
unloaded.

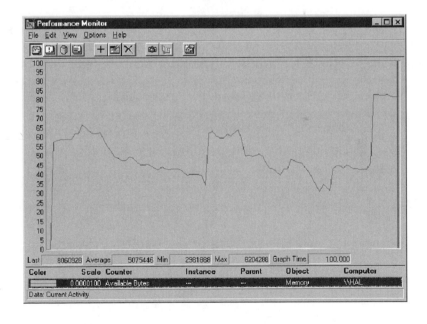

Zeroed memory is memory that the operating system has filled with all ASCII 0 values for the purpose of security and application integrity. The only memory that can actually be allocated to an allocation is zeroed. If there is not enough zeroed memory available, free or standby memory can be converted.

> If memory was not zeroed before being allocated to an application, one application could see the old data of another application. The other application may not be owned by the user that formerly used the memory area, and it may contain passwords or other sensitive data.

Free memory is memory that has been released to be reallocated to other applications, but has not yet been zeroed. *Standby memory* is application memory that has been removed from an application's working set and placed on disk, but is available to be reallocated to the application as demanded.

Commit Limit

Commit Limit is the total amount of memory on the system that can be committed to application requests. Figure 7.15 shows the current commit limit at 90918912.000. If the paging file can be extended further, this is a soft limit. In other words, when this limit is reached, the paging file is extended, and this limit is raised. Only when the paging file has reached its maximum is this limit a hard limit.

Figure 7.15.
*A Report view
showing the*
Commit Limit
*counter at a
typical value.*

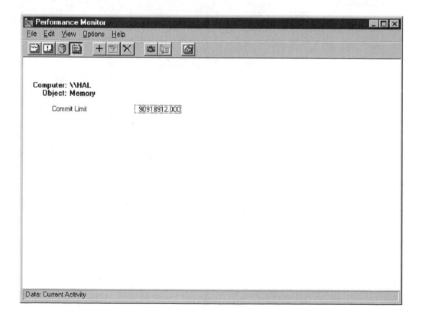

Committed Bytes

Committed Bytes is the total amount of memory that has been committed to application requests (see Figure 7.16). Notice that this does not represent the amount of memory that has been reserved by applications for future use, because it is not required to use physical memory to back up reserved memory.

Figure 7.16.
A sample Report view showing the Committed Bytes *counter.*

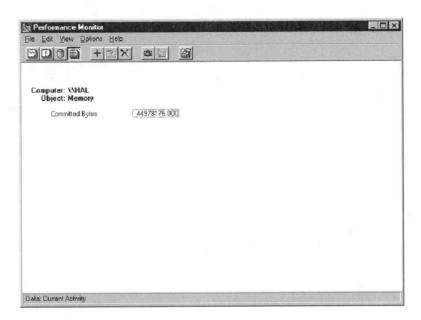

Percentage of CommhÁåed Bytes in Use

The % Committed Bytes In Use statistic shows the amount of committed memory in relation to the commit limit (see Figure 7.17). Remember that the commit limit is a soft limit and may be extended as needed until the maximum extension of the paging file is reached. When the paging file reaches its largest extent, this statistic becomes critical.

Cache Bytes

Cache Bytes is the number of bytes currently allocated to the system cache (see Figure 7.18). The system cache is used for buffering network and disk information, and is somewhat similar to the BUFFER parameter on DOS-based systems.

The *cache* is composed of memory that is not currently allocated to applications on the system. Readers familiar with the Novell NetWare network operating system should be familiar with this technique. All unallocated memory is used for caching purposes, so there is no wasted memory and performance is optimized.

Figure 7.17.
*A Report view
showing a sample*
% Committed
Bytes In Use
counter.

Figure 7.18.
*A Report view
showing a sample*
Cache Bytes
counter from the
Memory *object.*

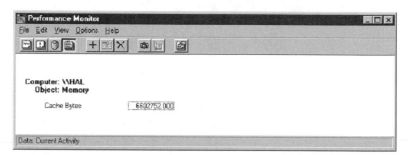

The PhysicalDisk Object

The PhysicalDisk object represents statistics regarding performance of the disk system hardware (see Figure 7.19). This does not represent logical drives because there may be many logical drives or partitions on one physical disk.

Figure 7.19.
*The Add to Report
dialog box
contains the
counters available
from the*
PhysicalDisk
object.

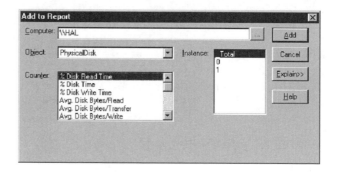

These statistics are greatly affected by the speed of disk hardware. Poor performance by the physical disk drives causes poor performance in the system. In order to increase the speed of disks, disk hardware must be upgraded. Alternatively, cache space can be increased to lower the number of requests from disks. Although this technique does not speed up the actual use of the disk drives, it does lower the number of disk accesses, thus raising system performance.

Percentage of Disk Time

Percentage of Disk Time is the percentage of time that the selected disk has spent servicing disk requests during the elapsed time interval. Recall that the elapsed time interval is the polling interval in Performance Monitor. If there is an exceptional amount of time spent in disk request-servicing during a slow time on the system, it could represent slow disk hardware or a lack of disk cache memory.

Disk Reads/sec

Disk Reads/sec is a representation of the read performance of a disk. It is the number of read operations completed by the disk drive per second during the sample time.

Disk Writes/sec

Disk Writes/sec is a representation of the write performance of a disk. It is the number of write operations completed by the disk drive per second during the sample time.

Disk Transfer/sec

Disk Transfer/sec is a combination of the Reads/sec and Writes/sec. This is the best representation of the absolute performance per second of a disk drive during that second.

Average Disk Bytes/Read

Average Disk Bytes/Read is the average number of bytes transferred from the disk during a read operation. This number is greatly affected by the application that is running. For instance, SQL Server works with a device page size of 2KB, so it will be transferring data from a disk at 2KB per operation. If a device is dedicated to SQL Server, this statistic will probably be that page read size.

It is generally better for this number to be high rather than low. The more that is being read per read operation, the better the performance is going to be. Data-intensive applications can take advantage of this by reading large block sizes. Indeed, the OS/2 High Performance File System, which is supported by Windows NT, has a large file-allocation mode that will read 16KB per read operation and 8KB during a standard file read.

Average Disk Bytes/Write

Average Disk Bytes/Write is the number of bytes that are being written to the disk during each write operation. Disk drives are much slower at writing than they are at reading, for understandable reasons. If an application is writing large blocks of data on a continuous basis, system performance may be degraded.

Average Disk Bytes/Transfer

Average Disk Bytes/Transfer is a combination of the Average Disk Bytes/Read and Average Disk Bytes/Write statistics. This statistic gives a good overall representation of how much data is being read from and written to the physical disk during each operation.

The LogicalDisk Object

Logical drives are data spaces that are allocated on physical drives. Network drives are also logical drives, but they cannot be viewed with Performance Monitor. To view a network drive, select the system it resides on to view, and then select this object. See Figure 7.20 for a listing of some of the counters available for the LogicalDisk object.

Figure 7.20.
The Add to Chart dialog box that shows some of the counters available for the LogicalDisk *object.*

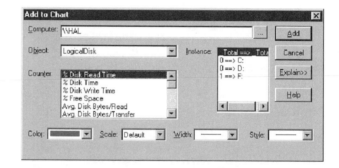

Percentage of Free Space

% Free Space is the percentage of disk space that remains free on a given drive. This % parameter is a good candidate for alerts, because a drive filling up can cause application errors. This parameter remains fairly steady, so tracking over time is not necessary to get needed information.

Free Megabytes

Free Megabytes is the absolute number of megabytes that are free on a logical drive. This statistic is useful for determining software for user placement, as well as monitoring its usage in a system. This is another candidate for an alarm, because there is probably a minimum number of free megabytes that should be maintained on a logical drive.

Disk Reads/sec

Disk Reads/sec is the number of read operations being completed by a disk every second during the sample period. Unlike physical disk parameters, logical drives can be striped volume sets, and performance across several physical disks can be monitored.

Disk Writes/sec

Disk Writes/sec is the number of write operations being completed on a logical drive per second during the sample period. Write operations are generally much slower than read operations, so there will be considerably fewer write operations being completed per second than read operations.

Disk Transfers/sec

Disk Transfers/sec is a combination of Disk Reads/sec and Disk Writes/sec. This is the best overall picture of how well the logical disk is performing under the workload. If this number is exceptionally high, it means that disk thrashing is taking place, and applications should be checked for errors or overburdening.

Avg. Disk sec/Read

Avg. Disk sec/Read is the average time in seconds that it is taking to complete disk operations. This number will usually be much less than a second. If this number is too high, it usually indicates a slow disk. A hardware upgrade or disk striping should be considered.

Avg. Disk sec/Write

Avg. Disk sec/Write is the average amount of time, in seconds, that the system is taking to complete write operations to disks. The amount of time to write data is generally higher than the amount of time to read data from a disk. If this number is too high, it could indicate the need to form a stripe set or upgrade hardware.

Figure 7.21.
A Report view showing the counters for the LogicalDisk *object.*

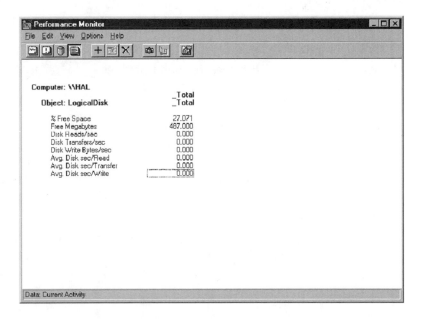

Avg. Disk sec/Transfer

Avg. Disk sec/Transfer is a combination of Avg. Disk sec/Read and Avg. Disk sec/Write. This is the best overall indication of the amount of time that a logical drive is spending to complete disk operations. If this number is too high, either a hardware upgrade or disk striping is probably in order.

The Server Object

Windows NT server acts as a file server, print server, and application server. Although these operations do not have direct effects on the operation of BackOffice, their load on the system does take processing power away from BackOffice. Because of this aspect of the BackOffice server functions, the relevant server-monitoring parameters are being presented here (see Figure 7.22).

Figure 7.22.
Some of the counters available under the Server *object, as shown by the Add to Report dialog box.*

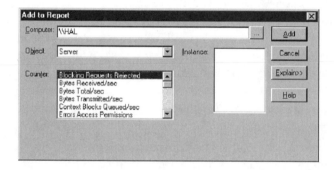

Logon Total

The Logon Total is the total number of users that have logged onto the system since the last time the system was rebooted. This includes all interactive logons, network logons, and service logons that are on the computer. It also includes a count of all logon attempts, both successful and failed.

Logon/sec

Logon/sec is the number of logon requests that a machine is processing per second during the sample period. This number will not be exceptionally high for a standalone server, but it will be for a domain controller. If a server is a PDC in the master domain of the master domain model, this statistic should be monitored closely. If a server has to process too many logons per second, the performance of logons for users could be degraded.

Files Open

`Files Open` is the number of files currently open by the system. This includes files opened by interactive users, network users, and services. This number is a good indicator of the overall activity of the system. Applications open and close files frequently, so a high number of open files over a long sample period indicates a busy system.

Each open file requires memory. This should be taken into consideration when sizing a system and dividing workload. This number should be monitored on all servers that will be doing file or application serving.

Bytes Received/sec

`Bytes Received/sec` is the number of bytes being received per second from the network during the sample period. This is a good indication of the activity of a network. No matter how fast a server is, only a certain amount of information can be accessed from the network interface per second. As users are added and services increase, this number will rise. If this number starts to curve out near a top mark and performance is degraded, the network interface is probably doing all it can.

Bytes Transmitted/sec

`Bytes Transmitted/sec` is the number of bytes being transmitted per second on the network interface. Like reading, there is only a certain number of bytes per second that can be put through the network interface. If this amount is exceeded, the network will need to be segmented and perhaps have more servers added.

Bytes Total/sec

`Bytes Total/sec` is a combination of the `Bytes Received/sec` and the `Bytes Transmitted/sec` parameters. This is the best overall indication of the current utilization of the network interface.

Remember that the network bandwidth is being shared by all applications on the Windows NT Server. A high amount of file serving can result in degraded SQL Server performance if data cannot be sent through or received from the interface by the SQL Server database processes.

Server Sessions

The `Server Sessions` parameter indicates the total number of active sessions presently on the server. This is a good indication of current server activity. If this number is exceptionally high, the server may be overloaded, and additional servers should be considered.

The `System` Object

The `System` object shows statistics about overall system performance and information. These statistics have a large impact on the BackOffice products, as well as on all other applications running on the machine.

During general browsing of server activity and utilization, these will be the most-queried counters. Most of these also make good candidates for tracking trends and viewing from remote systems (see Figure 7.23).

Figure 7.23.
Some of the counters available with the System object, as seen in the Add to Report dialog box.

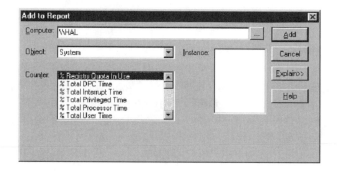

Unlike the `Processor` object, which stores information about activity on each processor separately, the `System` object stores information about all the processors as a unit. This is helpful, because the primary concern for performance is how well the processors are working as a unit and the total load across them.

Percentage of Total Processor Time

Percentage of Total Processor Time `% Total Processor Time` is the percentage of time all the processors spent executing threads other than the idle thread (see Figure 7.24). This is computed based on an average of all the processors over the sample period.

On multiprocessor systems, if this statistic remains high for too long, there is probably a system problem. This could be either a software or configuration error, or the system may be overloaded.

Context Switches/sec

Recall that a *context switch* is when the processor switches from User mode to Privileged mode. The switch is expensive, as far as processor time goes, because the processor must switch out control registers and do general housekeeping to accomplish the switch (see Figure 7.25).

Applications that are disk- or network-intensive will produce a lot of context switches because both disk and network operations require operating system services.

Figure 7.24.
This is a chart that shows the % Total Processor Time *counter for the* System *object.*

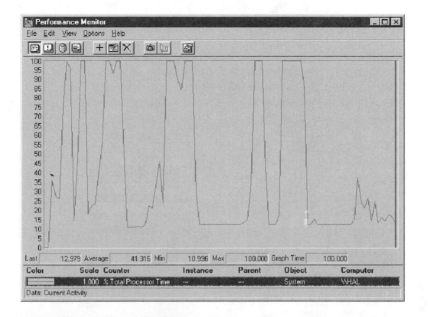

Figure 7.25.
An example of the Context Switches/sec *counter from the* System *object. The scale had to be changed from the default to get a meaningful graph.*

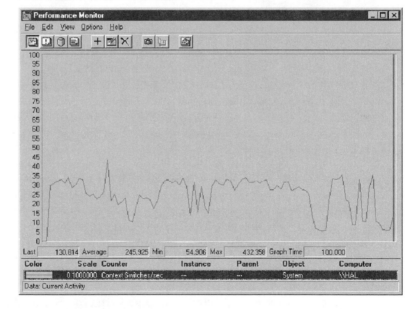

File Read Operations/sec

File Read Operations/sec is the number of logical-file read operations being processed per second during the sample period. This number is across all logical and physical disks on the system, and it gives a good view of the total file read activity on a system (see Figure 7.26).

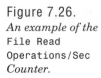

Figure 7.26.
An example of the
File Read
Operations/Sec
Counter.

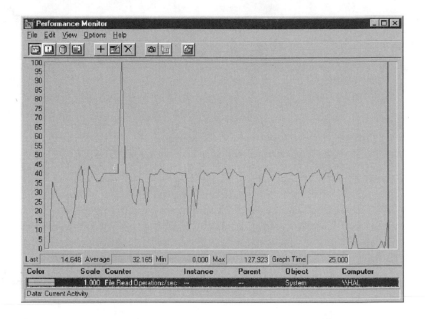

File Write Operations/sec

File Write Operations/sec is the average number of logical-file write operations being completed per second by the system. Like the File Read Operations statistic, this number applies across all logical and physical drives on the system. It takes longer to complete a write operation than a read operation (see Figure 7.27), so during normal workloads this number will probably be lower than the File Read Operations statistic.

System Up Time

System Up Time is the amount of time in seconds the system has been active since the last reboot (see Figure 7.28). A stable system, in theory, should never have to be rebooted. In practice, there are very few systems that can claim to never have to be rebooted. In my experience, Windows NT is a system that should be rebooted on a scheduled basis to maintain system performance and integrity.

Exception Dispatches/sec

Exception Dispatches/sec is the rate at which the processor is dispatching exceptions to the system. *Exceptions* are things like page faults and application errors. It is generally better for this number to be relatively low (see Figure 7.29). Exceptions are expensive operations, and high numbers of exceptions will result in lower system performance.

Figure 7.27.
There are fewer file write operations than Read operations, as is normal in a production system.

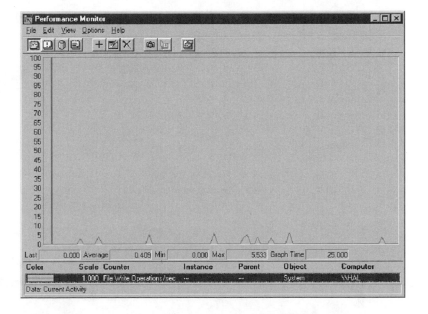

Figure 7.28.
This is a Report view showing the typical System Up Time *output for a system that has not been up for long.*

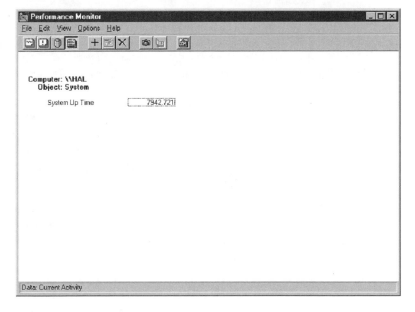

Figure 7.29.
An Exception
Dispatches/sec
display for a
system that is not
very busy.

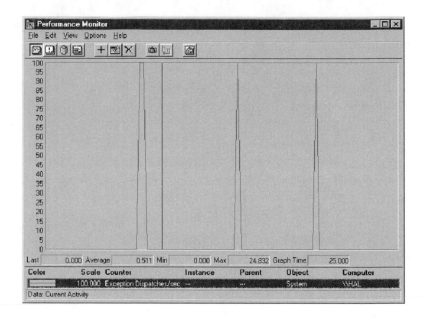

SQL Server

When SQL Server is installed, it installs several objects in Performance Monitor that allow monitoring of things that are specific to SQL Server. These objects are useful for gathering statistics and tracking trends both on the local machine and on machines across the network.

It should be noted that all information that is displayed under the SQL Server objects could also be retrieved using the built-in commands and stored procedures of SQL Server. This information would be presented in a text basis, so it would be nearly as attractive as its Performance Monitor counterparts. See Figure 7.30 for a partial list of the SQL Server counter list.

In Interactive SQL (ISQL), for instance, the sp_monitor command can be used to retrieve information about the status of the various SQL Server engines. sp_who can be used to show current logged-in users, and sp_lock will show information about locks.

Of course, Performance Monitor not only shows this data graphically, but allows tracking and storage as well. It will also allow reports to be designed that show this information. These and other features make Performance Monitor the preferred method of retrieving this information for most administrators.

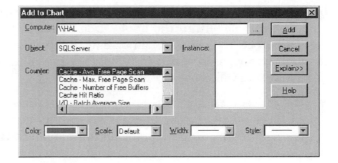

Figure 7.30.
*The Add to Chart
dialog box showing
the SQL Server
counter list.*

Cache Hit Ratio

One of the biggest single factors that affect the performance of SQL Server is the data cache. This cache is used to store data from tables, indexes, and other SQL Server objects so that it does not have to be retrieved from disk.

Unlike the operating-system cache, which usually uses the generic Least Recently Used method of cache management, SQL Server makes intelligent judgments. Sometimes SQL Server will use the Most Recently Used method for cache management, especially during sequential table scans. When testing a query from ISQL, the set showplan on command will instruct SQL Server to show a variety of information about the query in progress. One of the pieces of information shown will be the cache page replacement strategy.

> The operating system using a generic caching algorithm is not a weakness in the system, but instead a necessity. The operating system is written for any application that chooses to run on it, while SQL Server is a database application and is therefore optimized for database-style activities.

This statistic represents the percentage of time during which the requested data is in the data cache, as opposed to having to be retrieved from a disk. The better this ratio, the better performance that SQL Server will have. If this ratio is poor, increasing the size of the SQL Server cache will improve overall system performance. Memory additions to the computer may be required for additions to SQL Server data cache, because allowing the system to use virtual memory as the cache defeats the purpose of the cache—namely, avoiding disk hits.

Max Tempdb Space Used

Tempdb is the SQL Server equivalent of the \TEMP directory in Windows NT. In other words, it is a working space designed for temporary use. Like the \TEMP directory, Tempdb is vital to system operation.

Tempdb is used for a working space for user applications. This use is explicit and is usually configurable within the application. Tempdb is also used by the system during work processes, so its utilization may not always be apparent. Joined queries and order by statements result in temporary tables in Tempdb. If Tempdb fills, application errors will occur.

The Max Tempdb Space Used statistic represents the maximum amount of Tempdb space that has been used during the monitoring session. Unlike processor times, when peaks are normal, if the usage approaches the maximum, the action should be taken. This action could either be application and usage changes or increasing the size of Tempdb. Either way, filling Tempdb should be avoided.

Max Users Connected

The Max Users Connected statistic represents the maximum number of users connected at any one time during this monitoring session. This number should be checked against the total licensed connections to ensure the system is not approaching capacity. This statistic is a good candidate for an alert to prevent running out of license connections without warning.

NET-Command Queue Length

SQL Server does not handle every request at the moment the request is received from a client. When SQL Server starts up, it starts a certain number of working threads that define the number of clients that SQL Server may be servicing at any one time. Any requests that are received when SQL Server is already operating at capacity will be placed in the Command Queue.

This statistic represents the number of clients that are waiting in the Command Queue for SQL Server to service their requests. This should be monitored over time. If the Command Queue is long and slows over a period of time, corrective action should be taken.

This corrective action could be to increase the number of worker threads. There are two ways to do this. One is through ISQL, with the sp_configure command. The parameter to be configured is max worker threads. The default value on most systems is 255. To increase the number of worker threads with ISQL to 512, run this command:

```
sp_configure "max worker threads",512 <ctrl-E>
```

You will be prompted to run RECONFIGURE to make the changes take effect.

The preferred way for most administrators to work with the SQL Server environment is to use SQL Server Enterprise Manager (see Figure 7.31). To modify the max worker threads parameter, take the following steps:

1. Log on to the correct SQL Server.
2. From the Server menu, choose the SQL Server submenu.
3. From the SQL Server submenu, choose Configure.
4. Choose the Configuration tab.
5. Find the max worker threads parameter in the list, and change it appropriately.

Figure 7.31.
The SQL Server Enterprise Manager Server Configuration window can be used to modify SQL Server configuration values.

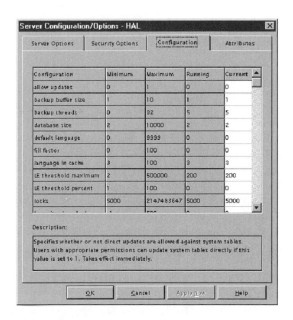

Raising the maximum number of worker threads is not always an option, because it will lower overall system performance. Adding more processors and memory to a system may have to be considered. Another option is using Replication to have a copy of the database on another server that some users can use.

User Connections

The User Connections statistic represents the total number of open user connections (see Figure 7.32 for this counter and others). Periodically checking this counter gives you a good indication of a system's usage over time. This parameter is also good for an at-a-glance view of system activity because it is a good overall indicator of SQL Server activity.

Figure 7.32.
*This is a Report
view showing the
SQL Server
counters.*

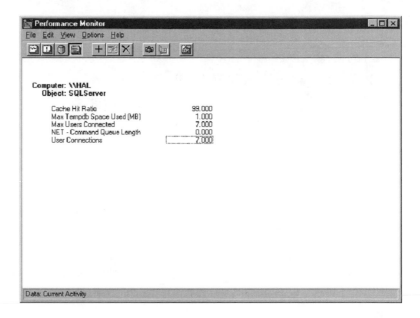

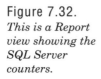

> A list of currently logged-in users can be obtained by entering this command at the ISQL command line:
>
>   sp_who <ctrl-E>

The SQLServer-Licensing Object

SQL Server licensing must be closely monitored. When available licenses are exhausted, users will be denied access to the system. Figure 7.33 shows counters that are available for monitoring the SQLServer-Licensing object.

Figure 7.33.
*The Add to Report
dialog box shows
counters available
in the* SQLServer-
Licensing *object.*

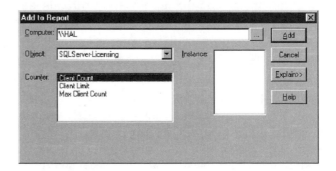

Client Limit

The Client Limit statistic represents the total number of clients that are allowed to connect to SQL Server. This statistic is for at-a-glance checking because it is not subject to change during normal operation.

Client Count

The Client Count is the number of clients currently connected to this SQL Server. This number is a good indication of the overall activity of the SQL Server. This statistic is also a good candidate for a counter, because users will be denied access when this number reaches the Client Limit.

Max Client Count

Max Client Count is the maximum number of connections that have been established at any one time during this monitoring session. Like all parameters that affect the monitoring session, this number is only useful if Performance Monitor is kept running over a period of time. If this number approaches the Client Limit under normal operating conditions, adding licenses to the SQL Server should be considered.

The SQLServer-Locks Object

Locks play a major role in the performance of SQL Server. No matter how many free worker threads there are, if a client request involves a table with an exclusive lock, it will be blocked until the lock is released. Statistics under this object sometimes make good candidates for alerts, especially when application software that uses SQL Server first goes online. See Figure 7.34 for a listing of some of the counters that can be monitored under the SQLServer-Locks object.

Figure 7.34.
The Add to Report dialog box shows some of the counters available with the SQLServer-Locks *object.*

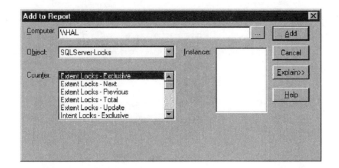

Total Exclusive Locks

Total Exclusive Locks is the total number of exclusive locks in the system at the time the sample was taken. There can be only one exclusive lock on a table at a time. In addition, when an exclusive lock is on a table, there can be no other activity on the table until the lock is cleared. The higher this number is, the worse the system performance is going to be.

> This number can be retrieved at the ISQL command line by entering this command:
>
>   sp_lock <ctrl-E>

There are several conditions that cause the establishment of exclusive locks. When a data page is being updated, an exclusive lock is placed on that page. If more than 80 percent of a table is going to take part in an update operation, an exclusive lock is placed on the entire table.

Total Shared Locks

The Total Shared Locks statistic represents the total number of shared locks that are in the system at the time the sample is taken. Shared locks are not nearly as damaging as exclusive locks.

A data page with a shared lock can still be read by other processes, but it cannot be updated. This is important because, generally, most SQL Server activities are reads, as opposed to writes. If there is an excessive number of shared locks on a page, insert and update operations can back up while waiting for the lock to clear.

Total Locks

The Total Locks statistic is a combination of the Total Exclusive Locks and the Total Shared Locks statistics. This number gives an overall view of the locks on the system. The total number of locks on a system cannot exceed the value specified in the locks parameter.

> To see the total number of allowed locks at the ISQL command prompt, enter the following:
>
>   sp_configure "locks"

The SQLServer-Log Object

The SQLServer-Log object deals with the various statistics concerning the transaction log. Figure 7.35 shows several of the counters that can be monitored to track the SQLServer-Log object. The transaction log is a fundamentally important part of the system and is responsible for not only tracking transactions, but storing the information necessary to do a ROLLBACK TRANSACTION. The transaction log can also be used to restore a database when a database dumps and the logs for all transactions since it occurred are available.

Figure 7.35.
The Add to Report dialog box shows the counters available with the SQLServer-Log *object.*

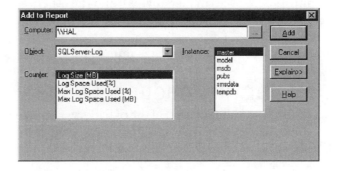

If the transaction log fills up, there cannot be any further database operations until there is space in the transaction log. It is recommended that the transaction log be dumped either to tape or to disk routinely to ensure this situation does not occur.

WARNING

> If the transaction log fills, it cannot be dumped to tape or disk because this action requires a transaction entry. If the log is full, it must be dumped with the command
>
>   DUMP TRAN <dbname> WITH TRUNCATE_ONLY
>
> After this is done, a DUMP DATABASE should be run to ensure recoverability.

The database to which the transaction log statistics apply is where they are stored. When selecting to view one, the database must also be selected.

Log Size

Log Size is the size of the current transaction log, in megabytes. This size will not increase dynamically, so constant monitoring is not necessary. The size of the transaction log can be increased through SQL Enterprise Manager or with the ALTER DATABASE command.

Log Space Used

Log Space Used is a percentage of the transaction space used on a particular database. Recall that if a transaction log fills, no new operations can take place on the database. Because the transaction log is so critical to the proper operation of SQL Server, this statistic is a good candidate for an alert.

Max Log Space Used

There are two parameters associated with the Max Log Space Used statistic. One is the maximum space used (in megabytes), and the other represents a percentage of total space, which is the highest point that a log reaches during the current monitoring session. Because of the nature of the transaction log, the log space used will gradually increase until the log is dumped.

SQLServer-Procedure Cache

Procedures are an integral part of the SQL Server architecture. They are preoptimized, preresolved queries, so they execute without the initial steps required with an ad-hoc query. See Figure 7.36 for some of the counters available for the SQLServer-Procedure Cache.

Figure 7.36.
Some of the counters available with the SQLServer-Procedure Cache *object.*

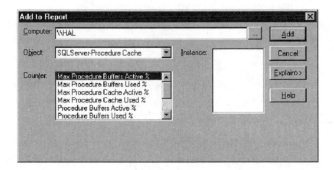

Because of their usefulness, there are usually many stored procedures in a SQL server. Indeed, most of SQL Server's built-in functionality is accessed via stored procedures, and, by default, only system stored procedures are allowed to access system tables.

The procedure cache is configured as a percentage of the total cache in the system. What is not allocated to procedure cache is allocated to data cache. The procedure cache uses a Least Recently Used page-replacement strategy, so frequently used procedures tend to remain in memory.

To see the percentage of cache being dedicated to procedure cache, enter

```
sp_configure "procedure cache" <ctrl-E>
```

If common procedures are swapped often from memory to disk, there will be a degradation in system performance. Because procedure cache is a percentage of total cache, raising the procedure cache will lower the amount of data cache.

Procedure Cache Size

SQL Server operates on a 2KB page size. All operations done by SQL Server use this page as the least common denominator. This statistic is the actual size of the procedure cache, expressed in 2KB pages.

1 kilobyte (KB)=1024 bytes; 1 megabyte (MB)=1000KB.

Procedure Cache Used

The Procedure Cache Used statistic represents the percentage of the total procedure cache that has been used. As this cache fills up, procedures have to be removed from memory to be reloaded from disk later. If this cache stays near capacity for a large percentage of the time, disk trashing is probably taking place, which lowers performance.

Procedure Cache Active

Running procedures are stored in the procedure cache, along with procedures that recently ran. This percentage represents the amount of procedure cache that is active at the time the sample was taken. If this percentage reaches 100, active procedures will have to be removed from memory. This will seriously degrade performance. See Figure 7.37 for the Procedure Cache counters.

SQLServer-Users

The SQLServer-Users object allows an administrator to view various statistics per user. This can be very helpful for tracking the source of performance problems or other excessive resource usage. Figure 7.38 shows the counters available for monitoring the SQLServer-Users.

Figure 7.37.
*A Report view
showing the*
`Procedure Cache`
counters.

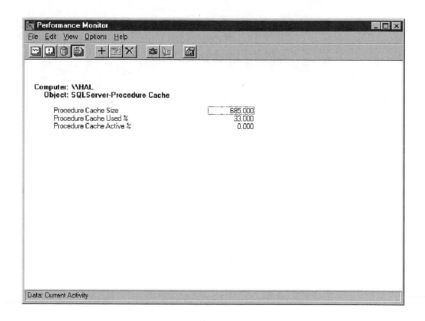

Figure 7.38.
*The Add to Report
dialog box shows
counters available
with the*
`SQLServer-Users`
object.

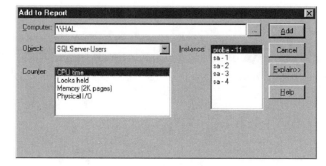

Because of their nature, these statistics are all stored by the user. When selecting them for monitoring, a user must be specified as the object for the query.

A list of users currently logged in to SQL Server can be seen from the ISQL prompt with the command:

```
sp_who <ctrl-E>
```

CPU time

The CPU time statistic represents the total amount of CPU time that a connected user has consumed during his connection. Excessive CPU time from an interactive user can sometimes mean the user is running bad queries or accessing data in a strange way.

Generally, any excessive CPU time should be investigated. The exception is batch-style jobs, such as data loads. There are also some "users" that are always shown as connected, such as sa for the database engines. For permanently connected users, CPU time will accumulate until the server is restarted. For batch jobs, judgment will have to be used to determine whether the amount of CPU time used is excessive.

Locks held

Locks held is the number of locks currently being held by a user connection. A lock on a page or table will prevent certain other transactions from taking place. If a process has a high number of locks over a long period of time, corrective action may be required.

Physical I/O

Physical I/O is the total number of reads and writes for the current statement. Because most statements finish quickly, this number is usually not very high. If this number is high, it usually indicates an improper query that involves too many jobs or is triggering a table scan. (See Figure 7.39 for an example of Physical I/O being used.)

Figure 7.39.
A Report view showing the SQLServer-Users *objects being monitored.*

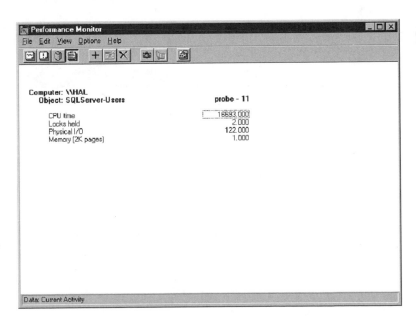

NOTE

The term *table scan* refers to what happens when SQL Server cannot find a direct path to data via an index. If a direct path cannot be found, SQL Server looks through every row in the table.

Monitoring Remote Systems

One of the most useful features of Performance Monitor is the capability to monitor remote systems. This feature enables constant monitoring of all systems on a network and can be helpful in diagnosing problems remotely.

Selecting a Remote System

To monitor objects on a remote system, that system merely needs to be selected to view. This is done from the Computer field in Performance Monitor. Pressing this button displays the Select Computer dialog box (see Figure 7.40). Choose a computer from this box, and, security permitting, access will be granted to view statistics from that system.

Figure 7.40.
Selecting a remote computer. Notice that computers are listed according to the domain they are in.

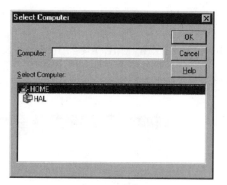

Network Implications of Remote System Monitoring

Monitoring a remote system generates network traffic. Monitoring many objects on several remote systems can generate an extremely large amount of network traffic and can skew the statistics, such as those that monitor network performance.

Generally, when monitoring remote systems, it is helpful to lower the polling interval from the default of 1 second to something more reasonable. Even changing the polling interval from 1 to 5 will lower the network traffic by a magnitude of five.

What Is Best to Monitor on Remote Systems

When monitoring remote systems, keeping down the number of things monitored is important. Things that are not prone to change often should not be monitored on a continual basis. Things that are critical to system performance should not always be monitored either, because an alert can be set up to warn of problem conditions.

Generally, the interactive monitoring of remote systems is for temporary troubleshooting and should not be a permanent monitoring method.

Tracking Trends

Tracking trends over time is the best way to know the overall performance of a system. There are many parameters that are meaningless for a single sample, but are helpful if an average is obtained.

The Report tool is very powerful for gathering statistics. With Report options, Performance Monitor can be programmed to track the counters of a certain statistic in an object. This report can be saved and used for analysis at a later date, a very powerful feature.

As mentioned previously, Performance Monitor is helpful in detecting bottlenecks. This is done by monitoring several objects and keeping track of their performance trends over a period of time. Figure 7.41 shows the Performance Monitor Report view monitoring several objects.

Figure 7.41.
A Report view that is monitoring several objects.

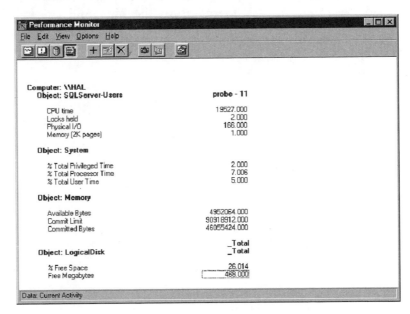

Summary

A proper plan for monitoring performance is vital to the successful operation of the network. Any system, no matter how well designed, must be tracked for problems. There are various third-party monitoring tools, but the built-in Performance Monitor tool is usually more than adequate, if configured properly.

Performance Monitor allows watching statistics on a variety of objects, including Windows NT OS objects, BackOffice objects, and objects added in by other software. Each of these sometimes relates to an *instance* of an object, such as a user.

Statistics can be viewed in Chart or Report views. A chart is a graphical representation of the data as it is happening. A report is a text view of statistics that may be exported for use in other applications.

Statistics can also be logged for viewing later on the same machine or another machine. This is helpful for diagnosing performance problems over a long period of time or gathering them from a machine that is not directly connected.

The most powerful feature of Performance Monitor is the capability to alert the administrator if certain conditions occur. Performance Monitor can be set to send alerts to the log on the same machine, or across the network to notify a remote administrator.

A proper monitoring plan is essential for the continued performance and usability of the network. An administrator should have a plan in place before users are placed on systems, and should maintain the plan and check logs for possible alert conditions. If the monitoring plan is effective and followed diligently, it will detect many potential network problems before they have a chance to grow into real issues.

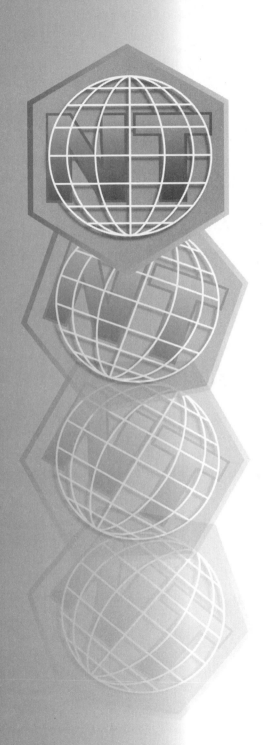

Part III

File System Resources

Data Access and Integrity

Data access and integrity are key areas of any system architecture, and they have become even more critical in BackOffice systems. Applications are changing from traditional midrange and mainframe environments to the client/server community; data access and integrity requirements are included as part of that transition. This section addresses Windows NT disk-management components and how these components are used to enhance BackOffice applications as well as general system performance and fault tolerance/integrity.

Volume Sets

Windows NT manages its fault tolerance and disk performance enhancements by using several variations of striped and mirrored volume sets. The volume sets also allow the system to better utilize areas of the physical disk(s). Windows NT allows system administrators to use these features without buying any special controllers or hard disks. Fault tolerance and performance enhancements follow the industry standards for Redundant Array of Inexpensive Disks (RAID) Levels 0, 1, and 5. These RAID levels have become commonly used in today's computing environments, with new variations emerging every day.

Volume Sets Explained

Volume sets are used within Windows NT to efficiently manage your hard disk resources. For purposes of this discussion, *volume sets* refers to the logical grouping of partitions, not to stripe sets or mirrored sets. The Windows NT operating system manages disk resources as either primary or extended partitions. The key to disk management is to understand the differences between primary and extended partitions, their functionality, and their limitations.

There are only four primary partitions and one extended partition allowed per physical disk. The extended partition actually counts as one of the four primary partitions; therefore, the physical drive makeup can be either a maximum of four primary partitions or a maximum of one extended partition and three primary partitions. If you need more than four drive letters or partitions, you need to create additional logical drives within an extended partition. Therefore, preplanning the layout of your physical drives is important. Any number of logical partitions can be created within an extended partition, but the practical limit is the number of drive letters, assuming standard BackOffice applications are going to be used. Volume sets can use all types of partitions except Active Primary partitions. Volume sets are used to maximize the utilization of free space on the disk(s) and provide a mechanism for extending the size of an existing partition.

> Active partitions cannot be extended. Only nonactive primary partitions, logical drives, and available free space can be used to create volume sets or to extend volume sets. Additionally, logical drives must be created in extended partitions. If you try to extend the active partition, the Disk Administrator will present the error message shown in Figure 8.1.

Figure 8.1.
*The Disk
Administrator
error message.*

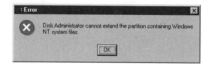

Windows NT uses volume sets to provide for better use of free disk space. A system with a single or multiple physical hard drives may have several areas that have been fragmented into smaller, less functional sections. This is seen in systems that have been divided up from different disk administration activities, such as striping disk sets, mirroring disks, and/or fragmented growth of the system's partitions. Without the feature of volume sets, the system would have to manage smaller partition fragments as individual drives. Volume sets can combine smaller partitions into a single, larger logical partition that is presented to the operating system as one drive letter. In addition, these smaller partitions of free disk space can be used to extend any existing volumes or volume sets on the system. The alternative is having many smaller drives, each with its own drive-letter assignment.

Figure 8.2 shows three "free-space" partitions that can be combined into one volume set and presented to Windows NT as one drive letter. All three partitions are highlighted at once by holding down the Ctrl key and clicking each partition once with the mouse. Once the partitions have been highlighted, select Create Volume Set from the Partition menu (see Figure 8.3). You will be prompted to include the size of volume set you want to create (see Figure 8.4). Once you select the size, the volume set will be created, but it will be unformatted (see Figure 8.5).

Figure 8.2.
Highlighting the free-space partitions is the first step in creating a logical volume set.

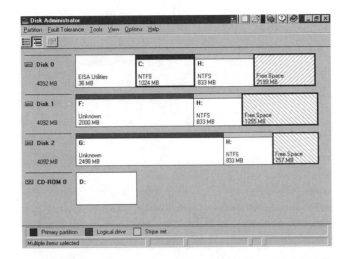

Figure 8.3.
Creating a volume set through the Partition menu.

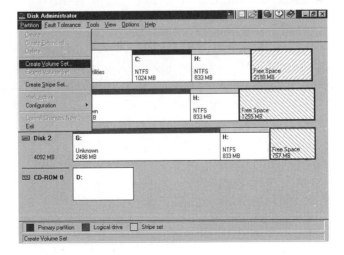

Figure 8.4.
The Create Volume Set dialog box.

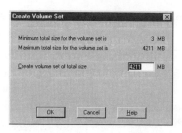

Figure 8.5.
The volume set is created.

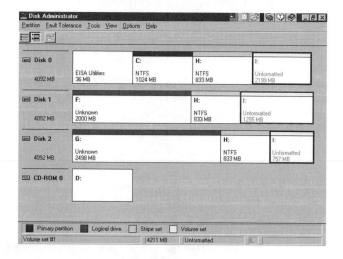

The volume set can be formatted as either FAT or NTFS; however, Disk Administrator requires that the changes be saved first. This is done by selecting Commit Changes Now from the Partition menu (see Figure 8.6). Now the volume set is ready to be formatted. In this example, NTFS is specified as the file system and the quick format option is selected (see Figure 8.7). Formatting begins after the Start button has been clicked. Disk Administrator will indicate that the formatting is complete (see Figure 8.8). Disk Administrator will then reflect the newly created volume set as it appears in Figure 8.9.

Only NTFS file systems can be extended.

Figure 8.6.
*Changes to the
disk configuration
must be saved
before formatting
can take place.
This is done by
selecting Commit
Changes Now from
the Partition
menu.*

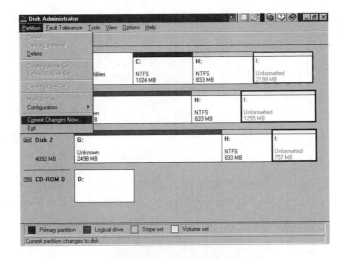

Figure 8.7.
*The Format dialog
box. Select the
Start button to
commence the
formatting process.*

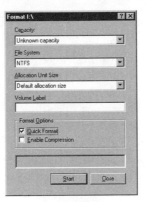

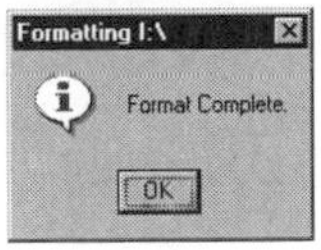

Figure 8.8.
*The Format
Complete message.*

Requirements for Volume Sets

Volume sets can be created from 2 to 32 areas of free space on a single or multiple physical hard disk(s). Volume sets cannot include striped, mirrored, or system partitions. NTFS format is not required in order to create a volume set; however, it is required in order to extend an existing volume set.

Figure 8.9.
*The volume set
creation process is
complete.*

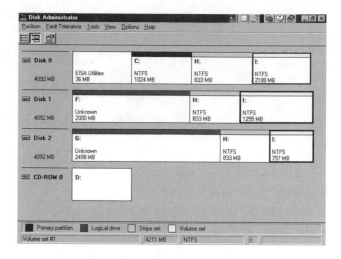

Practical Implementation of Volume Sets

One area in which volume sets can be used effectively is in file and print server environments. Traditional file servers are set up with an Applications area or drive and a Users area or drive—P: and U: in Figure 8.10. However, most administrators, when setting up this drive arrangement, will split up all the available space between these two areas, which doesn't allow for any flexibility in the future, short of adding physical drives to the system. The result is a Users drive with no available disk space and a Programs drive with plenty of available disk space. Unfortunately, the available disk space on the Programs drive cannot be assigned or used by the Users drive, and the space is wasted. Additionally, drives cannot be shrunk. The only way to reduce the size of a volume is to delete it and re-create a smaller one. The better way is to allocate disk space and create two logical drives from an extended partition, with ample space for each area, and leave the remaining space as extended free space.

In the preceding example, any of the logical drives can be extended, because the free space has been set up as extended free space, as noted in the bottom-left part of the status bar. This setup allows any drive to be extended multiple times with the use of the available free space and will not require reconfiguration of the disks. It is advisable to expand logical drives within the same physical drive. This will reduce the point of failure for the logical drives (that is, if drive U: were expanded using free space on Disk 0, that would cause the U: drive to exist on two physical disks; therefore, a failure of either disk would result in a failure of the U: drive).

Figure 8.10.
A sample logical drive setup within an extended partition.

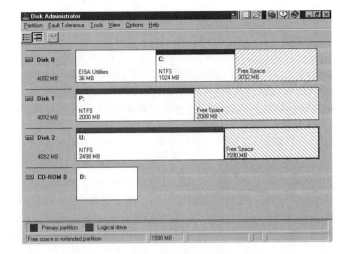

This type of drive setup also has one other benefit. As of this writing, there is no way to limit a user's disk space on a Windows NT file server without the use of third-party tools or some customization of some of the utilities in the NT Resource Kit. The drive setup described here keeps an end user from absorbing all the disk space on the server; he will just be absorbing all the disk space on the Users drive on the system. This will not affect other drives on the server, just the U: drive.

A drive at 100 percent capacity can have adverse effects on the NT Operating system if the swap file is located on the same drive. If the swap file is set up to expand if necessary and is unable to because of a lack of disk space, a system crash is the most likely result. This is seen on systems that have Users directories on the same drive as the swap file, which is typically located on C:.

Disk Striping

Disk striping is designed to address data-access issues, specifically performance. Windows NT uses two popular methods of disk striping called *disk striping* and *disk striping with parity*. Both of these methods closely follow the existing RAID standards. BackOffice applications can be demanding of the disk-storage system for both read and write operations, and striping data will significantly improve performance. However, disk striping without parity (referred to as just "disk striping" in Disk Administrator) does not have any fault tolerance and should not be used for applications that cannot tolerate disk failures.

Disk Striping Explained

Windows NT's implementation of disk striping closely follows the RAID Level 0 standard. (RAID is discussed later in this section.) Disk striping performs disk I/O transactions by accessing multiple disks at the same time. The term *striping* means that the data is spread across all drives in the stripe set. For example, when you save a document to a stripe disk set, the actual file is spread out over all the disks in the set. The function of writing data to disk is accomplished with greater speed when the data is written in smaller increments to multiple disks simultaneously.

However, disk striping does not account for or protect against disk failures. If one of the disks in the stripe set fails, all the data in the set is lost, and the only recourse is to restore the data from the most recent backup, once the hardware has been repaired. Although the performance gains can be significant, most application environments need fault tolerance for the hard disks, which disk striping does not provide; therefore, disk striping without parity protection is rarely used.

> Even greater performance is gained by spreading the disks onto multiple disk controllers.

Requirements for Striping

Windows NT can create stripe sets from a minimum of two areas of free space to a maximum of 32, all of which must be on separate physical hard drives. Only free space areas can be used; no existing partitions are allowed. Disk Administrator creates each partition to be approximately the same size in order to create the stripe set, equal to the smallest area of free space selected. For example, if three areas are chosen to create a stripe set, 500MB, 700MB, and 800MB, the set will consist of three 500MB partitions, for a total of 1.5GB of usable storage space. Stripe sets can be formatted with any file system supported by Windows NT (basically FAT or NTFS).

Performance Gains from Striping

In a single-disk environment, all disk I/O transactions happen through one reader head on the physical disk. The event of copying a large document means that every bit associated with that document must pass through the reader head of the disk and down the disk I/O channel to its destination. With a large amount of disk I/O, this part of the process can become the bottleneck of disk I/O transactions. Disk striping allows simultaneous reads and writes to multiple disks.

Suppose that in the preceding example of copying a file, only a fifth of the document passes through the reader head of all five disks in a five-disk stripe set. In theory, it should happen five times as fast as a single disk I/O, but there are many other components and factors that affect the speed of disk I/O transactions. Regardless of the other factors involved, however, the performance gains from doing simultaneous accesses to multiple disks are significant. In addition, the more disks in the set, the greater the performance gains, although there is a point at which the channel will become the bottleneck, and then multiple channels or disk controllers can be deployed for even greater performance gains. The art of fine-tuning disk I/O is a multimillion-dollar business, with some of the biggest companies in the world researching and developing better and faster disk solutions. The feature of disk striping, provided with Windows NT, is to facilitate this technology without the expensive and complex hardware configurations typically required.

Setting Up Stripe Sets

Stripe sets are easy to set up with the Disk Administrator's tool. Simply click each partition that is to be included in the stripe set with the mouse while holding down the Ctrl key on the keyboard. After each set has been highlighted or clicked, select Create Stripe Set from the Partition menu (see Figure 8.11). Disk Administrator will prompt you with a dialog box indicating the minimum and maximum size for the stripe set. In Figure 8.12, a smaller size was selected than the default. See how Disk Administrator appropriates the disk space from each of the selected partitions.

Figure 8.11.
Choosing Create
Stripe Set from the
Partition menu
(with free space
highlighted).

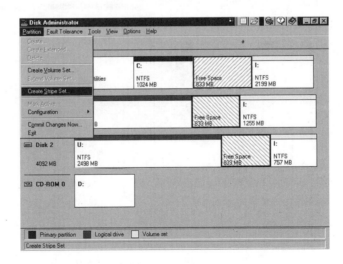

Figure 8.12.
*Total size of the
stripe set is
selected to be less
than maximum.
An equal portion is
used from each of
the highlighted
partitions to create
the stripe set.*

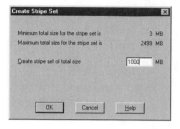

In order to format the newly created stripe set, Disk Administrator requires that the changes be committed (see Figure 8.13). Now the set is ready to be formatted. Select Format from the Tools menu (see Figure 8.14). Again, NTFS is selected as the file system type, and the Quick Format option is chosen, as seen in Figure 8.15. When these steps are complete, the stripe set is ready for use.

Figure 8.13.
*Choosing Format
from the Tools
menu.*

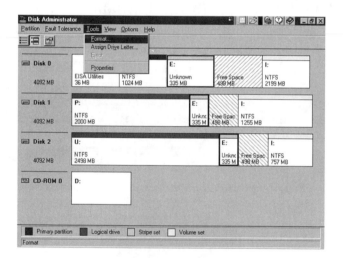

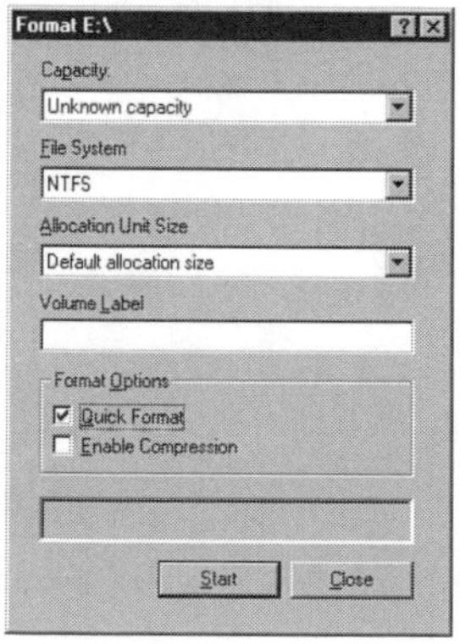

Figure 8.14.
*The Format
dialog box.*

Figure 8.15.
Disk Administrator shows the completed stripe set.

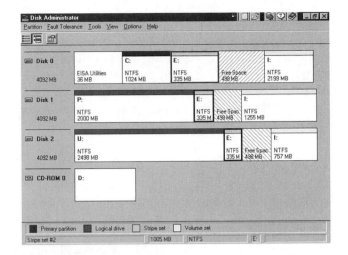

Disk Striping with Parity Explained

Disk striping with parity is an enhanced version of disk striping that closely follows the RAID 5 standard (which is discussed later in this section). As with disk striping, data is accessed simultaneously from multiple disks, but disk striping with parity includes fault tolerance on the stripe set. Fault tolerance allows for one of the disks in the set to fail without loss of data or disruption to operations. In the striping process, there is a parity stripe written to each of the drives. In the event of a disk failure, the data that was on the failed drive is determined by the parity stripes on the surviving drives. Therefore, there is no single point of individual disk failure with the stripe set as there is with disk striping without parity (described in the previous section).

However, until the failed disk is replaced, there is a single point of failure among the surviving disks in the set. There is some additional processing required by Windows NT in order to facilitate disk striping with parity; therefore, the performance gains are not as significant as disk striping without parity in an identical hardware setup. Additionally, performance is degraded during a single disk failure as the surviving disks re-create the failed member's data with the parity information.

Requirements for Striping with Parity

Windows NT can create stripe sets with parity from a minimum of three areas of free space to a maximum of 32, all of which must be on separate physical hard drives. As with striping without parity, Disk Administrator creates each partition to be approximately the same size in order to create the stripe set. The disks in the set are not required to be on the same disk controller; in fact, greater performance is gained with multiple disk controllers when implementing disk striping. Also, like striping without parity, FAT or NTFS may be used when formatting the stripe set.

Performance Gains from Striping with Parity

The performance gains of disk striping with parity follow the same theory of disk striping without parity. However, the additional processing required by Windows NT for striping with parity will affect the performance gains of striping; therefore, from a raw performance perspective, striping without parity will be faster than with parity. As with striping without parity, increasing the number of disks used in the set will increase the performance and the number of disk controllers.

Increased Data Protection

Windows NT is limited in its implementation of striping with parity in that, regardless of the number of disks used in the stripe set, the protection against data loss and service disruption is limited to single-disk failures. Multiple-disk failures will yield the same results as a single-disk failure in striping without parity. Statistically, increasing the number of disks not only increases performance, but also increases the risk of failure.

Setting Up Stripe Sets with Parity

The procedure for setting up stripe sets with parity is almost identical to setting up stripe sets without parity. Stripe sets with parity are easy to set up with the Disk Administrator's tool. Simply click each partition that is to be included in the stripe set with the mouse while holding down the Ctrl key on the keyboard. Next comes the step that is different from setting up stripe sets: After each set has been highlighted (or clicked), select Create Stripe Set with Parity from the Fault Tolerance menu (see Figure 8.16). Disk Administrator will prompt you with a dialog box indicating the minimum and maximum size for the stripe set (see Figure 8.17). Simply type in the desired size with the maximum/minimum range indicated; then press the Enter key or click the Create button. Disk Administrator must commit the changes in order to continue formatting the stripe set with parity partition. The formatting procedure is identical to the previous section; however, immediately after formatting, the lower status bar will display Stripe Set with Parity #N [INITIALIZING] (see Figure 8.18).

Windows NT 4.0 now identifies stripe sets and stripe sets with parity by different colors. By default, stripe sets without parity are light green, and stripe sets with parity are light blue. Previous versions were marked with the same color, with only the lower-left status bar as a way to differentiate between the two types of sets.

Figure 8.16.
Choosing Create Stripe Set with Parity from the Fault Tolerance menu.

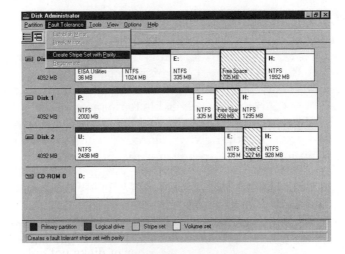

Figure 8.17.
Selecting the size of the striped set.

Figure 8.18.
Disk Administrator shows the creation of the stripe set with parity is complete.

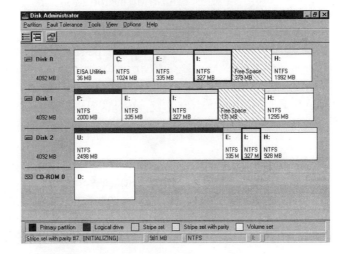

The maximum in this example would be three times the smallest partition selected, 327MB, which would allow for 981MB as the maximum size.

Recovering a Failed Stripe Set with Parity Volume

Windows NT will first attempt to remap failed sectors of the disk if remapping is supported by the interface. If this fails, Windows NT will log a high severity entry into the Event Log (Event Logging is discussed in Chapter 15, "Auditing"), indicating a disk failure in the set. All disk activity and system processes will continue to function as normal. It is advisable to replace the failed disk as soon as possible. As with all hardware-repair procedures, always make sure you have a recent backup of the data. Select the newly replaced disk and the RECOVERABLE stripe set with parity by holding down the Ctrl key and clicking on both within Disk Administrator (see Figure 8.19). Then select Regenerate from the Fault Tolerance menu (see Figure 8.20). In order for Disk Administrator to start the REGENERATING process, you must select Commit Changes Now from the Partition menu. When this step is complete, the status bar in the lower right will indicate the current condition (REGENERATING) of the stripe set (see Figure 8.21). The four status conditions are

● [INITIALIZING]—This is the status of stripe set generation immediately after the set has been created.

● [HEALTHY]—This indicates that the set is functioning normally.

● [RECOVERABLE]—This appears when one of the partitions is not synchronized with the rest of the partitions in the set or when a drive has failed, but the set is still functional.

● [REGENERATING]—This appears as the replaced drive is being updated from the surviving members of the set. No reboot is required to begin this process.

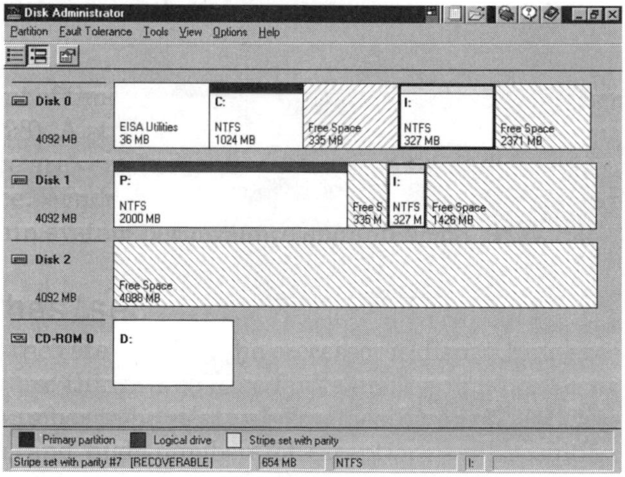

Figure 8.19.
A stripe set with parity in the Recoverable state.

Figure 8.20.
Choosing Regenerate from the Fault Tolerance menu.

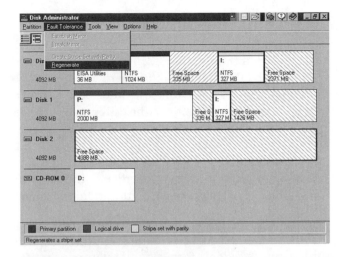

Figure 8.21.
The stripe set with parity is regenerating.

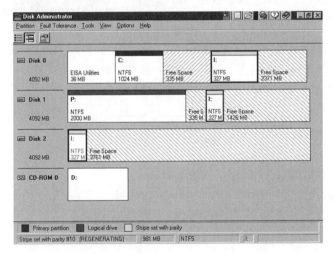

Stripe sets with parity are used most often because of their fault-tolerance capabilities, utilization of disk space, and performance. Stripe sets with parity provide a good balance for the different types of demands from BackOffice applications.

Disk Mirroring

Disk mirroring is another way to provide some performance enhancements as well as another level of fault tolerance. Although widely used, it is more expensive than other types of fault-tolerant disk implementations. Windows NT provides disk mirroring functionality as yet another tool for use in NT Server and BackOffice applications environments.

Disk Mirroring and Duplexing Explained

Disk mirroring and duplexing closely follows the RAID Level 1 standard (which is discussed later in this chapter). *Mirroring* involves two physical hard disks on the same disk controller, whereas *duplexing* involves two physical hard disks on two separate disk controllers. Duplexing adds both a level of redundancy and a level of performance increase. These are the differences between mirroring and duplexing. Mirroring and duplexing will be collectively referred to as mirroring in this discussion except where noted. Unlike striping, where pieces of the data are spread out over several disks, mirroring writes an exact duplicate of the data to other partitions on another physical hard disk of the same size. In the event of a failure, the surviving copy continues without data loss or disruption of services.

Requirements for Mirroring

Disk mirroring is the only form of fault tolerance that can be used on a system or boot partition. Mirrored partitions must exist on two physical hard disks. Disk mirroring does not require the same drive type, controllers, disk geometry, or disk size; however, the partitions must be the same size. Additionally, mirroring is supported by both FAT and NTFS. Only one instance of NT can exist on a mirrored partition; an attempt to install a second instance of NT will cause the installation process to indicate that the mirrored partition is damaged and unrecognizable and that it must be deleted in order to continue. Mirroring is supported only on NT Server, not NT Workstation.

Increased Data Protection

Mirroring maintains duplicate copies of all data in the mirrored set. In the event of a disk failure, the surviving member continues to function without data loss or disruption in service. Loss of a mirrored disk does not degrade performance, because there is no rebuilding of data on the surviving member; it is already there. Loss of both disks will result in a complete loss of data, thus limiting the protection of mirrored sets to single-disk failures.

Performance Implications

Performance with mirrored sets is mixed. Read operations are faster than they are with single-disk environments, because the FTDisk driver that supports mirroring is able to load balance read operations between the two disks. Write operations, however, are slower, but they are not a one-to-one relationship in that they do not take twice as long, because the data must be written to two separate disks. Write operations are asynchronous; therefore, impact is minimal in most application environments. However, in a duplexed environment, the write operations are not any slower than single-disk setups, and read operations are even faster. Additionally, there is greater protection, because both the disk controllers and the disks themselves are redundant. Like striping and striping with parity, the objective of mirroring is to achieve a performance increase and to add fault tolerance. The degree to which performance is increased will depend on the architecture of the hardware. Newer PCI buses will support greater sustained throughput than older EISA or ISA architectures.

Setting Up Mirror Sets

The procedure for setting up mirror sets is also done with the Disk Administrator's tool. Simply click on the primary partition (that is, the partition you want to mirror) and then, holding down the Ctrl key, click on the partition that will be mirrored. Now both partitions should be highlighted. Select Establish Mirror from the Fault Tolerance menu (see Figure 8.22). The status bar will change to indicate [NEW]. In order to begin the [INITIALIZATION] process, the changes must be committed from the Partition menu in Disk Administrator. Once the changes are committed, the mirror set begins initialization and will indicate the change in status in the status bar (see Figure 8.23). The following is a review of the different status indications associated with mirror sets:

● [NEW]—This is the status of the set after creation, but before the system has been shut down. This is required in order to initialize mirror set generation.

● [HEALTHY]—This indicates that the mirror set is functioning normally.

● [INITIALIZING]—This is the status of the mirror set generation after reboot of the system.

● [BROKEN]—This appears when one of the partitions is not synchronized with the other partition in the set or when a drive has failed, but the set is still functional.

Figure 8.22.
Choosing Establish Mirror from the Fault Tolerance menu.

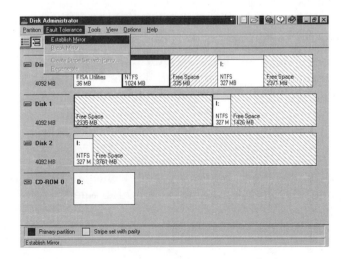

Figure 8.23.
The mirror set in the
initialization state.

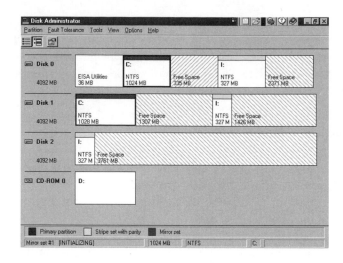

Recovering a Failed Drive in a Mirror Set

Disk Administrator will change the status in the status window from [HEALTHY] to [BROKEN] once there is a disk failure in the mirror set (see Figure 8.24). Although there is a failure, Disk Administrator will still represent the drives as mirrored. The repair procedure requires that the mirror set be broken, or separated, before it can be repaired. From Disk Administrator, break the mirror set from the Fault Tolerance menu (see Figure 8.25). This returns the system to a single disk structure that existed before the mirror set was created. Breaking the mirror set prevents problems when restarting the system. As a result of breaking the mirror set, the surviving drive receives the drive letter that was previously assigned to the complete mirror set. You can shut down the system and replace the failed drive. It is a good idea to use a drive as similar to the remaining drive as possible. This is most important if the mirror set contains the system partition. Once the failed drive is replaced, the re-creation process is the same as creating a new mirrored set (as illustrated in the previous section).

Mirrored sets provide good fault tolerance for hard disks. This is the only fault-tolerant scheme that can be used within Windows NT for the system/boot drive. It does provide good performance, although it is more costly than stripe sets.

RAID

RAID is a method of organizing disk devices to drastically increase I/O bandwidth and improve data availability. The concept of a RAID subsystem was originally postulated and described in the 1987 Berkeley paper, *A Case for Redundant Arrays of Inexpensive Disks*. Since the publication of this paper, extensions have been made to the original RAID standard.

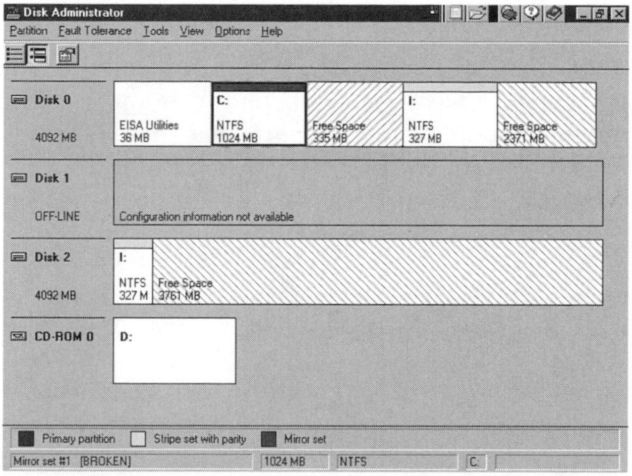

Figure 8.24.
A mirror set in the broken state.

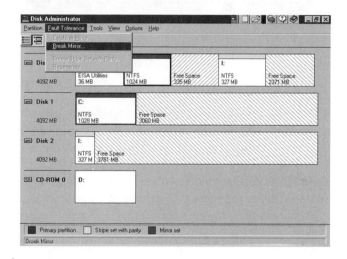

Figure 8.25.
Choosing Break Mirror from the Fault Tolerance menu.

The Berkeley paper described five levels of redundant arrays that are named RAID 1 through RAID 5. Each increasing level was defined by a different set of architectural features and an associated increase of some aspects of performance, capacity, and fault tolerance. The driving force for the Berkeley work on arrays was to address the differences between processor (CPU) performance and disk performance. This allows the implementation of high-performance disk subsystems to keep up with the demand to store more data and support an increasing number of online users, which in turn increases the amount of disk I/O requests. Each of the array types defined has some basic characteristics that sets it apart from the others.

RAID 0

RAID 0 consists of a disk array that implements data striping without any drive redundancy. It offers no fault tolerance and is less reliable than a single-drive implementation; its only advantage is speed. Data loss is subject to single drive failures across the entire RAID 0 array. RAID 0 is only useful in applications where system reliability is not critical.

RAID 1

RAID 1 is called mirroring. It duplicates the data onto separate physical disks. Performance is degraded during write operations because data must be written to two disks. However, to improve write performance and fault tolerance, duplexing is commonly used in NT-computing environments. *Duplexing* is a variation of mirroring that requires each disk to have a separate disk controller, thus providing better performance and fault tolerance. In the event that either the disk or the disk controller fails, the surviving partner continues system operations uninterrupted. This RAID level is the most costly, because only one half of the total disk space is usable. Windows NT Server supports both mirroring and duplexing.

RAID 2

RAID 2 stripes data across multiple data and parity disks. The parity information is striped onto several hard disks, while the data is striped onto separate hard disks. RAID 2 uses an interleaved Hamming code, which can be used to detect and correct single-bit errors and double-bit errors. RAID 2 is optimized for reading and writing large data blocks where smaller block reads are inefficient. Most client/server environments require small-block write operations, which would result in poor performance when using RAID 2. RAID 2 is not available with Windows NT Server.

RAID 3

RAID 3 uses a single parity drive. Data is striped at the bit level onto the data disks, while the parity drive receives all the check disk information. Performance is less than satisfactory in most environments because the data is striped at the bit level. This option is not available with Windows NT Server.

RAID 4

RAID 4 uses the same structure as RAID 3, but the data is striped at the block level. It performs better than RAID 3 in most operations; however, RAID 4 bottlenecks during write operations because of the single parity drive arrangement. RAID 4 is not available with Windows NT Server.

RAID 5

RAID 5 dedicates the equivalent of one entire disk for storing parity but evenly distributes the parity information over all the drives in the group. Because of this arrangement, RAID 5 requires a minimum of three drives. There is some overhead involved in writing parity information across all drives, however. Performance is better suited for today's client/server environments. This is the preferred option when setting up fault tolerance in Windows NT Server; it is known as *stripe sets with parity* (discussed earlier in this chapter).

RAID Implementation Discussion

RAID features of Windows NT are limited to Levels 0, 1, and 5. Level 5 is the preferred method for Windows NT. However, hardware-level RAID technology offers even greater performance, because it is not dependent on the speed of the operating system. In addition, maintenance and serviceability have been simplified, in that all the RAID overhead is managed by the hardware of the system, and is therefore transparent to the administrator and the operating system. Although hardware-level RAID implementations are more costly, they are also easier to manage and are able to achieve higher performance than software-level RAID implementations on Windows NT.

Summary

Volume sets are an integral component of effectively managing your Windows NT disk resources. They are able to address several areas of data access and integrity. Better utilization of disk partitions and fault-tolerance mechanisms are all incorporated into the Windows NT Server platform. A thorough understanding of how volume sets are used, including the limitations and functions of each type of partition, are critical components of the system performance and utilization. Testing and planning should be a part of any system deployment.

As more business-critical applications are deployed on BackOffice platforms, data access and integrity become even more important to system architecture. The different RAID levels supported by Windows NT Server are complements for the different fault-tolerant strategies used in today's client/server environments. Although there are superior solutions available from hardware vendors today, Windows NT Server has the necessary components to allow any application or organization to utilize RAID technology to provide enhanced data access and integrity.

Backup and Recovery

Windows NT Backup Tools

Data recovery is a necessary component for most computing environments. For most organizations, the real value in information systems is not in infrastructure or computer hardware, but in the data itself. The cost of gathering, manipulating, and supporting the data is far more expensive than any other component of information management. Backing up data is done as a precautionary measure to protect it against any type of loss. Additionally, complete disaster-recovery procedures, which are not discussed in this section, should be explored.

Windows NT Server and BackOffice applications are complex in their design and require testing and planning before final deployment. A critical part of that testing and planning should be in a backup strategy and procedures. These procedures should be documented and tested on a periodic basis to ensure the data is protected and the procedures are effective. This section discusses the different components and tactics used to back up and secure accurate copies of application data for Windows NT Server and BackOffice products.

Windows NT Server includes a useful backup utility (NT Backup) that is functional, yet lacks many standard features available from third-party software vendors. Any production environment should seriously consider its requirements and determine whether NT Backup will meet its needs. Some of the more common features missing from NT Backup include a tape-scheduling interface, tape-rotation software support, and a robust cataloging feature. One of the advantages of NT Backup is that it is a common data format that can be used to transport and share data between departments and companies; everyone who has access to Windows NT will have the software needed to read a tape from another NT machine. With some third-party software, both parties have to have the same backup software in order to access data via backup tapes.

Backup Media

Backup media have made some impressive advancements in just the last couple of years. The most advanced media form currently available is *digital linear tape* (DLT) technology. DLT drives place data in longitudinal tracks compared to the slanted stripes of helical scan technology, which is used in some of the older tape drives. The longitudinal recording approach is more suitable for adding read/write data to the head to significantly increase data transfer rates. Although quite expensive, it is extremely fast and has very high capacity. Its cost per gigabyte is very competitive with the older, slower, smaller media formats such as 4mm and 8mm tapes and tape drives that have been in the marketplace for many years.

Backup Methods

Each type of backup method has specific features that can be used as part of the backup strategy. Once the strategy is outlined, the backup types can be incorporated to support the backup architecture. There are five backup methods supported by NT Backup:

- Normal—Sometimes referred to as *Full*, a Normal backup backs up all files and marks them as such by resetting or clearing the Archive bit. The Archive bit can be seen from within File Manager or Explorer by selecting "details" from the View menu. This will display the file attributes, along with all the other file details. Those files that have been added or changed since the last Normal or Incremental backup will have the Archive (a) bit displayed, along with any other file attributes.

- Copy—A Copy backup is the same as Normal, but the Archive bit is not reset.

- Incremental—An Incremental backup backs up only those files that have been added or changed since the last backup or that have the Archive bit displayed. Incremental backups will reset or clear the Archive bit.

● Differential—A Differential backup backs up only those files that have been added or changed since the last backup and that have the Archive bit displayed. Differential backups will *not* reset or clear the Archive bit.

● Daily—A Daily backup backs up only those files that have been modified on the same day that the backup is executed. Daily backups will not reset or clear the Archive bit. Windows NT documentation indicates that the daily backup type is useful when you want to quickly select the files that you have worked on that day.

Developing a Backup Strategy

Developing a backup strategy is the key to securing your server data. The backup strategy should address two primary issues: disaster recovery and file restorations. Cost will also be an influential factor in choosing your strategy.

Disaster recovery has many components. Although all components of disaster recovery are not discussed here, the components of disaster recovery should be reviewed and documented. The backup strategy is one of the key components of a disaster-recovery plan, and performing Normal backups each day facilitates disaster-recovery plans. As discussed in the previous section, a Normal backup will back up all the data and reset the Archive bit. When this is done on a daily basis, recovering the entire server is completed from one tape or tape set. The steps to recover a server are minimized when working with a Normal backup of the server from the previous day. In a recovery scenario, this type of strategy will significantly reduce the amount of time required to restore a complete server.

However, depending on the applications and the amount of data, Normal backups may be quite costly. For example, if the server has 24GB of data, you will need a fast tape drive to back up all the data in a timely manner. Also, backing up the data will degrade performance of the server, which may affect mission-critical applications served from that server. As illustrated here, cost is a determining factor in the backup strategy, because in order to do a normal backup of 24GB, the more expensive tape drive hardware is required.

NOTE

Some of the newer third-party backup devices are using RAID technology to stripe data to multiple tape drives simultaneously, achieving performance levels to support backing up large amounts of data in a very short period. As of this writing, some of the published performance data is as high as 70GB per hour.

File restoration is another key component of the backup strategy. Windows NT does not have any type of "undelete" feature that is commonly found in other types of operating systems. Therefore, the ability to get to individual files from tape can be very important. NT Backup does not have a way to store copies of the catalog to disk, so before a file can be found, the catalog of the tape must be loaded from the tape. This can be time consuming, depending on the speed of the tape and the size of the catalog. Incremental backups are typically much smaller than full backups. This type of backup only backs up the files that are new or have been changed since the last backup. Because the backup sets are smaller, finding individual files with the backup sets is faster, because it takes less time to load a smaller catalog set. Incremental and Differential backup options will better support individual file-restoration procedures.

CAUTION

One commonly overlooked consideration associated with Incremental and Differential backups is that doing a complete restore does not account for files that have been deleted since the last Full, or Normal, backup. Doing a complete restore will also restore files that were deleted between the last Normal and Incremental or Differential backup.

Tape Rotation

Windows NT Server does not have any built-in tape-rotation support. There are several types of tape rotations that can be used, including Generational (sometimes called "Son," "Father/Son," or "Grandfather") methods. Other rotation schemes include features that prevent tapes from being overused, such as "Tower of Hanoi," which is used by some of the third-party vendors that market backup software for Windows NT. The advantage of tape-rotation software is that the backup program keeps track of which tapes are used. This reduces mistakes in the rotation scheme and prevents tapes from being overused, thus lengthening the life of the media and reducing the chances of media failure. The rotation scheme must support the backup strategy. Additionally, the length of time the data needs to be stored will determine the rotation scheme used.

Testing the Backup

Testing the backup may seem straightforward, but some of the features of the backup-and-restore process should be tested as well. For example, does the backup successfully backup file permissions, and does the restore successfully restore those permissions?

Doing a Manual Backup

Manually doing a backup means that the backup is done interactively from the backup console interface (see Figure 9.1). Simply select the drives and/or files you want to back up from the Drives window. (There are only two windows in the NT

Backup console interface: Drives and Tapes.) Next, select Backup from the Operations menu or just click the Backup button on the toolbar, and NT Backup presents the Backup Information dialog box, shown in Figure 9.2.

Figure 9.1.
The Drives window of the NT Backup console interface is where files and/or directories are selected for backup.

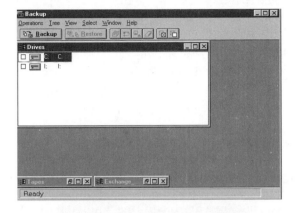

Figure 9.2.
You can select the different backup options in the Backup Information dialog box.

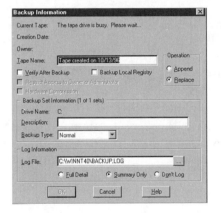

The following are the options available for backing up files:

● Tape Name—This one is self explanatory. The default is `Tape created on current date`. Depending on the rotation scheme used, the tape name could be the day of the week (for example, `Monday`).

● Verify After Backup—This option compares the data written to tape with the data on the disk. It is useful in determining the accuracy of the backup procedures.

● Backup Local Registry—This option is one of the supported ways to back up the Registry. It is highly recommended for disaster-recovery support.

● Restrict Access to Owner or Administrator—This option secures access to the tape by requiring the appropriate level of security in order to restore the data.

- Hardware Compression—This option allows the tape drive to compress the data onto the tape, if it is supported by the tape hardware.

- Append or Replace—This is where most accidents happen. Replace will overwrite the data on the tape, and Append will add it to the existing data on the tape. NT Backup will prompt you, if you have selected Replace, with a dialog box that indicates that data loss will occur if you continue.

- Description—This is a description of the backup set. Each set on the tape can (and should) have a different description.

- Backup Type—Normal, Copy, Incremental, Differential, and Daily, all of which were discussed earlier in this chapter.

- Log File—If logging is selected, the location of the file and the file name must be put in this field.

Automatic Backups

Automatic backups are facilitated via batch files and the scheduler service that is included with Windows NT. The Schedule service allows different command and batch files to be scheduled by day of the week or day of the month and by the frequency. This service must be started with an account on the server or a trusted domain that has Backup Operator privileges on that system. The correct syntax for the Schedule service is seen at the command prompt by typing at /?. (Figure 9.3 is an example of how to enter a scheduled backup command at the command prompt.) The first command in the figure is net start schedule, which starts the Schedule service. Next is the actual command to schedule the backup. This particular command will run the fullback.bat command, Monday through Friday, at 11:00 p.m., interactively. The final command is the at command, which displays the current jobs. Figure 9.4 is a copy of a sample batch file that can be used to automate backup routines.

Figure 9.3.
A sample Schedule management / syntax window.

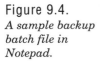
Figure 9.4.
A sample backup batch file in Notepad.

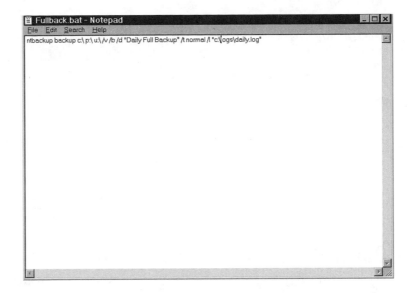

The sample batch file in Figure 9.4 will back up the C:, P:, and U: drives of the Windows NT computer from which the batch file is run. It will also verify (v), backup (b) the Registry, add the description (d) Daily Full Backup to the backup set, do a Normal backup (t), and log (l) the backup information to c:\admin\logs\daily.log.

There is a GUI interface available in the NT Resource Kit for the Schedule service.

Batch files cannot use wildcards in the path, nor can they be used to back up individual files. Only drives and directories can be specified.

The drives available in the Drives window can be physical drives on the system or mapped network drives assigned to those drive letters.

For a complete list of options that can be incorporated into the batch file, choose Help from the menu within NT Backup, select Contents, and then select Backing Up Files to Disk. There is a subcategory that lists and describes all the options available (see Figure 9.5).

Figure 9.5.
*The Help file
location for
creating batch
files.*

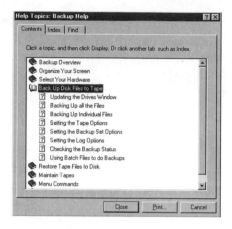

Restoring Data with NT Backup

Backup strategy and planning are done for one thing: restoring the data. Unsuc-
cessful restores negate all the backup activities. File restores are also an area where
accidents can happen, by restoring over valid data or by not restoring permissions
properly. You should plan and practice restoration procedures, to become familiar
with the different features and their functionalities.

Restore Considerations

Restore considerations are governed by the options that can be selected with the
Restore Information dialog box, shown in Figure 9.6.

Figure 9.6.
*Selecting restore
options.*

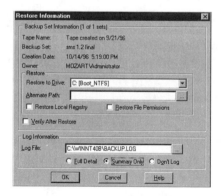

Restore Local Registry should be used only when doing a complete recovery of a
system, or if the Registry has become corrupt or damaged.

Restore File Permissions is usually required in a network server environment
where directory and file permissions are important to the security of the data.

Selecting this option will restore the data with the file permissions that were in place when the data was backed up.

Verify After Restore simply verifies that the data that has been restored matches the data that is on the tape. For long restore jobs on a network, some verifies will fail because the data has been changed by users by the time the backup job returns to verify those files.

Restoring Specific Files

Restoring specific files requires that the tape be cataloged. This can be a time-consuming process, and NT Backup has no feature that allows for storing of tape catalogs on disk (which would be much faster), only on the tape itself (see Figure 9.7). Basically, each tape that is used to restore files must be cataloged first, by backup sets and/or sets and files, depending on the type of restore required. There is no cataloging requirement if the restore is requested from the most recent backup and NT Backup has not been closed, because the catalog is already loaded. The same options are available for single file restores that are listed in the previous section.

Figure 9.7.
*Catalog loading
from a tape.*

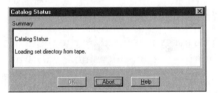

When you insert a tape to be restored, only information about the first backup set is displayed in the right panel. If you want to restore the entire tape, you need to load the tape catalog, to display a list of any other backup sets. If you want to know which files are in each backup set, you need to load the individual catalogs for each backup set.

Performing a Complete Restore

Complete restores can be complex; however, there is a simple procedure to follow, assuming the complete restore is on the repaired original server or on an identical hardware platform. Install Windows NT Server on the server. The objective is to get NT Server functioning on the box in order to perform the complete restore from NT Backup. The complete restore cannot begin until NT Server is installed and functioning. It is advisable to install Windows NT into a different directory than the one that is going to be restored. For example, the restored instance will probably be in C:\WINNT40, so install this temporary installation into C:\WINNTBAK. When the installation is complete, simply run NT Backup and select the necessary drives to restore. (Depending on your backup plan, you may need to restore the last Normal backup plus any Incremental or Differential backups since the last Normal backup. See the backup plan discussion earlier in this chapter.) Also be sure to select Restore Registry and Restore File Security from within the Restore dialog box for a complete restore. Once the restore is complete, the box can be rebooted and the second instance of Windows NT can be deleted, if desired.

Restore operations are critical to the success of any backup strategy. Different types of file restore operations have different requirements. Security and Registry options are the most important and can also be the most damaging. As part of the backup strategy, different procedures should be documented and tested, based on the requirements of the environment.

SQL Server Data

SQL Server in Microsoft's relational database application program is designed to support mission-critical client/server applications in today's ever-changing distributed computing environment. Like Windows NT Server, a solid backup strategy is a key factor in supporting SQL Server. Many of the same principles apply in designing an appropriate backup strategy, as discussed earlier in this chapter.

The backup strategy is guided by the requirements of the computing environment. For some client/server applications, backups take place hourly, in order to ensure the minimum amount of data is at risk. Other environments are well suited to doing daily transaction log backups and weekly database backups. You should consider the time required to recover from hardware failures and irreparable database corruption. Keeping in mind the value of the data and the cost of being without that data will help in designing the correct backup strategy.

Backup Devices

Backup devices are used to store dumps of databases and/or transaction logs. (*Dump* has the same meaning as backup in SQL Server terminology.) Devices are easily created from within SQL Enterprise Manager. Simply locate the SQL Server on which you want to create a dump device and right-click on Backup Devices (see Figure 9.8). If a tape device is chosen, it must be attached to the SQL Server on which the dump device is created. Disk dump devices can be either local or network based. Diskette drives, however, cannot be created as dump devices with the SQL Enterprise Manager. Once the device is created, it is ready to participate in backup routines.

Figure 9.8.
The SQL Enter-
prise Manager
pull-down menu
for backup devices.

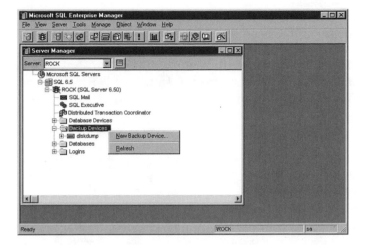

Tapes cannot be shared between SQL Server and NT Server backups. The header is written in a different format, which will result in data loss. Tape drives can be shared between NT Server and SQL Server, just not between the tapes.

Backing Up with the SQL Enterprise Manager

SQL Enterprise Manager is designed to help system administrators easily locate and execute the different features of SQL Server. Once the dump device(s) has been created, any database on the server is ready to be backed up. Simply locate the database you want to back up and right-click it. A list of available actions appears where you can select Backup/Restore (see Figure 9.9).

Figure 9.9.
The SQL Enter-
prise Manager
pull-down menu
for databases is
presented by right-
clicking the
database itself.

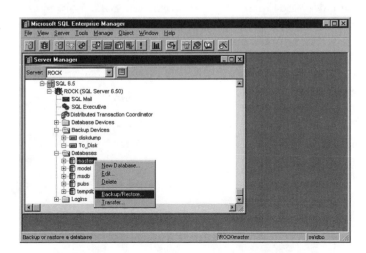

The next dialog box is tab oriented; both backup and restore operations can be accomplished from this point (see Figure 9.10). Backup options include Initialize Device, which is required to prepare the device and apply a label to it for backup routines. SQL Enterprise Manager will present an error dialog box if the device has not been labeled and the Initialize Device option has not been selected (see Figure 9.11).

Figure 9.10.
Database Backup/
Restore dialog
boxes are selected
from the tabs at
the top.

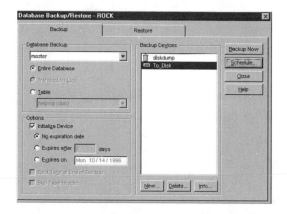

Figure 9.11.
The device
initialization
warning message.

At this point, regularly scheduled backups can be set up by selecting the Schedule button in the upper right of the dialog box. The Backup Volume Labels dialog box appears first; you can change it if desired (see Figure 9.12). The Schedule Backup dialog box has several options that will support any type of backup strategy that has been decided on for any database on SQL Server (see Figure 9.13). Recurring schedule will activate the Task Schedule dialog box with all the necessary options needed to support the backup strategy (see Figure 9.14).

Figure 9.12.
The Backup
Volume Labels
dialog box is a
good method of
identifying
different backup
sets.

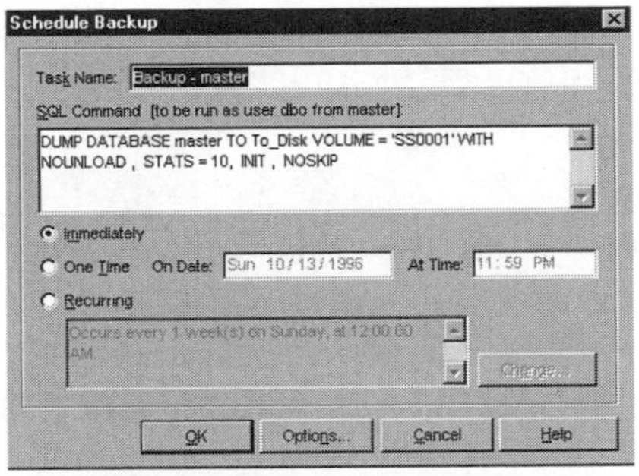

Figure 9.13.
*The Schedule
Backup dialog box.*

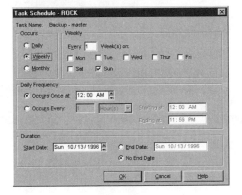

Figure 9.14.
*Simply select how
often the backup
routine needs to
run.*

Once a schedule has been set up, it can be monitored via the Scheduled Tasks option found in the Server menu. When Backup Now is selected instead of Schedule, SQL Enterprise Manager displays the progress of the backup process (see Figure 9.15).

Figure 9.15.
*The Backup
Progress status
window lists both
the database name
and label.*

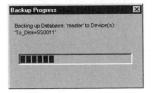

Restoring with the SQL Enterprise Manager

The procedure to restore a database has been intuitively set up within SQL Enterprise Manager to easily guide the system administrator through a restore process. This section follows the process of restoring the database that was backed up in the previous section. The Restore screen is the same as the dialog box presented during the backup, except only the Restore tab is active (see Figure 9.16). There are no scheduling options with Restore; there is only the device to restore from (which is selected with the Device button), which presents the administrator with the Restore Device dialog box. Once the device and backup are located, click the Restore Now button in the upper-right corner. The Restore Progress status window is displayed (see Figure 9.17).

Figure 9.16.
Use the same procedure to perform the backup of this database.

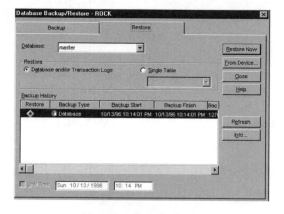

Figure 9.17.
The Restore Progress status window.

In this example, the Master.dat database was restored. There are special procedures outlined in the SQL Administrator's companion for restoring the Master database. The procedures for restoring the Master database are unique to the Master database and are not required for other database restore procedures. The example discussed in this section outlines the procedure for restoring a standard database with SQL Server.

Summary

Data backup and recovery are key aspects of managing today's complex computing environments. Windows NT Server and BackOffice applications are responsible for supporting mission-critical environments where backup and recovery become paramount in the systems-management strategy. The most valuable asset in systems management is the actual data that the backup and recovery strategies are designed to protect.

You have reviewed the different components of backup and restore procedures and how those procedures work to support data-recovery strategies. The most effective way to ensure that the strategies are effective is to test the documented procedures. The success of any systems-management effort is dependent on a planned and executed data-recovery architecture.

CHAPTER 10

Product Specifics

This chapter reviews the file system resource requirements and configuration techniques associated with the BackOffice product suite. Some of the disk resource management techniques are discussed in Chapter 8, "Data Access and Integrity," which reviews some practical implementations of volume sets and file system resources. The material reviewed here is in general terms; you should understand that each computing environment has a different set of requirements that will impact how file system resources are used with each BackOffice product implementation.

Your file system resource allocation will have different requirements, depending on the BackOffice products being used. Although most implementations of BackOffice products are done as a single application per server, it is important to be familiar with the different requirements of each product and how they may affect each other when installed on the same physical server. Adequate testing and planning are invaluable when managing file system resources for BackOffice applications.

Exchange

Of all the BackOffice products, Exchange has the most unique set of requirements. Microsoft has made a quantum leap from the previous mail server platform, Microsoft Mail Server, to Exchange Server. Exchange has its own set of requirements that are important to understand before deploying an Exchange Server. For example, depending on how Exchange is used, the Information Store (discussed in the next section) can become quite large. Additionally, the transaction logs are written sequentially, and better performance is gained by using a FAT partition instead of NTFS. Because messaging platforms are mission critical for most companies, Exchange Server can benefit from the more advanced implementations of RAID technology, in addition to other forms of hardware redundancy.

The Information Store

The *Information Store* (IS) is where all the mail messages are stored and managed. The format of this database is actually a Jet-type database, which is the same type used with Microsoft Access database applications. There is a utility included with Exchange called EDBUTIL.EXE that allows for periodic maintenance of this database. It is designed to recoup the space created in the database when messages are deleted. Although the process of database fragmentation is much more complex, this is what this utility is designed to do. The EDBUTIL database-maintenance tool can have a significant impact on file system resources (see Figure 10.1).

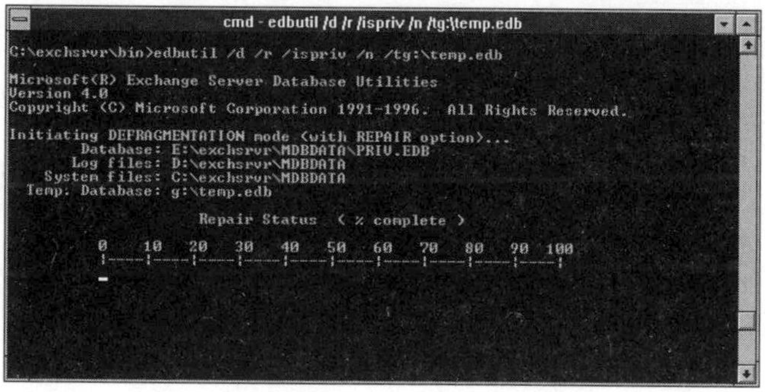

Figure 10.1.
EDBUTIL *displays both the parameters of the command issued and the progress of the database maintenance.*

```
                    cmd - edbutil /d /r /ispriv /n /tg:\temp.edb

C:\exchsrvr\bin>edbutil /d /r /ispriv /n /tg:\temp.edb

Microsoft(R) Exchange Server Database Utilities
Version 4.0
Copyright (C) Microsoft Corporation 1991-1996.  All Rights Reserved.

Initiating DEFRAGMENTATION mode (with REPAIR option)...
           Database: E:\exchsrvr\MDBDATA\PRIV.EDB
          Log files: D:\exchsrvr\MDBDATA
       System files: C:\exchsrvr\MDBDATA
     Temp. Database: g:\temp.edb

                        Repair Status  ( % complete )

           0    10   20   30   40   50   60   70   80   90  100
           !----!----!----!----!----!----!----!----!----!----!
           _
```

NOTE

The IS is similar to an Access database, but it is not possible to use Access utilities to view or manipulate the IS. Doing so may result in irreparable damage to IS.

In order to run the EDBUTIL maintenance utility, there must be a disk with at least as much space as the database itself. For example, if the size of IS equals 3GB, there must be at least 3GB of free space on the server in order for EDBUTIL to function. EDBUTIL will actually copy the existing IS to a temporary location, complete the maintenance routines, and then copy the IS back to the production location. As of this writing, the Exchange IS has a limitation of 16GB, which in theory would require a minimum of 32GB of disk storage on the Exchange server in order to accommodate the EDBUTIL maintenance process.

Disk space requirements can be estimated by multiplying the number of planned mailboxes for the server by the size of the average mailbox on the system. Mailbox sizes can be limited with the Exchange Administrator; therefore, the estimation can be made more accurately by multiplying the number of users times the maximum limit set on each box (see Figure 10.2). In addition to disk space requirements, file system resources can be addressed through the type of disk systems used to run the EDBUTIL. Greater performance can be gained by using hardware-level Redundant Array of Inexpensive Disks (RAID) disks. RAID Level 0 will yield the best performance, and the need for recovery is not as critical because EDBUTIL uses only a copy of the IS, so a failure of a disk during the process would not result in data loss. The key points for planning are the amount of disk storage needed to accommodate maintenance functions and the speed (or RAID setup) of the disks themselves. Each Exchange Server will have different requirements, and each situation should be approached with the proper testing and planning.

Figure 10.2.
Setting a limit on mailbox size with Exchange Administrator.

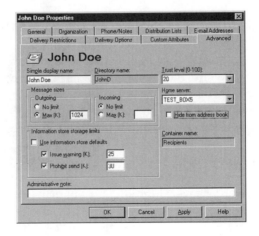

Transaction Logs

The *transaction log* is a copy of what has been written to the IS database. As each transaction takes place, a record of that transaction is kept in a transaction log. The process of creating this transaction log involves a writing process in which the data is written to the disk in a sequential fashion.

Disks formatted with the FAT file system perform better than NTFS when data is written sequentially, so that is the preferred format for this process. Even greater performance is gained when the disk used for the transaction log has a dedicated disk controller. Planning an Exchange Server hardware platform can be a detailed process. The key to transaction logs is proper maintenance—and, more importantly, placing the transaction log on a FAT-formatted disk.

The requirements for Exchange can be quite detailed. The environment reviewed here is one in which Exchange availability is mission critical, and performance and maintenance are very important. Each component of the file system resources is designed to provide maximum uptime, while making scheduled maintenance easier to manage and maximizing performance. Each environment has a unique set of requirements for Exchange deployment. Understanding those requirements is the key to properly managing the file system resources within an Exchange Server.

Disk Considerations with Internet Information Server

Microsoft has designed the Internet Information Server (IIS) in such a way that the file system resources are not a critical component of the system. Space, speed, and security can be addressed by moving components of IIS (that is, Web pages) off the IIS server and onto more robust or secure servers via the virtual directory features of the IIS. This is accomplished by changing the alias representation and thus causes no disruption to the client community. IIS is a very forgiving product for server design and setup, including file system resources.

Database Replication with SQL Server

SQL Server has several options for ensuring database integrity and redundancy. The options include mirroring segments with SQL Server, mirroring the database itself, and database-replication techniques. Although the first two are helpful, they can be more easily managed by just mirroring the physical volume itself, either via the hardware or within Disk Administrator, as discussed in Chapter 8. Database replication actually keeps a copy of the database on a separate SQL Server.

This section reviews the file system requirements associated with database replication from within SQL Server. The practical implementations for database replication are not discussed in detail; rather, this section focuses on the disk requirements for the different implementations of this feature.

Each type of SQL Server database-replication scheme has similar requirements. The key is that the database is being copied from a *distribution server* to the *subscribing servers*. The distribution server is usually the *publishing server*, which is where the database updates originate. Space considerations are especially important on the distribution server. Should the replication fail, the transaction log files will continue to grow until the replication is either executed or disabled. Each subscribing server will need enough space to accommodate the database being replicated, in addition to any expected growth. In Figure 10.3, the publishing server requires disk space three times the size of the published database. Each subscribing server requires enough disk space to accommodate the published database plus room for growth. Excluding special types of RAID configurations, this feature of SQL Server requires the greatest amount of planning and configuration testing regarding file system resources.

Figure 10.3.
The SQL database-replication topography. Each server has a brief description of its role in the replication scheme.

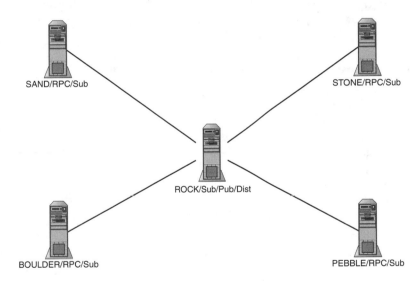

SAND/RPC/Sub

STONE/RPC/Sub

ROCK/Sub/Pub/Dist

BOULDER/RPC/Sub

PEBBLE/RPC/Sub

SQL Server database management requires that the file system resources be tuned and sized appropriately for the applications using the databases. Each type of application has a different set of requirements. Database replication adds to those requirements, and proper planning should be part of any deployment. Each participating member of a replication scheme will have different requirements that affect file system resources.

SMS Configuration

Systems Management Service (SMS) has complex file system resource requirements. As a site grows and as child sites are added to parent sites, the flow of inventory and client-configuration information will affect the requirements of the file systems. Preplanning an SMS deployment will identify the different areas that can (and will) affect the hardware requirements of an SMS deployment. Unlike Exchange Server, which has complex disk requirements, SMS is not a real-time application that affects end users immediately when there is a problem, in most environments. Software distribution and inventory management are the key components, and neither has real-time client/server processing requirements. Therefore, SMS is somewhat more forgiving when changes or alterations need to take place within the site, which includes file system resource management. This does not, however, excuse any of the planning and testing required for SMS deployment efforts; it is only an indication that certain types of alterations to an SMS site or server will not affect the user community at large.

SMS has five main components: software distribution, hardware/software inventory, network monitor, remote control, and shared application support. The three areas that have the most impact on file system resources within an SMS site or server are software distribution, inventory, and shared application support. The other two components have a disk requirement, but in standard installations, it is no more than the disk space required to install the components. The three primary areas should be reviewed and tested within each environment, to better gauge the total disk requirements within the sites and/or servers.

File System Requirements for Packages

Packages are used to distribute software for sharing network applications and local workstation software installations. All these will affect file system resources. The general rule for package distribution is that a package will require three to four times the size of the package "source" directory. For example, Microsoft Word may have a source directory size of 60MB. The site server would then need anywhere from 180 to 240MB of contiguous available disk space to support this package. The range in size is as follows: If the site server is also the distribution server, the rule is four times; if the distribution server is on a separate server, it is only three times the size of the source directory.

The space requirements for a receiving site server are slightly different. This is the process by which a parent site sends a package to a child site. The receiving child site server requires three times the size of the package source directory if it is also the distribution server, and only two times the size of the source directory if it is not the distribution server. Depending on the size and quantity of packages distributed within the SMS architecture, the space requirements can be quite large. Proper planning is very important when installing SMS. The disk space requirement can become quite large, depending on the SMS architecture and site requirements.

NOTE

If SMS is installed on the active boot partition, that partition must be large enough to store and manage the package distribution components, because an active boot partition cannot be expanded.

Packages are compressed, and they remain on the site server until they are removed. Removing them manually is detrimental to the health of the SMS configuration, so they must be removed with the Remove Package from Server job (see Figure 10.4).

Figure 10.4.
Setting up the
Remove Package
from Server job.

Requirements for an SMS Database with SQL Server

SMS database requirements within SQL Server are not on the same scale as the requirements of package distribution. However, planning the site does require some calculation for the SMS database size within SQL Server. During the site installation, SMS provides the option to change the database and log device default sizes; therefore, some preplanning is necessary in order to properly size the database and devices (scc Figures 10.5 and 10.6). The general rule is that the SMS database should be sized at about 35KB per workstation. Certainly for smaller installations this is not an issue, but for larger enterprise sites, this should be calculated and planned for, according to the estimated number of workstations. For example, if the site is expected to be 15,000 workstations, the SMS database size should be about 525MB, as a general rule.

Figure 10.5.
*Click the Device
creation option to
get the dialog box
that changes the
default sizes.*

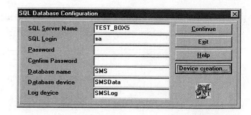

Figure 10.6.
*The size selection
dialog box for
Database and Log
devices.*

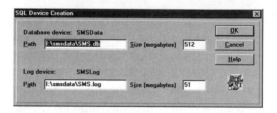

In addition to the database-size requirements, the Log device, Tempdb database device, and Tempdb Log device are all multiples of the SMS database (see Table 10.1), and should be accounted for when calculating space requirements. These SQL devices are critical to the functionality of SMS. Should these devices become inoperable due to sizing problems, the SMS system performance will suffer, or SMS may quit functioning altogether. Proper management and capacity planning are critical for these SQL components.

Table 10.1. SQL Server space requirements for SMS.

SQL Server Device	Multiple Applied	Total
SMS database size	35KB × 7500	512MB
SMS dB Log device size	.1 or 10% of SMS database size	51MB
Tempdb database size	.2 or 20% of SMS database size	102MB
Tempdb Log device size	.2 or 20% of Tempdb database size	20MB
Total disk space required		685MB

The size of each device is estimated as a multiple of the database itself. This example uses an estimated 7,500 desktops to calculate the space requirements.

Package Compression

Package compression is one of the features of SMS. The functionality is that software distribution can be compressed into smaller packages and distributed throughout the SMS system until it reaches the distribution servers. This makes transporting the software more efficient, especially when WAN links are part of the SMS site organization. Compression does require significant disk resources, but not in capacity, as with software distribution. Rather, the requirements for compression are in disk speed. The speed of the disk(s) and any associated RAID implementations affect how quickly jobs can be processed.

The function of package compression is done as part of the job-submission procedure. The level of compression is controllable, with progressing levels of compression from 7 to 1. Level 7, the default setting, provides the least amount of compression and is therefore the quickest. Level 1 is the slowest, because it will compress the source distribution files to a greater degree than Level 7, with each level proportionally slower or quicker. Because the compression process is disk-intensive, high-performance disk subsystems will provide quicker compression times than single physical disks. As discussed in Chapter 8, RAID Level 0 provides the best performance overall. Furthermore, hardware-level RAID implementations with advanced disk/drive channeling coupled with RAID Level 0 or 5 will significantly reduce the compression times.

Once the package has been compressed, it remains in a compressed format until it is removed from the site with the Remove Package from Server job, as referenced earlier in this chapter (refer back to Figure 10.4). Therefore, the file system resource considerations for package compression need to be reviewed and tested, based on the expected level of package-creation process activity. Because the packages are stored in compressed form on the site server, they will have a tendency to build up over time and should be regularly maintained. This maintenance process will also affect how often packages are compressed (or, rather, re-compressed) for distribution. All factors should be considered during the design phase of an SMS project, especially when designing files system resources.

Systems Management Server has several components that will affect file system resources. As sites grow and change, the requirements will change. Having a full understanding of SMS component flow will be a great asset in managing an SMS site, and more specifically in handling the different demands placed on the disk resources.

Summary

BackOffice applications can become quite complex in their file system resource requirements. Each application has different demands that are placed on disk resources. Many production environments are isolating most BackOffice applications onto single NT servers, but for organizations that are combining applications onto single-server platforms, the disk systems can become even more complex. BackOffice products are customizable and can be used in any number of capacities. Each environment has unique requirements, and there is no one "right" solution for every installation. Each situation should be tested and reviewed before final deployment into production environments.

CHAPTER 11

Monitoring File System Usage

This chapter takes a brief, but important look at some elements of monitoring the file system.

The file system is arguably the most crucial component in your computer system. It is the area where your valuable data is permanently stored. Naturally, it's an important system to keep an eye on.

After you've got your system up and running, you'll want to be able to watch over the file system and make sure nothing weird is happening. Of course, the idea is that you want to do everything possible to *keep* the system up and running, because it can keep you employed if it's your job to keep the server up. At the very least, it can make you look good for your boss.

There are few points you might want to consider when planning how to monitor the file system:

- File system utilization
- Database utilization
- Archiving to conserve space
- Data access performance
- Monitoring disk performance with Performance Monitor
- Using Performance Monitor Alert view to warn about filling devices

One more thing before you get rolling. I'd classify this chapter as a "miscellaneous" chapter. In other words, there are key topics relating to the subject of the file system that are covered in more detail in other chapters. For example, Chapter 8, "Data Access and Integrity," is devoted to the disk subsystem. Chapter 9, "Backup and Recovery," is dedicated to tape backup concepts. This chapter is reserved for topics that are important, but that don't warrant an entire chapter.

File System Utilization

The way your file system is used can take several forms, but in the end, it's all about files taking up bytes on a storage medium.

Specifically, this chapter focuses on disk file systems. Although there are multiple types of file systems—CD-ROM, tape, disk, and so on—it makes the most sense, in the context of Microsoft BackOffice products, to concentrate on the disk file system.

What would you say is the most common type of file encountered with BackOffice products? What is the most *crucial* type of file? It would have to be the database. SQL Server is centered around a relational database, a file. Exchange Server is built around two central databases—the public and private message stores. Again, each is a file. Microsoft Systems Management Server (SMS), SNA Server, and Internet Information Server (IIS) each have database and storage files of their own. Even the Windows NT Registry itself is a database. I hope you understand that comprehending storage and management of databases is important to the successful implementation of BackOffice.

Database Utilization

I've established that databases are the topic of the day. So what about database utilization?

If you think about the different files installed with a typical BackOffice application, what is the one that will be most likely to change size? You guessed it—the database.

For example, let's say you have installed Microsoft Exchange Server. The files that now exist on your system most likely consist of Exchange executables, Windows NT executables, NT page file, Exchange transaction logs, and Exchange databases. Of that list, the database, logs, and page file are going to change in size. Of those three, the database is the one likely to increase in size the most. In fact, if you have 500 users, each taking up 30MB of disk space, suddenly you're at 15GB! By contrast, even if you have 512MB of memory in the system, it's likely the page file will never need to exceed 1GB, and the database logs are usually somewhere less than 2GB, depending upon how long you let them accumulate between backups or whether you have enabled circular logging.

Although the focus here is on the database, the database logs also must have some attention. Transaction logs are typically not erased over time; they simply keep growing. Certainly, in the case of Exchange Server, you can get around this by enabling Exchange's circular logging feature to prevent the logs from growing continuously. However, if circular logging is not an option, you must figure out something to do with the logs to prevent them from eventually eating all the disk space. Speaking of disk space, that brings us to my next topic: conserving disk space.

Conserving Disk Space

These days, a gigabyte of disk space comes pretty cheap. However, if you have spent any time around client/server environments—particularly BackOffice—you will know that you never seem to have enough of those gigabytes, no matter how cheap.

That's one good reason why knowing ways to conserve disk space is a good thing.

With that in mind, let's go over two ways to approach the idea of conserving disk space. These ideas can go a long way toward helping you successfully manage the files and disk space on your file system.

Archiving

Without repeating everything you learned in Chapter 9, I would like to comment about archiving files in the context of conserving disk space.

The transaction logs are an obvious target for this operation. However, keep in mind they are crucial to database integrity, so you have to be precise about how you handle them.

In Exchange Server, you can backup the logs along with the database, or just backup the logs alone. Exchange ensures that the data in the logs is committed to the database before the backup is done, so after the backup, you can remove the old log files. If a database failure occurs afterward, you can restore your current database by replaying the logs into the last good version of the database.

Another target for archiving is the database. However, because databases usually contain active data, it is sometimes difficult to archive live databases. You have to judge for yourself the best way to proceed.

For example, after SQL Server data is a certain age, it is no longer of use, so it can be archived and later purged. Or in the case of Exchange, maybe you impose a size limit on the mailboxes, forcing the users to archive e-mail to their own local storage medium so the server itself doesn't run out of storage.

Compressing

Let me state that in this section I am not talking about on-the-fly disk-compression products. While this may be fine for a user's desktop, there is no place on a production database server for disk compression of this type for several obvious reasons, not the least of which is performance and reliability.

Having said that, what I am talking about could more accurately be thought of as *reclaiming* unused space inside the database.

Back to the example of Exchange Server, there is a utility included with the software that provides a way to compress the database. The utility goes through the database and reclaims lost space by putting all the data fragments together and squeezing out the unused areas in between. The net result is that the database size will shrink if it is badly fragmented. That's good news for your file system because you have recovered some valuable space with very little trouble, and the price is right, too!

Of course, there's a limit to the usefulness of this kind of utility, but it's always worth a try.

Data-Access Performance

After all this talk about file systems and databases, let's touch on the idea of performance. It's one thing to have data available to users. It's another thing completely to configure your system for good data-access performance. However, in a production environment, you must be able to both maintain the data and configure it for optimal performance. There are a few things that will directly impact data access performance in Windows NT or any BackOffice application:

- The size of the Windows NT system Cache
- The size of the application data cache
- The location of log files and databases
- The implications of RAID performance

The first item that can affect data-access performance is the size of the NT system Cache. The system Cache is a chunk of memory set aside to buffer data for both the disk and LAN subsystems of NT. The memory used for the Cache is memory that is not used by active system processes. Fortunately, you don't have to worry about setting the Cache size because it is dynamically managed by NT. The actual size of the Cache fluctuates depending upon how much memory is available in the system, how much disk I/O is being requested, and other variables that NT manages. If you graph the `Memory:Cache Bytes` counter with PerfMon, you will see this dynamic sizing as disk activity occurs. However, BackOffice applications do not have to use the system Cache. Often, they supply their own caching mechanism.

This brings us to the second item that can affect data-access performance—the size of the application data cache. SQL Server and Exchange Server are two perfect examples of BackOffice applications that do not use the NT system Cache for their database access operations. Rather, they supply their own for better performance. There are other non-BackOffice applications that also supply their own cache—in some cases, even their own file system—to enhance performance. However, just as with the NT Cache, the size of the application data cache is important to data-access performance with that application. Depending on the application, this may or may not be accessible for tuning by the user. For example, the Exchange Server database and directory buffer caches are initially configured by Exchange Optimizer. However, you can go in and adjust the size of these caches manually if you want to. As with anything, you should know what you're doing before tweaking these types of parameters, or else you can really degrade the performance of your system.

A third item that can affect data-access performance is the location of the log files and database files. I touched on the existence of two files earlier in the chapter, but it is important to note that with applications that employ a database and log files, it is important to have the files located in the proper place. For example, if you have a SQL Server installation, the log files should be on a separate physical disk from the database itself. The reason is that the log files are written to sequentially, and the database is read from and written to randomly. First, you want to separate the random read/write activity of the database from the sequential write–only activity of the log files. Secondly, in a database environment, no transaction can be committed until the log file is assured to be written to disk, so you want to keep everything out of the way of writing to the log files. This concept also applies to Exchange Server and to any other application—BackOffice or not—that employs a database and log file.

Finally, a fourth item that can impact data-access performance is the use of striped volumes and Redundant Array of Inexpensive Disks (RAID) controllers. Chapter 8 covers these topics in detail, but it's suffice to say that you can see major performance benefits by using striped volumes or RAID disk controllers. Windows NT Server itself includes the ability to configure multiple disks as stripe sets. The reputable systems hardware vendors offer RAID disk controllers as components of their computers. These controllers handle disk striping and fault tolerance in hardware, which results in extremely efficient performance and reliable fault tolerance with arrays of disks. Note that I mentioned fault tolerance. When one of your disks dies, a RAID controller is the most reliable means to manage rebuilding your valuable data. If you have a large system, or are considering implementing one, you should definitely use a RAID disk controller for best performance and maximum data availability.

Now you have all these ideas about data-access performance swimming around in your head. But how do you monitor the performance of your disks so you know things are performing nicely? I'm glad you asked.

Monitoring Disk Performance with Performance Monitor

Anyone who has used Windows NT for any length of time has probably used the Windows NT Performance Monitor (PerfMon) program. PerfMon depicts system performance by displaying counters contained in performance objects; each object contains one or more performance counters. If you've never looked at the PerfMon objects and counters, I encourage you to do so because there are many, and they provide a wealth of information about what is going on inside Windows NT and the BackOffice applications running on top of it.

This section covers some objects and counters that should serve as a good starting point. Because they are installed when NT is installed, these counters prove useful when monitoring usage and performance of your file system, regardless of the BackOffice application you are running.

The exact counters you use vary with your exact implementation, and some counters may not be useful to you at all. For example, you may not be interested in information on the threads running under NT. So while the Threads object is always available, the thread-specific counters contained in that object won't be useful to you.

Conversely, when you install BackOffice applications, such as SQL Server and Exchange Server, there are usually several PerfMon objects loaded that relate performance data specific to those applications. These are usually quite useful, and they warrant some investigation. I'm not going to go into them here, but you should know they are there anytime you install a BackOffice application.

Regardless, the general principle is the same—you can use the objects and counters to monitor performance of your file system. With some practice, you will start using these counters to begin exploration on your own.

Tables 11.1 and 11.2 list a few of the many objects and counters available.

The PerfMon disk counters are not turned on by default, so you must manually do it. There is a slight performance impact incurred—probably less than 5 percent—when they are active. However, if you are trying to analyze disk performance, the trade-off is well worth it.

To activate the PerfMon disk counters, you must run the command diskperf -y from the command prompt. If you try to use the Logical Disk (and Physical Disk) objects beforehand, they will all show zero values.

Alternatively, you can activate the PerfMon disk counters using the Device applet in the Control Panel as shown in Figure 11.1. After opening the applet, find Diskperf in the list. Its Startup Type, by default, is set to Disabled. Set it to Boot. Click the OK and Close buttons to save the change. You must then restart Windows NT for the counters to be active.

Figure 11.1.
You can enable the PerfMon disk counters through the Control Panel.

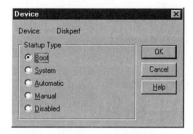

Table 11.1. Disk-related Performance Monitor objects.

Object Name	Description
Cache	The object that contains counters pertaining to the Windows NT system Cache.
Logical Disk	The object that contains counters pertaining to the *logical* disk drives in the system. The counters in this object are usually preferred over Physical Disk.
Physical Disk	The object that contains counters pertaining to the *physical* disk drives in the system.
Memory	The object that contains counters pertaining to memory usage in the system.
Paging File	The object that contains counters pertaining to the status of the page file.

Table 11.2. Disk-related Performance Monitor counters.

Object Name	Counter	Description
Cache	Data Map Hits %	The percentage of successful references to the in-memory system data cache.
Logical Disk	% Disk Time	The percentage of time the disk is busy servicing I/O requests.

continues

Table 11.2. continued

Object Name	Counter	Description
Logical Disk	Avg. Disk Transfers/sec	The average number of seconds it takes the disk to satisfy a disk transfer (could be a read or a write).
Logical Disk	Disk Bytes/sec	The rate at which data is transferred to or from the disk during I/O operations.
Memory	Cache Bytes	The size of the NT system Cache. Note that the system Cache is for both disk and LAN.
Memory	Pages/sec	Indicates overall paging activity— the rate at which pages are written to or read from the disk.
Paging File	% Usage	Shows what percentage of the page file is in use. If high, it could indicate that you need to increase your page file size.

Be careful about how you interpret the Logical Disk:% Disk Time counter, especially when using hardware RAID disk controllers.

This counter is designed to report the percentage of time during the sample interval that the disk queue length is greater than zero. In the case of a single disk system, the result is valid. However, in the case of a RAID controller, the result may not be valid. With a RAID controller, it is fine if the disk queue length is greater than zero because the controller is designed to process multiple disk I/Os at the same time. Usually this counter either shows 0 percent or 100 percent. When it shows 100 percent, it does not mean the controller cannot handle more load. It simply means the queue has something in it 100 percent of the time, and that's fine.

With RAID controllers, a better counter to monitor is Disk Transfers/sec or Current Disk Queue Length. These two counters provide a more realistic picture of the throughput on the RAID controller. You can calculate the maximum theoretical throughput of your disk subsystem, and use that as the upper-throughput limit to see how close to disk saturation you are.

To give you a feel for these counters, Figure 11.2 shows a sample run of PerfMon, monitoring some common disk-related performance counters.

Figure 11.2.
The average disk throughput for the logical drive C: *was almost 1MB/ sec during the 100- second sample period.*

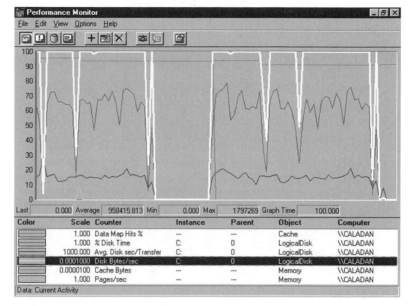

The counter highlighted is showing data for the number of bytes/sec on the logical drive C:. In this case, the graph shows a 100-second frame of data. During this 100 seconds, the disk was at rest part of the time because the Min (minimum throughput indicator) shows 0. Conversely, at one point, the drive peaked out at 1,797,269 bytes/ second. PerfMon calculates the average bytes/sec during this frame to be 958,415 bytes/sec.

Hopefully, you can see the usefulness in PerfMon when analyzing this sort of data. In fact, PerfMon proves to be an invaluable tool when measuring performance of an NT system. However, it has another feature: It has the ability to alert you if a counter exceeds a threshold.

Using Performance Monitor Alert View to Warn About Filling Devices

One thing that might have come into your mind while reading through this is how to know when the disk is approaching full. It's great to have the capability to monitor disk performance counters, but it would be nice to have the computer tell you when the disk drive is nearing capacity.

It just so happens that someone at Microsoft felt the same way. Fortunately, you don't have to sit and watch the disk counters yourself. In the prior section, you saw the Chart view of PerfMon, which is arguably the most useful of its four views. However, PerfMon has the capability through its Alert view to post alerts when any performance counter exceeds or falls below a preset threshold.

Figure 11.3 shows an example of what Alert view looks like after posting several alerts.

Figure 11.3.

The Event Monitor in Alert view can be used to post a warning when a disk device has filled beyond a predefined threshold.

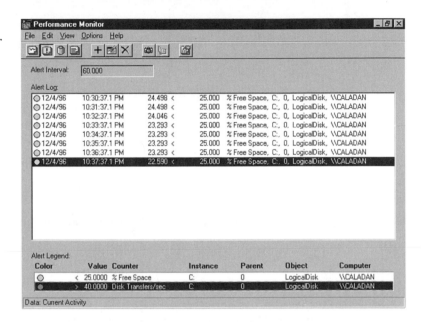

In Figure 11.3, two counters are being monitored for threshold violation—the percentage of free space and the number of disk transfers per second.

Let's say you want to know when your disk drive is more than 75 percent full. To watch for that, make sure % Free Space does not fall below 25 percent. If so, an alert is sent. Furthermore, you know your disk can handle 50 I/Os per second, so you set a threshold of 40 I/Os per second. If PerfMon detects the throughput exceeding 40 I/Os per second, an alert shows up in the Alert view. The window in Figure 11.3 does not show any alerts for violating the throughput threshold.

There are some alert options you can set to help customize things. First, click Options | Alert to get a dialog box that looks similar to Figure 11.4.

In this case, the PerfMon view changes to the Alert view when one of these monitored events happens. Also, an event is logged to the application event log, which can be viewed using Event Viewer. The automatic update interval is set for one minute (60 seconds), but you can also configure it to allow manual updating. Finally, you can opt to send a network message to anyone running NT on your network. To me, this option is not very useful because you don't know if the message got sent, if the user received it, whether you have the Net Name correct, or anything else about it.

Figure 11.4.
Setting options in
the Alert view.

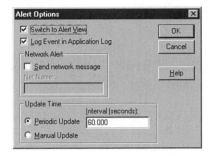

Play around with it. For any counter you can monitor in Chart view, you can set an alert associated with it.

NOTE

Some readers may be interested in taking this idea of monitoring a server to the next level of sophistication. Fortunately, this idea of being alerted when a counter exceeds a threshold is not a new one. There is an entire segment of the software market dedicated to what is called system-management software, which addresses these very issues. Companies, such as BMC Software and Computer Associates, all provide software solutions specifically for this purpose.

For example, you can configure BMC's Patrol Application Management product to monitor your server to ensure the drives are not getting too full. When that happens, you will be notified. Now, compared to what you have just reviewed with PerfMon's Alert view, that may not seem too impressive. However, consider what you would do if you wanted to monitor a few dozen servers at once. Maybe hundreds, maybe thousands—all from a single console. Or maybe you want to know when an NT service has stopped running. Perhaps you would like to be paged or sent e-mail rather than having to always rely on watching PerfMon's Alert view console to see the alert. These requirements are clearly outside the reach of PerfMon. You need software specifically designed to provide these features.

As computer systems grow in complexity, it becomes more important to be able to manage the systems rather than just deploy them and hope they stay up and running. System-management software is designed to provide you with the powerful features required to help you stay on top of things. If you haven't already, I recommend taking a look at some of the vendors' product offerings.

Summary

In this chapter, you learned about several topics related to the BackOffice file system.

First, this chapter discusses the topic of file-system utilization. The most important type of file system is the one found on the disk drives. From that you jumped to database utilization on the file system, with the idea that databases are an important element to manage on any disk file system. After that, you learned about archiving data and performance ideas pertaining to accessing data on your disk drives. Finally, you looked at the capabilities of Windows NT Performance Monitor with respect to monitoring disk performance and alerting.

The file system is much like any other resource in the system. It has to be managed properly or else it will eventually encounter problems. That means it will cause you problems. This chapter provides some guidance on how to manage your file system so you can keep it up and running.

Part IV

Network Resources

CHAPTER 12

Bandwidth Issues

Whenever you build an application that provides services to your end users, there should be a process for preparing that application for distribution that involves optimizing its performance so that the end user's experience is a good one. If you build an application on a single, standalone PC, performance becomes an issue of optimizing resources on that system alone. Characteristics such as memory utilization, processor utilization, and graphical performance become all-important.

However, in most environments today, that single PC is likely to be a server connected to a network that provides services to many client PCs. Windows NT Server was specifically designed as a network operating environment. In addition, the Microsoft BackOffice products that run on Windows NT Server take full advantage of its built-in networking features to provide services such as e-mail, mainframe connectivity, and intranet and Internet access. Optimizing performance and the end user's experience then becomes an issue not only of the resources on one server, but of those network resources connecting that server to each client. Despite the vast majority of networked computers in operation today, understanding and evaluating the role of the network in an application's performance is often the most overlooked area of system tuning.

This chapter is dedicated to understanding these issues as they relate to rolling out a Windows NT solution in a networked environment. It discusses the available topologies out today that Windows NT supports and evaluates their strengths and weaknesses. Then it discusses different types of network traffic management—routing, bridging, and switching—and their merits. Finally, I'll tell you about some network problems specific to client/server computing in Windows NT and how you can optimize for them.

Throughout this chapter I'll refer to a model for how the network's functionality is layered to provided different types of service. Figure 12.1 shows the OSI seven-layer model, the basis for most protocol stacks in use today. This chapter starts at the bottom of the model—in the Physical and Data-Link layers—building a foundation for the understanding of higher-layer client/server networking issues.

Figure 12.1.
The OSI seven-layer model.

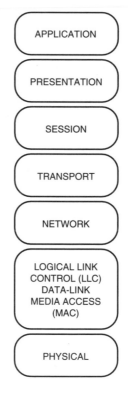

Network Topologies

This section discusses the various topologies available for connecting clients and Windows NT servers together at the Physical and Data-Link layers. It looks at *local area network* (LAN) technologies, which include those protocols confined to networks of a smaller scope (less than two kilometers from end to end). It also looks at *wide area network* (WAN) technologies, designed to connect resources separated by much greater geographic distances—even thousands of miles—and usually at slower transfer rates than LAN-based networks.

LAN Technologies

The *network interface card* (NIC) that connects your Windows NT server to the rest of your network is one of the most critical pieces of hardware you can buy. That is why your choice of LAN technologies has a great impact on the performance of your Windows NT server and its services.

There are basically two types of LAN technologies to consider for your network—deterministic and opportunistic. *Deterministic technologies* include Token Ring, Fiber Distributed Data Interface (FDDI), and 100VG-AnyLAN. Deterministic technologies are so called because traffic is carried over the wire in a determined, orderly way. Each node—be it a server or workstation—gets its turn to transmit a packet, and each gets an equal chance to access the medium. *Opportunistic technologies*, such as Ethernet, however, cater to a first-come, first-served mentality. If a station wants to transmit a packet, it checks to see if the medium is busy, and if not, it sends a packet. To top it off, all stations might be doing this at once, constantly checking the medium for others and then trying to transmit.

There are advantages and disadvantages with both types of technology. Opportunistic technologies such as Ethernet have a tendency to be less efficient (that is, they have a lower maximum effective transfer rate), but they are much cheaper in price. Deterministic protocols are very efficient, often achieving transfer rates very close to their maximum signaling rate. They're also very robust—one node with a problem is not likely to bring down an entire network. However, deterministic technologies like Token Ring and FDDI are usually much more expensive. This section looks at the technologies supported by Windows NT Server, and the advantages and disadvantages for each in a robust, high-performance BackOffice environment.

Ethernet

Standard 10 megabits per second (Mbps) Ethernet is easily the most ubiquitous network technology installed today, with more than 50 million installed nodes. 10Mbps Ethernet supports a variety of physical media, including standard Category

3 copper wire, which is commonly used in home phone wiring. Ethernet over copper is referred to as *10Base-T*, which stands for 10Mbps Baseband over Twisted Pair. *Baseband* refers to the fact that the specification for 10Base-T supports only a single signaling rate—10Mbps.

The Ethernet specification is maintained by the Institute of Electrical and Electronics Engineers (IEEE), as are most of the major network technologies in use today. Standard 10Mbps Ethernet is referred to as IEEE 802.3. The 802.3 standard defines the format of the Ethernet *header* within a packet. This header contains standard information—such as source and destination addresses—for an Ethernet packet. An 802.3 packet, including header and data, can be no more than 1,518 bytes in length. As far as physical media goes, 802.3 not only supports several categories of copper wire, but also thin and thick coaxial cable and even fiber-optic cable. Referring back to the OSI model, the Ethernet header corresponds to the Data-Link layer, and the physical media—be it copper or fiber—corresponds to the Physical layer.

Depending on the physical media used, Ethernet can use either a bus or star topology. Older, coaxial-based Ethernet networks generally use the bus model (see Figure 12.2), which can be thought of as a single cable connecting all nodes together and terminating on each end.

Figure 12.2.
A bus-based
Ethernet network.

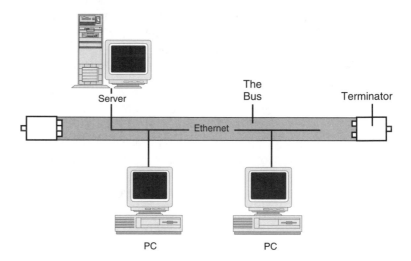

Star-based networks, like those used with 10Base-T, are networks in which the cable to each node emanates from a central hub, or *concentrator* (see Figure 12.3). Star-based Ethernet networks are definitely the most commonly used today because the cost for material and installation of coaxial cable per node is much greater, and a bus network is more difficult to troubleshoot than a hub-centric 10Base-T network.

Figure 12.3.
*A star-based
Ethernet network.*

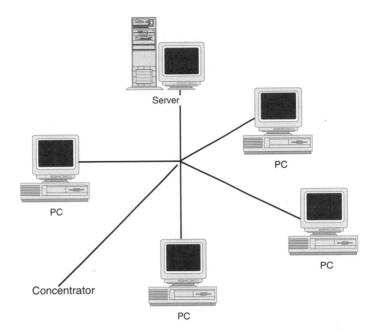

As previously mentioned, 802.3 Ethernet is an opportunistic protocol. It uses a method called *Carrier Sense Multiple Access/Collision Detection* (CSMA/CD) to allow nodes access to the network. Because only one node can transmit on the medium at a time, CSMA/CD attempts to guarantee that the wire is clear before a station sends a packet.

It's important to understand the effects of CSMA/CD as you optimize your network for your Windows NT servers. Basically, a node connected to an Ethernet segment takes the following steps when it wants to transmit a packet on the network:

- Listens on the *wire*—the physical segment—to see if anyone else is transmitting.
- If no one else is transmitting, it transmits the packet. If someone is transmitting, it backs off for a random period of time and then listens again.

If this carrier-sense mechanism, described in the first step, fails to detect another signal on the wire, and two workstations transmit at once, CSMA/CD detects a *collision* of packets, and the nodes involved back off for a period of time. Collisions are probably the biggest limiting factor on the maximum effective transfer rate of Ethernet. When a collision happens, the node trying to transmit has to resend the data. As a result, less data actually gets sent for a given time period. Because collisions are an inevitable by-product of a busy Ethernet network, the maximum effective transfer rate is no where near 10Mbps. In fact, Ethernet segments consistently at 30 percent to 50 percent utilization are considered heavily utilized— or *saturated*.

Collision problems are exacerbated by a couple of other factors. Ethernet segments—or any other network technologies—that span large distances can experience *propagation delay*. This is a phenomenon that's particularly noticeable on low-transfer-rate networks or WAN links. On 10Mbps Ethernet, the maximum allowed distance between two nodes on a given segment is 2,500 meters. When an Ethernet segment approaches this diameter, it's possible that nodes at far ends of the network may complete the process of listening on the wire for another signal and then transmit data without hearing each other in time. (That is, the time it takes for a signal from one node to propagate across the segment may exceed the time it would take for the other node to back off.)

Because collisions are inevitable on busy and large Ethernet networks, 10Mbps often makes a poor choice as a server NIC technology. When you think about it, the server is most likely to be the biggest talker on a given network, because many nodes are vying for its resources at once. Therefore, a server will suffer the most from the effects of collisions and propagation delay. For that reason, there are better choices for server-side NIC technology that are supported by Windows NT server today. Specifically, higher-bandwidth Fast Ethernet solutions as well as switched networks can provide relief for heavily used servers.

There are two competing fast (that is, faster than 10Mbps) LAN technologies that emerged at roughly the same time. 100Base-T (or IEEE 802.3u) is the 100Mbps version of 10Mbps 802.3. The 100Base-T specification uses the same CSMA/CD contention method to arbitrate access to the wire. The primary difference is simply one of signaling rate. 100Base-T packs 10 times more bits within a 1-second time slice. 100Base-T, like the 10Mbps version, is available over a variety of physical media including two pairs of Category 5 copper wire (also called 100Base-TX), four pairs of Category 3 or Category 5 copper wire (100Base-T4), and one pair of 62.5/125 micron fiber-optic cable (100Base-FX). Because of the greater signaling rate, however, the effective diameter for copper-based 100Base-T was reduced. On 100Base-TX or T4 segments, no two nodes can be greater than 205 meters apart, or roughly one-tenth the diameter of 10Base-T segments.

100Base-T makes an excellent high-bandwidth choice for server environments. In a server *farm*, where you have multiple servers on a single segment providing services to many clients, 100Base-T provides greater throughput for each node than 10Base-T ever could. 100Base-T NICs are now also comparably priced to 10Base-T adapters. It's not uncommon to find 100Base-T adapters in the $100–$200 price range. 100Base-T also uses the same cabling plant already in place for millions of 10Mbps nodes.

On the downside, however, 100Base-T is still subject to collisions; therefore, its effective throughput is still no more than 30 percent to 50 percent of the maximum transfer rate—between 30Mbps and 50Mbps. The rest is simply wasted on collisions and contention. It also has a limited network size—205 meters end-to-end. This means that it's not meant for large networks of physically diverse clients and servers. Rather, it's a better choice for the small, concentrated server farms you find in data center environments.

100VG-AnyLAN is a relatively new standard. This technology—championed mostly by Hewlett-Packard and AT&T—has not won the market acceptance that 100Base-T has, primarily because it uses new and untested methods for achieving greater network throughput and has greater cabling requirements. 100VG really falls into the category of a deterministic technology rather than Ethernet's opportunistic CSMA/CD model. It uses a mechanism called *Demand Priority Access* (DPA) to arbitrate a node's access to the medium. DPA not only requires the interaction of the NICs in the servers and workstations, but also of the 100VG hubs connecting the nodes together. The 100VG hub plays a key role. Because each node connects to the hub directly, it's the hub's responsibility to arbitrate access to the network. The hub polls each of its ports in a round-robin fashion. When a node connected to a port wants to transmit data, it does so when the hub polls its port. In this way, all ports get equal time, and all nodes can transmit as they need to.

In addition to this DPA scheme, 100VG supports two levels of priority—normal and high. This is a unique characteristic among LAN topologies. This prioritization mechanism is a key requirement for LANs that need to accommodate traffic of a time-sensitive nature, such as video or multimedia presentations. On Windows NT Server, for example, you might have a video-on-demand application that provides movies to clients on their PCs. On a normal Ethernet network, there is no guarantee of a timely arrival of the video packets to their destination; they may experience collisions that delay their arrival. This often results in multimedia applications at the client that skip or jitter as they play. With 100VG, the hub port connecting your Windows NT server—providing real-time video—could be configured at a higher priority than other ports. This would guarantee that your video server would be able to transmit its real-time data before other time-insensitive data got sent.

Despite its more flexible access method as compared to Ethernet, 100VG suffers from several disadvantages that make it applicable in only a small number of environments. First, the technology has not gained wide market acceptance. While this in itself should not doom the technology, it significantly narrows the choice of vendors for hardware and support, as well as resulting in a higher cost per port. In addition, 100VG requires four pairs of Category 3, Category 4, or Category 5 copper wire to operate. This is a big problem for the vast numbers of cabling plants already installed that are using two pairs of the existing three-pair Category 3 cable for 10Base-T, or are sharing a four-pair cable for voice and 10Base-T. The significant wiring costs associated with installing 100VG make it less appealing for many users, driving down the demand further and again raising the costs.

The bottom line for this technology is that if you have time-sensitive traffic like video or multimedia that requires high-bandwidth, real-time availability in a server environment, 100VG-AnyLAN is a good choice, provided you're willing to accept the relatively few vendor choices for hardware on the market.

Token Ring

Token Ring got its start from IBM and was traditionally used as a LAN topology to provide access to SNA-based mainframe systems. Token Ring is a deterministic technology, and its name describes how it works and how it's laid out physically. Each node is connected to a logical ring. Physically, this may actually be a concentrator into which all nodes plug directly, but the concept of the ring comes into view when you look at how nodes transmit data on the network.

One node on the ring is designated as the *Active Monitor* (AM). The AM generates a *token*—a special packet that passes from one node to the next in a circular way. When a station wants to transmit data, it has to wait until it receives the token. The node then transmits its data and releases the token to continue circling the ring. In this way, each node that wants to transmit gets the token, transmits data, and then releases the token.

The IEEE came up with a Token Ring specification similar to IBM's and called it 802.5. Today, in practice most Token Ring networks are said to be IBM Token Ring–compatible, as opposed to 802.5. The differences, however, are so minor that most NICs support both. Token Ring is available in both 4Mbps and 16Mbps transfer rates. Token Ring packet sizes can be up to 4,500 bytes, about three times that of Ethernet. Because Token Ring is deterministic, it has a very high, effective throughput. Most Token Ring networks can sustain transfer rates of 75 to 80 percent utilization without experiencing excessive congestion. (*Congestion* is the condition on Token Ring networks where the NIC or the attached PC can't process data fast enough to keep up with the network. This is usually seen on nodes that receive a lot of data, such as servers.) With Windows NT Server, congestion is exacerbated by the NIC's capability to buffer incoming packets, the speed of the Server's bus that transfers the data off the card, and the speed of the processor that processes the data for the operating system.

Token Ring can be run over a variety of physical media, including shielded and unshielded copper twisted pair (16Mbps Token Ring requires Category 5 UTP), as well as fiber-optic cable and IBM Type 1 cable. Another benefit to Token Ring is its built-in capability to isolate problem nodes from the ring. Through a process known as *beaconing*, a special packet circles the ring when a node detects a problem. When the problem node sees the beacon packet, it removes itself from the ring, does a self-test, and determines whether to remain isolated. In this way, Token Ring is more robust than Ethernet, because it has the capability to fix itself when there are problems. In a Windows NT Server environment, 16Mbps Token Ring provides a good mix of a high data transfer rate, fault isolation, and efficiency and can be a good alternative when choosing network technologies.

Token Ring, however, does have a downside: It has historically cost about $300–$400 more per port than Ethernet. Its fault-isolation characteristics can also be a liability. When a node on an Ethernet network is bad, you usually find out about it right away—the network simply stops working. However, Token Ring's beaconing process can go on, undetected, for a while, causing degradation of throughput while still providing a mostly functioning ring. Token Ring requires good monitoring and management tools to take advantage of all its built-in fault-isolation features. Finally, Token Ring is a complex protocol. It requires experienced network administrators who understand how it works in order to adequately support it. It's not as plug-and-play as Ethernet is today.

Fiber Data Distributed Interface

Of all the technologies I've discussed so far, Fiber Data Distributed Interface (FDDI) probably provides the best combination of time-tested operation, high throughput, fault tolerance, and high efficiency of any shared media technology. It's also one of the most expensive—commonly running $1,000 or more per NIC. For this reason, FDDI is best suited to a server or network backbone environment, where high bandwidths and high availability are key.

The FDDI protocol is based on the same token-passing technology that drives Token Ring. It also utilizes the same beacon-based fault-isolation techniques. However, the FDDI spec calls for two counter-rotating rings connected to each end device—be it a server, router, or hub. This dual-homed technology provides for fault tolerance in the event that there is a cable break in one of the rings. The primary ring detects the break and re-routes traffic to the secondary ring around the break. Because FDDI uses a deterministic token-based access method, it is very efficient, approaching the same 75 percent to 80 percent maximum sustainable utilization of Token Ring. The technology has also been around for quite a while, and there are a number of FDDI NICs available for Windows NT Server–based configurations.

Because FDDI is based on fiber-optic cable, it supports a maximum of 2 kilometers between any two stations. There is a 500-node limit for any FDDI ring. FDDI also accommodates larger packet sizes than either Ethernet or Token Ring, with packets up to 8KB as the maximum.

On the downside, FDDI is very expensive as compared to Ethernet or even Token Ring. It's also much more complex to troubleshoot problems on FDDI rings; you need to have special monitoring and analyzing tools to manage the ring. Additionally, FDDI's fiber-optic cable requirement makes cabling installation and maintenance costs much greater than those of the standard, copper-based Ethernet. Overall, FDDI makes a good limited server- or backbone-based solution, where the increased costs of cabling and NICs are outweighed by the need for fault tolerance, high bandwidth, and efficiency.

WAN Technologies

WANs are a necessary part of most larger networks. Most large networks span geography that exceeds the limit of LAN-based protocols like Ethernet and even FDDI. Enter the WAN. A good example is the Internet, which is simply one large WAN connecting millions of nodes together across the world. The most interesting challenge of using a WAN today is the relatively small transfer rates that users must deal with. Most WAN link transfer rates are on the order of one-tenth as great as the LAN protocols we've been discussing. It's important to understand the effects of this limitation on your server-based applications. First, however, let's look at the different WAN technologies in use today, including their advantages and disadvantages.

Leased-Line WAN Technologies

When you think about leased lines, you might automatically think fast and big, like the well-known T-1 rate. However, you could just as easily have a 9600bps leased line for some applications. There are several characteristics that distinguish leased lines from either analog or digital dial-up lines. Typical analog communication using a phone or modem establishes a call by setting up a switched virtual circuit between the source and destination. What this looks like is analogous to having a single piece of wire running from your phone or computer, all the way to the person or machine on the other end. This so-called SVC is built up by the intervening switches when you place the call, and torn down when the call is complete. This is generally how all switched services operate. Virtual circuits are created and destroyed as needed.

In this context, leased lines can be described as *permanent virtual circuits* (PVCs). PVCs are always "up"—that is, when you set up a leased line between two destinations, say your corporate headquarters and a branch office, this line is always open and available to transmit voice, data, or whatever you want to send down it. For this reason, leased lines are said to be fixed—there is no call setup or teardown. When you order a PVC between location A and location B, if you then want to call location C from A, you have to order a new leased line between A and C. Leased lines can be analog, digital, or both, and you can order them in a variety of transfer rate combinations. Because they use a synchronous signaling scheme, leased lines are capable of greater transfer rates, and because there is no call setup or teardown, you don't get many of the problems associated with switched services, such as delays or failures as the call is switched from one location to another.

As mentioned, leased lines can be ordered at any number of transfer rates. Generally, however, the standard unit for measuring a leased line is called a *DS0*, which is equivalent to 64Kb per second. A T-1 line is made up of 24 DS0s and equates to 1.544Mbps of transfer rate. You may also hear about fractional T-1s, which represent some subset of the 24 DS0s. And, just as dial-up analog lines require a modem to connect between your computer and the phone line, so too do leased lines need some hardware to connect between, for example, a server and a T-1 circuit. These devices are called *Data Service Unit/Channel Service Units* (DSU/CSUs) and are basically synchronous modems, converting digital data into analog or another kind of digital signal to be carried on the leased line. There are also some DSU/CSUs that provide additional functionality, like multiplexing.

A multiplexor (also referred to as a *mux*) is a device that allows you to divide up, for example, a single DS0 into lesser pieces. A multiplexor can take as its input, in this example, six 9600bps lines connected to perhaps six PCs with modems or six dumb terminals. On its output, it would connect to the DSU/CSU, which is in turn connected to the DS0 circuit. The multiplexor then has the job of taking in data from the six ports and feeding it onto the line in such a way that all six 9600bps streams can share the 64Kbps pipe. The multiplexor will do this using a variety of methods. One of the more popular methods is called *time division multiplexing* (TDM), which allots incoming bandwidth into discrete time slots, one after the other, that can be carried on the single DS0 to its destination.

One of the challenges you will have to face as you roll out Windows NT BackOffice solutions in a WAN environment is the limited bandwidth of most WAN links. Whether it's a 56Kbps line to your branch office or a T-1 between your IIS server and the Internet, the transfer rate of the line can have a profound effect on your end-node applications. Just as with LAN technologies, you should be aware of the propagation delay inherent in WAN media. This is the time it takes a data packet, or signal, to traverse the media. Indeed, this problem becomes more acute on WANs because of their relatively low transfer rate. And because propagation delay varies as to the size of the data packet—where larger packets take longer to get from one end of the link to another—you may get different results from an application that uses mostly small packet sizes as compared to one that requires many packets be sent at the *maximum transmission unit* (MTU). The MTU for most WAN links is 1500 bytes, but this can often be tuned.

Integrated Services Digital Network

The Integrated Services Digital Network (ISDN) standard has been around for quite a while. It was defined by The International Telephone and Telegraph Consultative Committee (CCITT) as a digital service that would allow different types of traffic—specifically voice and data—to be carried on a single wire. ISDN has been used for quite a while in Europe, but has only recently started to see wide acceptance in the

United States. Indeed, many regional Bell operating companies (RBOCs) are doing everything they can now to encourage people to move to ISDN, including pricing it as close to the same rates as regular analog voice lines.

ISDN has a number of features that make it exciting—not only in remote access solutions like Windows NT's Dial-Up Networking, but in the ease with which it can integrate the voice, video, and high-bandwidth data applications that are becoming prevalent. Chief among ISDN's features is its end-to-end digital pathway. Data is sent from an end device—for example, either an ISDN-capable phone for voice or video conferencing, or a PC capable of attaching to the ISDN network—all the way through the phone company's switched network, to an end station, with only digital signaling. There is no analog conversion along the way, neither at a user's home or remote office, nor along the way in the phone company switches. What this means is that a whole new infrastructure was required to accommodate this digitally switched network. Phone companies have been upgrading their central office switches for years to provide accessibility for users to high-bandwidth digital services like ISDN. Unfortunately, not all central offices everywhere have done this upgrade, so availability of ISDN or other switched digital services varies from location to location.

Another advantage of ISDN is its higher signaling rate. As compared to today's PC modems, ISDN has the capability to provide over five times the bandwidth of a V.34 modem. It accomplishes this by using several features. First, all asynchronous and many synchronous types of communication use *in-band* signaling—that is, signaling is encoded within the data stream so that, for example, every 8 bits of data on an asynchronous modem may have one or more signaling bits describing where the data begins and ends. With ISDN, data and signaling are channelized.

ISDN comes in two types of rate levels. The first, called *Basic Rate Interface* (BRI) is comprised of two B channels, each with a transfer rate of 64Kbps, and one D channel of 16Kbps for signaling. BRI is generally what a home user would order to access your corporate network. The aggregate bandwidth available using both B channels bonded together is 128Kbps. Also, some applications allow for use of part of the D channel for additional data transfer. The other type of rate level available for ISDN is called *Primary Rate Interface* (PRI) and is comprised of 23 B channels of 64Kbps and one D channel of 64Kbps for signaling. As you might have noticed, PRI has 24 64kbps, equivalent to a T-1. What this means is that PRI can provide 1.472Mbps of data throughput, not including the 64kbps D channel. And, if you add an additional PRI to the first, you can use the D channel on the first PRI to provide signaling for both, allowing use of the full 24 channels on the second PRI.

PRI is primarily used to aggregate numerous incoming BRIs. For example, you might have 20 remote users with ISDN BRI in their homes, and one PRI connected to your corporate network to provide access. If all 20 users were bonding both B channels together, each attaining 128Kbps, only 11 of them would be able to access your network at any one time (11×2 B channels each = 22 B channels, where PRI provides access for 23 B channels). If each home user is using only one B channel, you will be able to accommodate 23 users with your single PRI. The advantage of ISDN's channelized approach is that while one B channel may be used to connect to your data network, the other could be attached to a video phone or other ISDN-capable voice device simultaneously. This, of course, assumes you have the proper hardware to interface with the ISDN network.

When ISDN is extended by the phone company to a customer's premises, it requires a number of interfaces to connect to your computer, ISDN phone, or even regular analog phone. The point at which the local loop from your phone company's central office (CO) terminates at your premises is called *Network Termination type 1*, or NT1. NT1 simply provides the interface between the phone company's local loop and your internal equipment. It might be a PBX at your corporate headquarters or simply a junction box at your user's home.

In either case, the NT1 presents ISDN services to your premises, at which point it connects to the NT2 that can switch the available ISDN channels for voice or data use. In practice, the NT1 and NT2 may be in the same physical box—again, for example, in your PBX. The PBX may break out each B channel for use by ISDN on non-ISDN devices. Additionally, you may have some multiplexing capability for purposes of breaking down a single B channel into smaller channels, as I've discussed. If you're trying to connect a non-ISDN device to your ISDN service, you will need a device called a *terminal adapter* (TA). In the case of a PC, where the data is already in digital format, the TA performs rate adaption to prepare the signal for the B channel's 64Kbps. In the case where you are attaching an analog device like a normal phone to the ISDN network, the TA performs the conversion from analog to digital, as well as the rate adaption.

Switched 56

ISDN is an important new digital service for providing remote-access solutions that were never possible in the old days of analog. However, in areas where ISDN is not yet available, there are other options. Notably, Switched 56 service provides similar switched digital service, at bandwidths approaching one ISDN B channel, and because Switched 56 has been more widely deployed, it can often be found in areas where ISDN is not yet in place. Switched 56 provides 56Kbps worth of bandwidth, but unlike ISDN, it uses in-band signaling, reducing your effective throughput. Switched 56 is a synchronous service, similar to DS0, and requires a DSU/CSU, just like a DS0 or T-1, to connect to your data device. Network providers are also providing switched synchronous services at higher bandwidths, including switched T-1. These high-speed switched services are geared toward providing dial-on-demand backup to corporate networks where leased-line services have failed. Indeed, Switched 56 is less likely to be found on a user's desktop for remote access, but it may be useful for providing switched backup from your remote office to your corporate network.

Bridging

So far I have discussed the various LAN and WAN technologies you can use to connect a Windows NT server to your clients, either locally or remotely over the Internet. Now I'll talk about the technologies available for connecting LANs and WANs together over wide geographic, departmental, and campus environments. The task of designing a network to manage your traffic is much more complex and important than choosing the correct network topology for your applications. It's often the connecting technology—poorly designed—that can reduce your high-bandwidth server to a server-in-waiting as the rest of your network tries to keep up.

To discuss these connecting technologies, let's start at the Data-Link layer of the OSI model with bridging and work our way up.

Explanation

Bridging technology has been around for quite a while. Before there were routers and routed networks, there were bridges. Bridges operate at the Data-Link layer of the OSI model, and specifically at the Media Access Control (MAC) layer. To understand how a bridge works, it's important to understand the concept of segmented versus flat networks. These two terms refer to the fact that a physical network segment, such as a length of Ethernet with 10 nodes attached, can be connected to another Ethernet segment of, say, Windows NT servers in one of two ways. The first way is to connect the two segments via a MAC layer bridge. In this case, the bridge does as its name implies—bridges the two segments into one. Because bridges operate at the lower MAC layer and make very few decisions about where to forward a packet, they are generally very fast and efficient, with the capability to pass tens and even hundreds of thousands of packets per second.

From a MAC layer—that is, from an Ethernet perspective—the segments appear as one. If you expand this to include other Ethernet segments and even some WAN links, you've suddenly built one large physical segment bridged together without any kind of physical differentiation between nodes in San Francisco and nodes in Cleveland. Bridges also provide a way to overcome inherent limitations in a given network topology. For example, 10Base-T has a maximum network diameter of 2,500 meters, but two 2,500-meter Ethernet segments can be bridged together to effectively increase the size of the network beyond its limits.

Now, if those same two segments are connected by a router, which operates at the Network layer of the OSI model, you have segmented the network into two parts. At the MAC layer, Ethernet traffic goes as far as the router interface it's connected to and no farther—for all intents and purposes, the router is interested only in the Network layer protocols and ignores the Ethernet. Traffic is not automatically bridged to the other segment. However, through Network layer routing of packets, data does flow from one segment to the other. Again, if you connect together many segments including Token Ring, Ethernet, FDDI, and WAN links via routers, you create a large, segmented network.

The distinction between bridges and routers—flat and segmented—is an important one as you look at how to get the most network performance out of your BackOffice solutions. Because a bridge connects multiple segments together at the MAC layer, it does not discriminate among different types of MAC layer traffic. For instance, Windows NT uses the NetBIOS Session layer interface to provide many services, including file, print, and SQL Server access. One feature of NetBIOS protocols is that they often deliver services using broadcasts.

A *broadcast packet* is one whose destination is every node on the same physically connected segment as the sender. That is, every node on the segment receives the broadcast packet and processes it, regardless of whether the data is destined for that node. This process turns out to be efficient on small networks, where a greater percentage of the total traffic is likely to be destined for the few nodes. However, on large networks, broadcasts can quickly consume all available bandwidth, NIC buffers, and server resources. Bridges normally transmit broadcasts just like any other network. If broadcasts make up a large percentage of traffic on your network, bridging is not likely to help.

Most bridges support the concept of *filtering*. Filtering provides a way to either forward or discard a packet that reaches a bridge, based on the packet's source or destination MAC address or which bridge port it arrived on. Filters are administratively managed and can be used to prevent certain nodes from accessing other nodes or networks.

Different Bridge Types

There are primarily two types of bridging methods in use today: transparent and source routing. There are also translational bridges that connect two networks that use different bridging methods, and there are source route transparent bridges that combine the best of these two methods.

Transparent bridges are so named because a packet destined for a node does not know or care how it gets to that node. It passes from one bridge to another, with the decision being made at each bridge where to pass the packet next. In order to make this decision, the bridge maintains a bridge table that has information about other bridges in the network as well as MAC address-to-bridge port mapping for each node on the network. The most common transparent bridge algorithm in use today is the Spanning Tree protocol.

Spanning Tree prescribes the method for how bridges exchange information about each other and the best path to a given destination. It is described in the IEEE 802.1d specification. It is most often used for Ethernet networks, but can accommodate Token Ring as well. It uses a hierarchical model for building a bridge table. You administratively determine which bridge or bridges will become the root and backup root bridges for the network. You also administratively set the cost for each port on each bridge in your network. This cost information can be a function of the speed of the link to which the port is connected, or simply a reference to a preferred route you want traffic to take. The lower the cost, the more preferred the route. A bridged network can have multiple paths to the same network, but only the path with the lowest cost will be used. The other, higher cost paths are considered standby, until the primary path goes down.

The root bridge's function is to send out packets called *bridge protocol data units* (BPDUs) to discover information about other bridges on the network. From this information, each bridge builds its bridge table. When a workstation connected to the bridge starts up, it will—as a function of its upper-layer protocols—broadcast its MAC address on the network. The bridge captures this address, along with the port it came from, and fills the bridge table. When a bridge receives a BPDU from the root, it places information about its bridge table in the BPDU and forwards it to other bridges. In this way, all bridges in the network have a complete picture of where devices are located.

The other type of bridge—source routing—was invented by IBM for the exclusive use of Token Ring networks. The idea behind source-route bridging is that every node in the network maintains a complete route table—usually held in a special buffer in memory—that describes the path to a given destination. This information is kept in a special field in the Token Ring header portion of the packet, called the *routing information field* (RIF). When a Token Ring node wants to send data to another node on a source-route bridged network, it sends a route-discovery packet onto the network. When the packet reaches a bridge, the bridge adds its bridge ID to the RIF field and forwards it out of all its ports. The packet reaches the next set of bridges and eventually finds its destination node. By then, the RIF field of the packet contains information on each bridge the packet has passed through. The destination node then sends the RIF information back to the source node, which places it in its routing table and is then able to communicate with the destination. If there are multiple routes to a destination, only the first one returned to the source node will be kept.

This results in a source-route bridge network having a longer *convergence time*—or time taken for the network to discover a new route after a failure—than with Spanning Tree, which can have standby routes available as needed.

Reducing Traffic

As I've mentioned, the nature of a bridge is that it transparently connects two or more network segments in order to appear as one. This is both good and bad. The good part is that you can extend the limits of your existing Ethernet or Token Ring networks. The bad part is that a network segment that experienced heavy utilization, now connected to a bridge, afflicts other network segments with the same problem. This is especially true in a Windows NT environment where, even on a TCP/IP-based network, Windows NT uses broadcasting for services, such as name resolution, browser announcements, and elections.

Bridge filtering is generally the only way you can restrict traffic from one part of a bridge network to another. You can generally filter on a given MAC address or a broadcast address. Suppose you have a Windows NT server segment where you have loaded the NetBEUI protocol for communications between servers on that segment, and TCP/IP for intranet access on the other side of a bridge. Because NetBEUI is broadcast-based, you can use a bridge filter to block the NetBEUI traffic from passing the bridge while allowing unicast-based TCP/IP traffic to pass through to its destination.

Outside of bridge filters, the best way to reduce traffic on a bridged network is to simply reduce the network traffic generated by each node. Because broadcasts are, by default, forwarded by bridges to all nodes on a network, they are the first thing to look at. For example, if you've installed Windows NT servers, make sure you've loaded only the protocols you need. Ideally, if you can run with a TCP/IP-only network, you can reduce the number of broadcast packets required. Additionally, if you configure your Windows NT nodes to use DHCP and WINS for name resolution, you can practically eliminate the need for broadcasts beyond those required for the browsing function.

Routing

Routers and routed networks have been all the rage for the last six years, if not longer. The Internet is basically a giant routed network. Routers have gotten quite sophisticated and offer sophisticated filtering mechanisms, routing of multiple protocols, and even bridging functionality. Until switching became popular in the last year or so, segmentation of a network with routers was the standard practice for building robust, scalable networks.

How Routers Function

Routing is a Network layer function in the OSI model. Routing relies on Network layer protocols like IP, Novell's IPX, or Apple's AppleTalk to provide addressing of nodes on a network. For the purpose of this discussion, I'll focus on IP routing. You may already be familiar with IP addresses, because TCP/IP is the chosen protocol for the Internet. Indeed, every device that connects to the Internet needs an IP address before it can communicate. The IP address is a four-part, 32-bit address, composed of two sections—the network part and the host part. Depending upon whether the address is Class A, B, or C, and whether the address is *subnetted*—or broken into subnetworks—the network section may be as few as 8 bits or as many as 24 or more.

It is the network portion of the address that is used by routers to determine the source and destination of a packet. That, in conjunction with the node's subnet mask, determines whether an outgoing packet is meant for a node on the same network segment or for one across a routed network. Because the IP address of a node has to ultimately be associated with the node's MAC address for the packet to be delivered, the router keeps a mapping from the Network layer to the MAC layer for each connected node. In the IP world, this is accomplished using the *Address Resolution Protocol* (ARP). To understand the process, it's helpful to trace the path an IP packet takes from a server to a destination workstation:

- The destination IP address of a packet is evaluated against the server's own IP address. Is the packet destined for a node on the same subnet?

- If so, is there an ARP entry for the node? If not, the server sends an ARP request broadcast on the local segment.

- If the destination node is not on the same subnet, the server forwards the packet to the default gateway defined on the server. The default gateway is the IP address of the router interface to which the server segment is connected.

- The router then examines its routing table and sends the packet out of the appropriate router interface toward its destination.

Because routers must disassemble a packet's Data-Link layer first, then examine the Network Layer address, and then make decisions about the packet's destination based on its routing tables, routers generally forward packets much more slowly than either bridges or switches. However, they have more robust filtering functionality than most bridges or switches and, through product evolution, have better management interfaces. They also support some sophisticated routing algorithms for managing traffic flow.

Routing Types

The routing protocol is responsible for determining where to send a packet when it's received by the router. The protocol builds a table—depending upon the routing method it employs—to determine where other networks are located and how far they are. There are two major types of routing methods in use today: distance-vector and link-state. Examples of distance-vector routing protocols include the IP-based Routing Information Protocol (RIP), Novell IPX-RIP, and Cisco System's proprietary IGRP. Examples of link-state protocols include the Open Shortest Path First (OSPF) protocol and, again, Cisco's proprietary EIGRP.

The primary differences between the two methods of routing center around their view of the network and how quickly they recover in the event of a router failure—that is, their ability to converge quickly. *Distance-vector routing protocols* work just as their name implies—if I want to get to Network A, tell me how far away it is (distance) and which direction (or port) I need to go (vector). More specifically, protocols like RIP build a table on the router that contains a list of destination networks, which router port a packet should use to get to its destination, and how many *hops*, or router steps, away the destination is.

RIP routers on a network build their routing tables through a process of broadcasting to other adjacent routers, the networks that are connected to their ports directly. For example, in Figure 12.4, Router A has Networks 1, 2, and 3 connected to it directly. The information it passes to Router B includes Networks 1, 2, and 3 as well as the number of hops away they are—in this case, because the three networks are directly connected to Router A, they are given a *metric*—or distance—of one hop.

Figure 12.4.
RIP-based routers exchanging routing information.

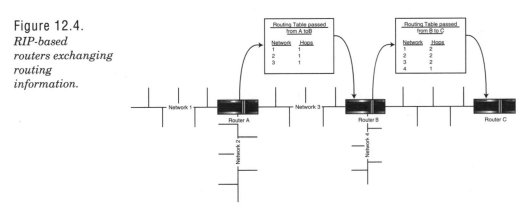

When Router B gets the information from Router A, it adds the port number that the routes came from and puts the entries in its routing table. Router B then broadcasts its routing table to other adjacent routers on the network. As part of this process, Router B will add one hop to the hop count on the entries from Router A and forward the table to Router C.

With most IP-RIP implementations, the broadcasting of routes happens every 30 seconds. IPX-RIP broadcasts every 60 seconds by default. Windows NT Server includes the IP/IPX routing service, which makes your Windows NT Server act as an IP or IPX router using RIP only. This may be useful if you don't want to spend a lot of money on a dedicated router but have multiple network segments you want to connect together. In this case, your Windows NT Server acts as an RIP router for each segment connected to it (see Figure 12.5.)

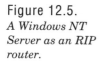

Figure 12.5.
A Windows NT Server as an RIP router.

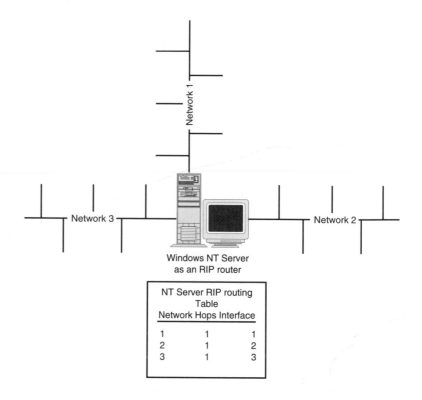

Windows NT Server
as an RIP router

NT Server RIP routing Table

Network	Hops	Interface
1	1	1
2	1	2
3	1	3

Distance-vector routing protocols like RIP are simple to manage and are well suited for small, routed networks. However, they generally don't scale well for large networks. Large networks generate large routing tables, which can require a large number of system resources on the router. RIP also does not use the concept of an administratively maintained cost for a given route. It only knows about hops, and most RIP implementations are limited to 16 hops—a significant constraint on the maximum network size supported.

The nature of RIP is that it does not provide quick convergence in the case of a router failure. This has to do with the way RIP removes routes that are no longer valid from the routing table. A router will give another three chances to send its every-30-second routing update before it marks the route unavailable. At that point, there is an additional period of time you can set before completely flushing the route from the routing table. This mechanism ensures that, on unreliable networks or for links that frequently go up and down, routes do not get prematurely flushed from the routing table. However, it means that, unless you tune down these timeout parameters, it can take several minutes for your routers to discover that a router is down. All the while, any packets destined for the down network will try in vain to follow the path in the routing table. For large networks where the routing tables on many routers need to be updated, this process can actually take much longer to reach all parts of the network. This can result in *routing loops*, where routers in different parts of the network advertise a contradictory path to a given destination that results in packets bouncing from one router to another in an infinite loop.

Link-state routing protocols were designed to overcome some of the limitations of distance-vector protocols like RIP. Rather than broadcasting entire routing tables from router to router every so many seconds, link-state protocols send updates only when something changes—a router goes down or comes up, or a new route is added. Outside of this occasional updating, routers exchange very small "hello" packets at short time intervals (usually about every 5 seconds).

These hello packets are designed to keep all routers in the network informed about each other's health. If a router goes down, and neighboring routers don't hear hello packets from the down router at an administratively configured number of hello intervals, that router is marked as down and the state of the down router is noted by its neighbors.

Additionally, while protocols like RIP keep one simple table listing destination networks, hops, and ports to use, link-state protocols, such as OSPF, have one table for dynamic routing and hello updates and another table that is computed dynamically, which builds a network-wide view of the best path to each network. This best path information is generated by spinning any one of a number of routing algorithms against the information in the dynamic routing table that describes networks that a given router has heard about and the metrics or cost to get to those networks. In a nutshell, one table holds the raw information about networks, metrics, and availability, and another table is built by taking that raw information and forming a logical picture of the full network for the router to use in making routing decisions.

Although link-state protocols converge more quickly than distance-vector protocols, they do have some associated costs. They are generally more complicated to set up and maintain. They also require more processor and memory resources of your routers, because they are doing more work to create and keep track of the best routes for the whole network.

Overall, your choice of routing protocols has to be driven by balancing the size of your network and the need for quick convergence, with ease of management and lower resource requirements for your routing devices. However, as a routing device, Windows NT Server supports only distance-vector routing (RIP) out of the box today.

Reducing Traffic

The popularity of routed networks grew partly out of the need to reduce traffic on large, bridged networks. Because bridges forward all traffic around the network, a problem in one area can quickly become a problem everywhere. Broadcasts and contention were an especially big problem. Because routers do not forward broadcasts (or collisions, in the case of Ethernet networks), they form a barrier to these types of traffic problems. Routers help define broadcast and collision *domains*, or limits. An Ethernet segment with 20 servers on it—when connected to a router— becomes a broadcast and collision domain. If 10 of those servers were placed on another Ethernet segment and connected to a router, that new segment would form another domain. Then there would be 10 servers on a segment, each contending for bandwidth with only 9 other devices, as opposed to 19.

In the past, this process of segmentation by introducing routers was the main mechanism that existed for network designers to reduce network contention. The more contention you had, the more segmentation you created and the fewer devices per segment you had. Of course, this process has diminishing returns as the cost of adding additional routers overwhelms the benefits of segmentation. Other methods, such as using higher-bandwidth technologies like FDDI and 100Base-T, help balance these costs. Switching technologies, discussed in the following section, are the next generation of networking, and they help reduce the need for highly segmented networks.

It's also important to remember that while segmenting networks with routers reduces contention and defines smaller broadcast and collision domains, it also introduces additional latency in the network. (*Latency* is the time a packet takes to be processed by the various media and devices it passes through as it reaches its destination.) Because routers work at the OSI Network layer, they must process more of a packet's data to get to the network addressing information. Additionally, routing algorithms tend to be more complex than simple bridges that forward packets everywhere. Routers also come with advanced filtering capabilities; they often are capable of filtering packet information at the Network and even Transport layers. This filtering capability is important for networks that need to secure access at the packet layer, but again, the filtering process adds latency.

As a result, routers process packets that pass through in times measured in milliseconds, as opposed to microseconds for bridges and switches. This time difference, added up as packets passes through multiple routers, can result in significant latency, which, as you'll see in the section on client/server network traffic, can cause problems with end-user applications. When you look at a large, routed network that includes relatively slow WAN links, latency from router hops and propagation delay from WAN links can have a significant impact on application performance.

Switching

Switching as a technology is by no means new. Our worldwide telephone networks use switches to connect millions of people each day. LAN switching, however, is a fairly new concept. LAN switches have begun to gain popularity only in the last two years—although companies like Kalpana were selling Ethernet switches three to four years ago. LAN switches today represent an interesting evolutionary step in networking. First, there were bridged networks, which worked at the MAC layer and were fast but relatively feature poor. Then came routers, working at the Network layer, which were introduced to segment busy networks and reduce contention and broadcast effects. Additionally, routers provided sophisticated filtering for security applications, such as Internet firewalls.

On the downside, however, routers introduced significant latency, and increased segmentation resulted in a greater reliance on network-management tools to keep track of large, segmented networks and their complicated addressing. Enter switches, which again work at the MAC layer as bridges did, and indeed can be thought of as more intelligent, more specialized bridging devices.

Explanation

A LAN switch takes the concept of reducing contention to its logical conclusion: that a network of one device will experience the least amount of contention possible. When Ethernet, Token Ring, and FDDI protocols were invented, they were based on the concept of shared media. Every device connected to an Ethernet or Token Ring segment shared bandwidth with every other connected device (see Figure 12.6).

Figure 12.6.
*How a shared
media network
works.*

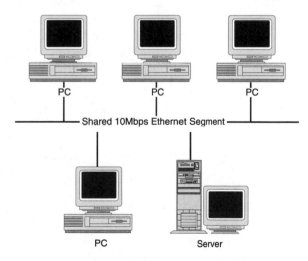

All devices transmit at once
and must share the medium

Contention increases—as do by-products like collisions and congestion—as the number of devices on the shared segment increases. A LAN switch looks like a shared-media hub with multiple ports into which you plug server or workstation nodes. However, instead of passively repeating each node's signal onto the segment, as a hub would, the switch is really a large bridge. Each port, and the device connected to it, is considered its own segment—be it Ethernet or Token Ring (see Figure 12.7).

Figure 12.7.
How a switched network works.

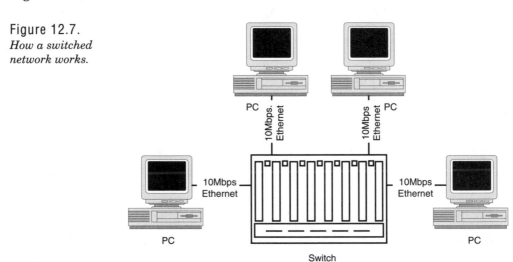

For example, if you have a server connected to a port on the switch in Figure 12.7 via 100Base-T Ethernet, that server is the only device on that physical Ethernet segment. Its collision domain is a domain of one, thereby greatly reducing the contention for bandwidth for that server. Remember, however, that because the switch is just a glorified bridge, broadcast traffic is still forwarded to all ports on the switch. Behind the scenes, what's happening in the switch is similar to how a bridge works.

When a device starts, its upper-layer protocols usually announce the MAC address to the network. The switch takes this information, and the number of the port it arrived on, and builds a bridge table in its memory. If it's an Ethernet switch, it uses the 802.1d Spanning Tree algorithm to build a table that defines paths to every device on the network that it knows about. If you have multiple switches on the same physical network, they each trade BPDUs, as do regular Spanning Tree bridges, so that they can build a full bridge table of the physical network. Switches are very high speed. Depending upon the size of the packets, a switch can forward hundreds of thousands to millions of packets per second. Latency in switches is low as compared to routers, because a switch works at the lower MAC layer and makes very simple decisions.

As I've alluded to, switches are generally just bridges with higher port density and better performance. However, there is a greater limit to port densities on switches than on standard shared-media hubs. This has to do with switches having greater backplane demands than a shared-media hub. For example, suppose you have a chassis-based shared-media hub with a 24-port 10Base-T card for workstations and a 12-port 100Base-T card for servers. Workstations send packets to the server card over the backplane of the hub.

The backplane is rated at some high aggregate throughput, based on the fact that it must accommodate many devices communicating with each other at the same time. Suppose all 24 workstations want to communicate with a server on the 100Base-T card at once. Because of normal Ethernet contention, at best 30 to 50 percent of them will be able to access the server at one time. This limits the upper throughput on the hub as a whole to something like 1.2Gbps. The throughput of the hub's backplane doesn't have to be as high as the theoretical maximum of all 24 workstations and 12 servers, because contention makes it impossible to approach this limit.

Now let's look at the same scenario on a switch, where each workstation is connected to one of the 24 10Base-T switch ports and the server is connected to its own 100Base-T switch port. Because the switch guarantees that each device connected to a port experiences no contention, you easily could have all 24 workstations transmitting at 100 percent of 10Mbps to a server, for an aggregate throughput of 2.4Gbps required on the backplane. If the backplane's throughput is greater than the maximum throughput for a given switch configuration, the backplane is said to be *nonblocking*. Most switches are not as port dense as a corresponding shared-media hub, because the cost to produce a nonblocking backplane under all possible configurations would be prohibitive.

Another interesting side effect of going from shared media to switched networks is the loss of certain network-management capabilities that shared media provides. Most notably, it becomes very difficult to perform captures of network traffic on switched networks. In today's shared-media world, if you have a network problem, you can connect a protocol analyzer like Network General's Sniffer to a port on shared-media hub and capture all the packets on the segment. Because switches can dedicate a port to each connected device and each port is its own network segment, you can no longer plug an analyzer into a switch port and expect meaningful results. The switch forwards traffic to the analyzer port only if the traffic is meant for the analyzer, which is rarely the case.

Vendors have come up with some inventive ways of performing packet captures, but none have yet proven as flexible as just plugging an analyzer into a shared-media hub. This is something to consider as you build your switched network. The ability to do good network management and analysis becomes critical as your network grows and spans geographic regions.

Reducing Traffic and Contention

The whole purpose of LAN switching technology is to reduce contention without segmenting via router ports, but you can still have one or more devices connected to a given switch port. If you have more than one device connected to a switch port, those devices share the media and contend with each other within the domain of that port. In a typical switched network, you might find several workstations on shared media, such as 10Base-T, and connected to a switch port. Then, on their own dedicated ports, there are several servers (see Figure 12.8).

Figure 12.8.
*A switched
network with both
shared and
dedicated devices.*

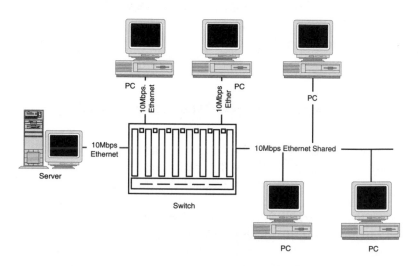

In this way, you can take advantage of a switch's ability to reduce contention for high-use devices like servers, while still reducing the collision domain for shared media workstations by having fewer workstations per segment. However, like bridges, while switches can reduce contention (and, on Ethernet, the collision domain), broadcast packets are still forwarded around the entire switched network. There are two ways to reduce this type of traffic in a switched network: place routers at the boundaries of the switched network or implement some kind of virtual LAN (VLAN) technology.

Just as routers help define broadcast domains within a shared media network, they also perform that function in a switched environment. In a switched network, contention is not an issue, so you're able to create larger, flatter networks, consisting of hundreds or even thousands of nodes on the same physical segment. However, because switches do not block broadcasts, switches become a big problem on a 1,000-node segment. You can use routers to connect switched segments together, defining smaller broadcast domains. You might then have two 500-node switched segments connected via a router that defines the broadcast boundary (see Figure 12.9).

Figure 12.9.
*A router acting as
a broadcast
boundary to two
switched segments.*

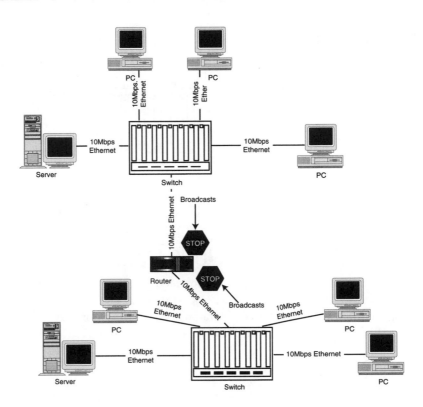

Another option for broadcast control is to use some new technology specific to the switching arena—VLANs. VLAN is a method of isolating certain groups of switch ports within a switched network from other ports. For example, you might have a switched network composed of Ethernet segments spread across an FDDI backbone. You might have a set of servers connected to one switch that provides services to a set of workstations on another switch. The purpose of VLANs is to group these like resources together within a broadcast domain. In Figure 12.10, you see that VLAN A spans several ports on two switches—Switch 1 and Switch 2.

Even though there are other devices connected to Switch 1, when a broadcast packet is sent from a server within the VLAN, it is not forwarded to any other port on that switch.

VLANs are a powerful way to manage traffic on a switched network. However, in today's market, there is no one standard for implementing VLANs. This makes interoperability between different vendor's switches difficult. VLANs can also get complicated to manage, because you have to keep track of which ports are members of which VLAN. If you're planning a multivendor-switched network, you should consider using routers to control broadcasts until an industry-supported VLAN standard is in place.

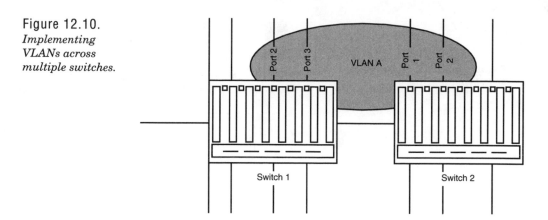

Figure 12.10.
*Implementing
VLANs across
multiple switches.*

Client/Server Network Traffic

So far in this chapter, we've focused on general networking technologies at the lower—Physical and Data-Link—layers of the OSI model. Now let's move up the model and look at the Transport to Application layers and how Windows NT BackOffice products and services use the network at these layers.

NT Server

From a network perspective, there are two types of services that a Windows NT server offers: file and print services and application services. File and print services are the traditional LAN services in which the server acts as a repository for binaries and data associated with an application, such as Microsoft Word. A client *mounts*, or maps, a server drive where the binaries reside—using the network redirector that's part of the client-operating system—to its local file system, and runs the application in local memory. The network redirector on the client ensures that the client PC responds to the server-based files as if they were loaded on its local C drive.

Windows NT file and print services are based on the OSI Session Layer NetBIOS mechanism called *Server Message Blocks* (SMBs). SMBs provide analogous functionality to Novell's NetWare Core Protocol (NCP). SMBs are a connection-oriented protocol. This means that in a Windows NT TCP/IP environment, SMB functionality is implemented over TCP. From a networking perspective, this ensures that in the event of network contention, SMB packets are sequenced and can be retransmitted if dropped or if they do not arrive in a timely manner. However, it's important to remember that while SMBs are connection-oriented and therefore robust on busy networks, the application code being served may not be able to tolerate excessive network timeouts.

If you're running Word from a Windows NT Server and the network experiences a period of excessive contention at about the same time you're running the spell checker, it's possible that Word will be unable to transfer the spell-checker code from the server in a timely manner, and you may get an error. Although this is an extreme case, many applications are even less tolerant of delays in the network around file and print services.

I've talked about problems related to network latency. It's also important to take into account server latency—the time it takes for the server itself to process incoming and outgoing packets. This is generally a function of how busy the server is with other tasks, and how many memory buffers are available to hold incoming and outgoing packets from the network. To minimize server latency problems on your network, there are several things you can do from a hardware standpoint. First, make sure your server has sufficient bandwidth to deal with the traffic load. Second, consider buying NICs that have onboard CPUs. These so-called *smart* NICs offload the processing of incoming and outgoing packets from the server's CPU, allowing it to do other more important work.

There isn't much in the way of tuning you can do to Windows NT Server to prevent problems on busy networks. What you *can* do is make sure that you monitor your Windows NT networks to ensure that problems don't arise (see Chapter 13, "Monitoring Network Utilization"). With file and print services, which tend to generate a lot of traffic, make sure you place your servers on high-bandwidth segments, co-located with the clients that plan to use them. It is never a good idea to place a server that you plan to use for file and print serving across a slow WAN link from multiple clients. This is a guarantee that you will have response problems. In this case, you will be better off copying the binaries and data to the local workstation's hard drive.

The other class of services a Windows NT Server provides are application services like SQL Server, Systems Management Server (SMS), Exchange Server, and Remote Access Services (RAS).

SQL Server

SQL Server 6.5 is Microsoft's most recent relational database offering. By default, SQL Server uses a NetBIOS connection–oriented protocol called Named Pipes to provide access to its services. You can specify other network protocols to use, such as TCP/IP Sockets, from the SQL Server Client Configuration Utility (see Figure 12.11).

Figure 12.11.
*Changing network
protocols in the
SQL Server Client
Configuration
Utility.*

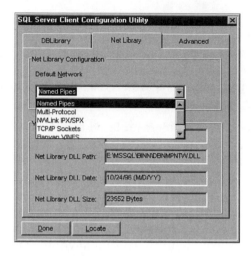

The nature of SQL-based databases is such that client interaction is minimized to a series of requests, or queries, and responses, or answers to queries. The query is sent from the client to the server; the server processes the query locally and returns the answer to the client. These answers usually arrive in the form of records or rows of the SQL database, and populate a form or report within the client application. Even though the data passing between the client application and SQL database is minimized, these types of applications are still sensitive to low-bandwidth networks such as slow WAN links.

Applications will often time out if responses to queries aren't received in a timely manner. SQL Server 6.5 provides the capability to alter the default packet size when communicating with the server via an application, the SQL Enterprise Manager, or the ISQL/w Query tool. In each case, you can set the default packet size to fit your available network bandwidth. If you are transmitting query results over a slow WAN link, smaller packet sizes are better. While less efficient at transferring data, small packets experience less propagation delay traversing the slow link and are less likely to cause application timeouts. You will need to test your application and network for the best combination. The challenge is to balance slow network response times associated with big packets with the wait time incurred by your client application as it receives many smaller packets.

Another mechanism you can take advantage of in SQL 6.5 to reduce traffic on slower networks is stored procedures. *Stored procedures* are frequently used queries or pieces of code that reside on the server and are called by name by the client application. Instead of the client repeatedly sending a frequently used query over the network to the server, the application simply calls the stored procedure, which executes the query and returns just the answer to the client.

SMS and Software Distribution

SMS 1.2 is Microsoft's current offering for software distribution, help-desk functions, and inventory and asset management. SMS uses a hierarchical site model for distributing software. A primary site server (PSS) holds all information about software packages available for distribution. Secondary site servers (SSS), running on Windows NT Servers throughout the network, serve as distribution points for these packages.

SMS uses services called *Senders* to perform the distribution to secondary sites and to receive inventory updates from secondary sites and send them to the primary sites. Depending on the network connection, there are several different types of Senders, including LAN, SNA, and RAS. The LAN Sender is the most common, covering both local and WAN links. Remote sites connected via RAS use the RAS Sender. Because software-distribution jobs can use up a lot of network bandwidth and have a significant impact on utilization of slower WAN links, SMS 1.2 includes a Sender Manager tool (see Figure 12.12).

Figure 12.12.
*Using the SMS
Sender Manager
tool.*

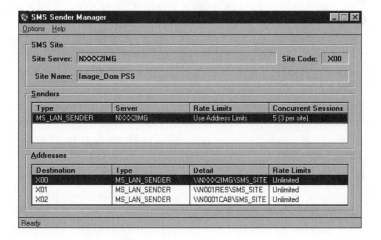

The Sender Manager tool gives you the ability to tell SMS how much of the available bandwidth it can use at a given time of the day on a per-site basis (see Figure 12.13).

For example, you might have a site across a slow WAN link that experiences high utilization during business hours. Using the Sender Manager, you can limit bandwidth utilization during business hours to some small percentage of the total link rate, and then increase it during the night when you initiate the software-distribution job. For other sites that are local to the PSS on Ethernet or other high-speed topologies, you can provide SMS with unlimited bandwidth access, allowing it to distribute as much as possible, as quickly as possible, with no regard to bandwidth usage.

Figure 12.13.
Configuring SMS bandwidth and time-of-day usage per site.

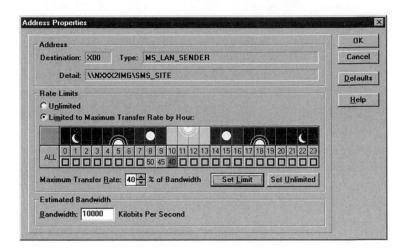

Exchange Server

Exchange is Microsoft's messaging platform, providing such functions as e-mail and group scheduling. There are several aspects of Exchange, including its use of the network, that you need to be aware of when planning an implementation. Exchange also uses the concept of sites, but they are implemented in a different way than SMS sites. An Exchange site is a collection of servers that share a *Global Address List* (GAL) and public folders, and contain a number of user mailboxes. The sharing of the GAL and public folder information happens automatically within the site between all servers. You normally have no control over this replication process. By contrast, if you build multiple sites, each containing its own GAL, public folders, and user mailboxes, you can configure what you want to replicate between sites, and how often.

The replication of information within and between sites can have significant impact on available network bandwidth. This is especially true within sites, because you have little control over how much or when information is being replicated. For this reason, it's a good idea to design your Exchange sites with network bandwidth limits in mind. For example, when building a site that traverses slower WAN links, you need to have at least 56Kbps of *available* bandwidth to accommodate intrasite replication. This guideline means that, if you only have a 56Kbps link between two locations, you should not install an Exchange site server on each side of that link. Rather, you should either upgrade the link or have your clients connect to an Exchange server across the link.

Another issue to be aware of when implementing Exchange in low-bandwidth environments is the effect of mail attachments. Users commonly attach files, documents, or pictures to mail messages. The impact of attaching a 1MB .gif file to a mail item at a location that's connected to an Exchange Server across a 56Kbps link is significant to the utilization of that link. The user will experience a significant slow-down in application response as he waits minutes for the attachment to be sent to the server. Take advantage of the Exchange Administrator feature that allows an administrator to limit the size of both incoming and outgoing attachments by user or by profile.

WAN Traffic

The section on WAN technologies discusses the different types of links for connecting devices across geographically disperse locations. In this section, I'll tell you about two services that Windows NT Server provides that interact with or provide access to WANs—the Internet Information Server (IIS) and RAS.

It's important to understand why LAN traffic behaves differently when it reaches a WAN link. WAN links are point-to-point links. That is, there are only two places on a WAN link where traffic can enter—at each end of the link. This differs from most LAN technologies, where nodes contend for access at any point on the network to which they are connected. Contention on a WAN link then becomes an issue of which packets arrive first at the input buffer at either end of the link. And, if the device buffering the input—a router or a Windows NT Server running RAS—cannot provide access to the link quickly enough, the packets get dropped and must be retransmitted by the end station.

WAN contention really becomes an issue of contending for buffer space, which is directly related to how busy the link is. When a packet does get placed on the link, it is given a time-slice—or discrete amount of time—of the available bandwidth, just as with LAN technologies. When all time-slices available are taken up for a given interval, packets must wait in buffers. If the wait becomes too long, some applications will time out. If the link is very slow (that is, 56Kbps or less), the combination of wait time to get onto the link and propagation delay traversing the link can cause many applications to time out.

Remote Access Service

RAS, also known as *Dial-Up Networking* in Windows NT 4.0, provides a cheap and easy way to create a WAN on your Windows NT network. RAS provides NetBEUI, TCP/IP, and IPX/SPX point-to-point connections using a variety of supported physical media, including 28.8 analog modems, ISDN, X.25, and frame relay. RAS, in conjunction with Windows NT Server's router feature, can provide a dynamic WAN connection to remote sites, via dial-up or leased connections.

Because RAS's primary function is as a dial-up provider, there are special issues to be aware of if you're implementing it to provide WAN connectivity between two or more Windows NT sites. Specifically, if you're using RAS as a dial-up WAN connection between Windows NT sites, there is a certain amount of background traffic that Windows NT generates for functions like browsing, domain controller replication, and NetBIOS session keep-alives. Additionally, if you have BackOffice services running on remote servers—such as Exchange site replication or SMS site inventory—you might require other background traffic to keep your sites consistent.

RAS has the capability to autodial connections when network requests are made to or from the remote site. If you frequently have background network activity, this autodialing can result in high costs on links using technology like ISDN or Switched 56, which charges you higher rates for initial circuit setup in the first minute of a call. You could end up having hundreds of these connections made each day for this background traffic.

In these cases, you will need to tune this background traffic as much as possible by reducing some of the periodic processes that Windows NT uses. For example, by stopping the NetLogon service on remote Backup Domain Controllers during daytime hours, you can prevent domain controller replication traffic. As long as no changes need to be made to the user account information, your remote users will still be able to authenticate to the domain.

Internet Information Server

Internet Information Server (IIS) is Microsoft's World Wide Web, FTP, and Gopher service for Windows NT Server. While you may have IIS servers providing these services for LAN users on your intranet, this section focuses on WAN-based access to IIS services.

If you're using Windows NT Server with IIS to provide Web services on the Internet, you need to be aware of the network issues and the tuning you can do to maximize the link. HTTP, the primary Web-based protocol, uses TCP to create connections between client and server. As I've discussed, connection-oriented protocols like TCP provide advantages and disadvantages on slower WAN links. TCP will sequence and retransmit packets that initially fail to reach their destination. This can be good for slow links or for busy links leading to your Web server. However, TCP's robustness can also result in diminishing available bandwidth for other, connectionless traffic.

With the goal of providing the best experience for users connecting to your Web site, there are several alternatives for managing available bandwidth for your IIS server. The first and most obvious is to segregate IIS-based traffic onto a separate WAN link from other Internet traffic. From a cost standpoint, this may or may not be a viable solution. Another option is to use some of the configuration features that IIS provides to provide acceptable performance for your Web users.

From the Internet Service Manager, you can set properties for each IIS service you employ. For example, each service—FTP, Gopher, and Web—provides you with the capability to limit the number of connections to your IIS server (see Figure 12.14).

Figure 12.14.
Limiting the number of incoming IIS connections.

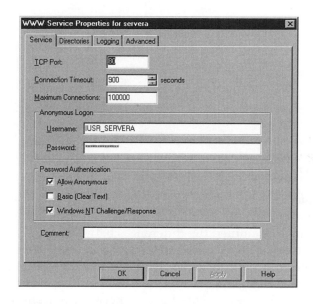

By limiting connections, you guarantee that most users accessing the server can experience reasonable response times. You can also reduce the connection timeout value. This guarantees that connections time out quicker, allowing other users to access the server. Another feature of IIS is the capability to limit the total bandwidth used by the IIS services. For example, you might have a slow 64Kbps ISDN line connecting your Web site with the Internet, and IIS services may be only a part of what you use the link for. Using the Internet Service Manager, you can tell IIS how much bandwidth to make available to its services (see Figure 12.15).

Limiting bandwidth in this way guarantees that your Internet link never gets overwhelmed with IIS-related traffic. Again, using this feature and limiting the number of users connecting to your IIS services allows your Web users the best combination of response time and access to your Web services with the available limited bandwidth.

Figure 12.15.
*Limiting the
bandwidth
available to IIS.*

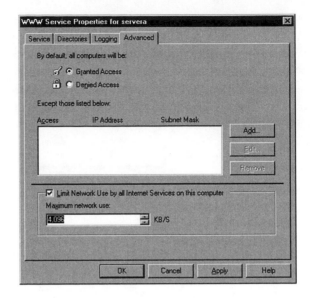

Summary

In this chapter, you looked at the most common LAN technologies available for Windows NT networks today—Ethernet, Fast Ethernet, Token Ring, and FDDI. You have examined the differences between deterministic and opportunistic network topologies and their respective performances under load. I talked about the various WAN technologies available and the effects of propagation delay. Next, I discussed bridging, routing, and switching—including the use of VLAN technology—and how each contributes to network contention, delay, and performance.

Finally, you examined the networking aspects of some Windows NT BackOffice products. I discussed how Windows NT Server uses SMBs for file and print services, how SMS uses LAN Senders to distribute software, and how you can tune LAN Senders for limited network bandwidth usage. You looked at the requirements for Microsoft Exchange sites on low-bandwidth networks, and examined how you can configure the IIS for maximized performance on WAN links.

CHAPTER 13

Monitoring Network Utilization

In Chapter 12, "Bandwidth Issues," you looked at the characteristics of the most common network topologies in use in the Windows NT environment today—Ethernet and Fast Ethernet, Token Ring, and Fiber Distributed Data Interface (FDDI). You also examined the various technologies used to bridge or route these topologies and their impact on performance. In this chapter, you'll use the tools that Windows NT provides to examine bandwidth usage and the effects of contention—collisions and congestion. Then, you'll take a look at what these numbers mean for the overall performance of your BackOffice solutions.

Network Monitoring Tools

Windows NT Server provides the tools you need, right out of the box, to troubleshoot most network problems. Between the Performance Monitor tool and the Network Monitor tool and agents, you can track protocol-specific statistics from the Data-Link layer to the Session layer. Statistics like network utilization, broadcast rate, number of discarded packets, or current IIS connections are valuable to have at your fingertips when you discover problems on your Windows NT network.

Performance Monitor

The Performance Monitor (PerfMon) is Windows NT's most indispensable trouble-shooting tool. From system or process-related statistics to network information, PerfMon provides a great way to discover what your server is doing. You can start PerfMon in one of two ways. From the Start menu of your Windows NT server, select **R**un, type PerfMon, and then click OK. Or, from the Start menu, select **P**rograms, Administrative Tools, and then Performance Monitor.

PerfMon has four views to the data—Chart, Alert, Log, and Report. The Chart view (see Figure 13.1) is the default view when you start PerfMon.

Figure 13.1.
The Chart view is the default in Performance Monitor.

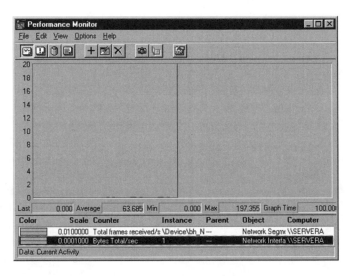

Chart provides real-time monitoring of objects and their counters. The Alert view allows you to set thresholds on specific counters and performs some action if these thresholds are exceeded. Log provides a mechanism for historical logging of data. You select a set of objects you wish to capture, select a capture file, and let PerfMon run. The log function is the best way to keep track of network resources on your system over the course of a day or more. This not only gives you good long-term data for troubleshooting possible network problems, but it also provides a baseline for future network capacity planning. Be aware, however, that the more objects you log, and the more frequently they poll the server, the larger your log file grows. Four objects polling every 15 minutes can generate two to three megabytes of log data a week.

Finally, the Report view provides real-time, at-a-glance statistics on chosen counters. It's useful for quickly viewing, in tabular format, key information about your system, such as network utilization, errors, and current connections (see Figure 13.2).

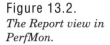

Figure 13.2.
The Report view in PerfMon.

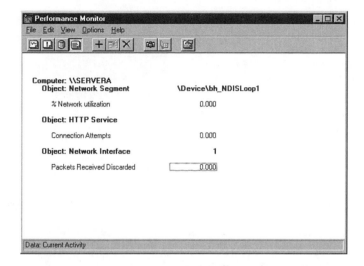

One advantage of using PerfMon is its tight integration with Windows NT Server and BackOffice products. All BackOffice products—when installed—add objects and counters to PerfMon for use in monitoring their performance. You can take advantage of this feature to capture product-specific statistics about these services. For example, in Figure 13.2, PerfMon is reporting not only on base network statistics, but also on HTTP server connection attempts. This counter was added to PerfMon by the installation of Internet Information Server (IIS).

The Network Monitor Tool

The Network Monitor (NetMon) tool has been a feature of Systems Management Server (SMS) since version 1.0. With Windows NT 4.0, it was added as a base tool in NT Server. However, the NT Server version is limited in functionality as compared to the SMS tool. Specifically, the Server version only allows you to capture network packets flowing to and from the server where the tool is running. The SMS version allows you to connect to remote "agents," or software-based collectors running on any Windows NT workstation or server anywhere on the network. The NetMon tool provides a software-based protocol analyzer similar in functionality to Novell's LANalyzer or Network General's hardware-based Sniffer tool.

To add the NetMon tool and agent to your Windows NT server, you need to add a network service. From the Control Panel, start the Network applet. Select the Services tab, click Add, and choose Network Monitor Tools and Agent (see Figure 13.3). You'll have to restart your system after installing the tool.

Figure 13.3.
*Installing the
Network Monitor
Tools and Agent
from the Network
Control Panel.*

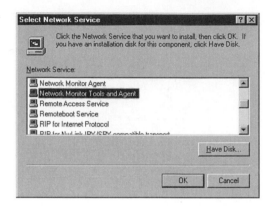

If you are using the SMS version of NetMon, you only need to install the Network Monitor Agent on your Windows NT Server. Note that in either case, the Network Monitor Agent is installed as a Windows NT service and can be controlled from the Control Panel Services applet. By default, it's installed with a manual startup type. This means you have to explicitly start it if you wish to use NetMon on your system.

If you've installed the Network Monitor tool, it is placed in your Start menu, under Programs | Administrative Tools | Network Monitor. When you start it, you're presented with a default view of four panes, each one capturing a different set of information (see Figure 13.4). These include Graph, Total Stats, Session Stats, and Station Stats. To start capturing packets on the server where the tool is running, select Capture from the NetMon menu, and select Start. If you have multiple NICs in your server, you can only capture one segment at a time. From the Capture menu, select Networks to connect to the desired adapter.

Figure 13.4.
*Viewing network
capture statistics
in NetMon.*

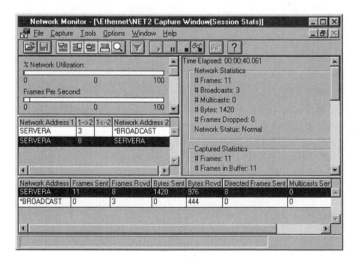

If you have installed Dial-Up Networking (DUN) for use on your server, Windows NT creates a virtual MAC address for your DUN device, and you can capture packets on this as well. This is a really useful feature, because you otherwise would need an expensive hardware-based WAN protocol analyzer to perform this kind of capturing on dial-up or leased wide-area connections.

Bandwidth Usage

What is bandwidth? That's a good question to ask if you need to understand the effects of an overutilized network. Some people say that bandwidth is the "speed" of the network or its transfer rate. Bandwidth is best thought of as an available time-slice on the wire. A 10Base-T network is said to be 50-percent utilized if a 10Mbps signal has transmitted some data within a half-second period.

Or, to think of it another way, if two nodes transmit on an Ethernet segment—one right after the other—and they each transmit for one quarter of a second at 10Mbps, they are utilizing 50 percent of the available bandwidth for one second. If you measure bandwidth utilization as a time-slice smaller than one second, the bandwidth utilization goes up, because you're using the wire for a greater percentage of the time-slice. Most tools available today for measuring bandwidth usage provide an average of the instantaneous bandwidth utilization over the time they are capturing.

Bandwidth usage is an important statistic to track on your Windows NT Server. The very nature of a server—providing services to many clients at once—means that its NIC(s) or WAN connections are likely to become a bottleneck eventually. Bandwidth usage is subject to a number of factors, and different usage rates are interpreted differently for a given network topology. For example, 10Base-T Ethernet on a shared segment would be considered overutilized if the *sustained* bandwidth usage is greater than 40–50 percent. You might see the effects of this overutilization in the form of excessive collisions or dropped packets. However, 10Base-T in a switched environment would be expected to perform close to its maximum available bandwidth. An FDDI network would also be expected to support sustained transfer rates in excess of 75 percent before experiencing congestion or dropped packets.

Both the PerfMon and NetMon tools provide facilities for capturing bandwidth usage over time. PerfMon's logging feature is the best tool for this. NetMon shows real-time network utilization for the segment you're monitoring in its Graph pane, but this information is not saved for future reference.

PerfMon provides several objects and counters for viewing bandwidth utilization and the amount of traffic on a given interface:

- ● Object: `Network Interface`; Counter: `Bytes Total/sec`—This gives the total number of bytes transmitted and received on the chosen instance (NIC) per second.

- Object: `Network Segment`; Counter: `% Network Utilization`—This gives the current percentage of bandwidth utilized for the chosen instance.
- Object: `RAS Port`; Counter: `Bytes Transmitted/sec` and `Bytes Received/sec`—This gives the inbound and outbound transfer rates for a given RAS (or Dial-Up Networking) port.

By default, you won't see the `Network Segment` object unless you install the Network Monitor Agent on your server. The agent doesn't have to be running to provide Network Segment statistics, but it does need to be installed. This object is recommended, because it uses the Network Monitor's software interface to the NIC to capture true bandwidth utilization from the chosen instance. There is also a counter associated with the `Network Interface` object, called `Current Bandwidth`, that provides no information other than the current transfer rate of the NIC you are monitoring. For example, an FDDI segment will always show 100Mbps as its current bandwidth.

Contention

Contention is closely related to bandwidth usage. When there are more devices needing to access the wire than there are available time-slices on that wire, you have *contention*. Depending upon the network topology, contention exhibits itself in different ways. For CSMA/CD-based 10- and 100Mbps Ethernet, contention results in collisions. For Token Ring or FDDI, contention results in congestion and sometimes beaconing (see the section on Token Ring in Chapter 12 for a discussion on beaconing).

As a result of many nodes contending for access to the media, you can end up with problems that manifest themselves at several different protocol layers. For example, if an Ethernet segment is busy and a server is trying to transmit responses to a number of workstations, the workstations may time-out waiting for a response and retransmit their original requests, adding still more traffic to the crowded network. This is an issue mostly with connection-oriented upper-layer protocols like TCP, and it can be a real problem for higher-layer protocols like named pipes, used in most SQL Server communications.

Of the tools available, neither PerfMon nor NetMon provides the ability to view MAC-layer problems, such as collisions or congestion, directly. However, there are ways that these tools can view the results of these problems. In NetMon, the following statistics can show possible contention problems:

- In the Graph pane, keep an eye on the `% Network Utilization`. If continuously high, you might have contention problems, especially on an Ethernet network.

- In the Total Stats pane, look at Network Card (MAC) Error Statistics. Too many dropped frames as a percentage of total captured packets or a continuously incrementing dropped-frame counter could mean than hardware or software buffers for packets are filling up because the NIC can't get access to the wire.

In PerfMon, you have a wide variety of objects and counters you can examine to determine if you have a contention problem. Because contention results from an overly busy network, and manifests itself in a host of lower- to upper-layer protocol problems, it's a good idea to choose a set of counters representing each layer, to determine if you have a contention problem. For example, the following counters might help discover contention problems on a server providing file services and SQL Server (connection-oriented) services:

- Object: Network Segment; Counter: % Network Utilization—This gives current bandwidth utilization.
- Object: TCP; Counter: Segments Retransmitted—This determines if you're experiencing excessive retransmissions.
- Object: Server; Counter: Sessions Errored Out—The Server service provides inbound network I/O for file and print service and other inbound network functions. This counter shows network errors related to the Server service servicing requests.
- Object: IP; Counter: Datagrams Outbound Discarded— This indicates that send buffers were unavailable to process the packet, potentially due to the server's inability to access the media in a timely manner.

Once the data is gathered, the next step is to interpret what you've collected and take steps to eliminate the network as a bottleneck, if needed.

Interpreting Performance Monitor and Network Monitor Indications

Once you've collected the data, how do you know whether you have a network problem? Bandwidth usage and contention are very much inter-related problems. The higher your usage levels, the more likely that contention will result in dropped packets, excessive retransmissions, or a host of upper-layer protocol problems. To make things more difficult, some applications are more tolerant of bandwidth shortages than others. For example, HTTP traffic uses User Datagram Protocol (UDP)—a connectionless protocol—to provide Web services. Web services are therefore very tolerant of congested networks, because they don't maintain a connection with the client and don't keep track of whether a packet reached its destination.

However, you might also have a TN3270 application provide mainframe terminal emulation. Because this is generally a TCP-based application and 3270 sessions are very sensitive to timing delays, your users might experience dropped sessions on the same congested network where your Web users are doing just fine.

Using the tools previously described—PerfMon and NetMon—you can determine whether you have a network problem and what you need to do about it. There are many types of network problems. Here are some general guidelines on interpreting the data that can make the troubleshooting process easier:

- If you're on a shared Ethernet (10- or 100Mbps) network and PerfMon is showing average % Network Utilization in excess of 40–50 percent, it's possible you have a capacity problem. Take a look at the TCP object at the same time and check to see if you're getting consistent retransmissions. Also, check the Network Segments object's % Broadcast Frames to ensure that you're not experiencing a broadcast storm that may be artificially elevating the network utilization.

- On wide area networks (WANs), it's often difficult to directly measure utilization or capture packets. A problem usually manifests itself at the end-station, whether it be a workstation running an application across the WAN or a server trying to access the WAN to send data. If the server is directly connected to the WAN, chart the Object: Network Interface, Counter: Packets Outbound Discarded. If this counter is incrementing continuously, it may indicate that the WAN is so busy that the network buffers on the server cannot keep up with the outbound flow of packets.

Summary

In general, if you use PerfMon's logging function to baseline your network initially, you will know what's normal and what's not during periods of heavy use. You can then use NetMon to capture traffic between problem nodes and examine what exactly is happening. If the problem indicates a bandwidth bottleneck, your choices are to provide more bandwidth or reduce the traffic. In the case of the former, it may be a matter of going from 10- to 100Base-T, moving from a routed to a switched network, or upgrading from a 56Kbps WAN link to a T-1 or fractional T-1.

In the case where you have to reduce traffic, use NetMon to capture traffic and ensure that you don't have any unnecessary traffic on a link. For example, Windows NT uses NetBIOS broadcasts for a number of functions. These might become excessive on a switched or bridged network, and might be prevented by installing routers or filtering on your switches or bridges.

By using PerfMon to baseline your network and NetMon for pinpointing problems, you can quickly anticipate and solve most network problems as they arise.

Part V

Security

CHAPTER 14

Product Security

One of the major features of the Windows NT networking architecture is the integrated security mechanisms that enable a user to log on only one time to gain access to other BackOffice components, such as the Exchange Server or the SQL Server (and BackOffice-compliant software). This does not mean that these other products do not have their own security mechanisms that control access to data or procedures, but you have to get through Windows NT security as a first step before you can access these other applications and their security mechanisms. The BackOffice suite is supposed to be a complete solution to office integration and security management techniques, which are common to most products and for which accountability can be audited.

In Volume 4, *Networking Windows NT 4*, several chapters discuss the inherent integrated security of Windows NT:

- Chapter 1, "The Windows NT Domain," covers the domain model(s) used in networking Windows NT. Domains are the main administrative unit (especially for security purposes) in the NT architecture.

- Chapter 8, "Understanding User Rights," gives you a greater insight into the rights and permissions and how they interact to allow the system administrator to establish procedures and policies for a secure network.

- Chapter 9, "Resource Shares and Share Security," gives a more in-depth discussion for those who need to know more about how Windows NT uses share security (similar to the method used by Windows for Workgroups) and how it also offers security using the native file system for NT (called NTFS) to provide security down to not just the directory level, but also down to the file level.

This chapter discusses other topics, such as encryption of data and password information and the security policies and mechanisms that are built into the BackOffice products, as well as continuing the discussion on basic Windows NT security.

When you refer to the Windows NT domain–based security in Volume 4, you will notice that each and every person (or machine) that logs into an NT domain must use a domain-based account. Because Windows NT runs some programs as background services, each of these needs a user account under which to run, so that each service can be restricted, just like a user, using rights and permissions.

These accounts are stored on a Primary Domain Controller (PDC) and one or more Backup Domain Controllers (BDCs). For example, the Exchange Server runs under Windows NT as a *service* and thus must have a *service user account* granted the appropriate rights the service needs, and the permissions set on files and directories must be accessible through this server account. Even the Internet Information Server (IIS) has three components: the WWW, Gopher, and FTP applications, which all run as individual services under Windows NT. You may find in other BackOffice products there is more than one service that runs, and you may find that some services are dependent on others. So, to sum it up, you should consider the basic NT security directory database as your starting point for implementing BackOffice security.

Encryption

Within the BackOffice environment, encryption comes into play several times, depending on which action you are performing and which product you are using. For example, when you log on to an NT server using remote access (or the Dial-Up Networking Client), you are given the opportunity to send passwords as clear text, which simply means that the ASCII characters are sent unaltered across the communications medium. Anyone with the advanced knowledge of how to use a network sniffer, or other device that can capture and display the data in network packets, can intercept your name and password. Obviously, this is not the preferred method for sending passwords and usernames across a network.

WARNING

If you plan to use FTP in your NT server setup, remember that FTP allows only two types of logons. The first is by using the clear-text method, which is standard for the FTP protocol. Under the IIS property sheet for the FTP service, it is always a better idea to run the service under an anonymous account and restrict the permissions on your files, directories, and other objects (such as printers) so that only the information you want anonymous users (actually, this is *anyone* who can access your computer) to have access to is granted. You wouldn't want to give anonymous users access to your entire computer system, because they could then wreak havoc by deleting system files or filling up your disks with useless files, among other things.

Workstation Password Authentication

When a workstation wants to log on to an NT server domain, it uses a challenge/response method that never requires the actual password to be transmitted across the network. This is done by using the following steps:

● The user's plain-text password is encrypted using a standard text key known to the workstation and the NT Server processing the logon. It is the same key generated by the NT Server when the user's account was first created.

A proprietary-encryption scheme developed by Microsoft (but similar to Data Encryption Standard, or DES) is used to encrypt the data.

● When the workstation attempts to log onto the domain, the domain controller challenges the workstation by returning the same standard text used as the key, but encrypted by using the server time as the key for this encryption.

● The workstation receives the challenge, and it then uses the same encryption method to encrypt the challenge it just received from the server. It uses the standard text pseudo-key from the first step in this process as the key to encrypt this data and returns the data back to the server.

● When the server receives this response, it knows that it has received an encrypted version of its original challenge to the workstation, using the stored plain-text password that both used as a key. If all matches, the user must have typed the correct information.

Note that by using this challenge/response method, no actual user password ever has to travel across the network.

NOTE

It seems that the French government does not allow the import of any type of data-encryption software. Therefore, the French version of Windows NT and other products that support encryption do not contain the necessary encryption-software modules.

Application Data Encryption

When sending data across the local area network (much less the Internet), you may find you need to encrypt not only your passwords, but also the data being sent. Windows NT and the BackOffice products supply several methods for this.

If you are part of a mixed network, that is, you have clients other than Windows NT and are running Microsoft Mail for PC Networks, encryption is used on the files with the extensions MAI, ATT, CAL, and MMF. In addition, the MASTER.GLB and ACCESS.GLB files are also encrypted. The reason that Microsoft has developed its own proprietary format for encrypting these files is that DES encryption is not allowed to be exported to countries outside North America. Microsoft's method is similar, but it uses 40-bit keys.

Data Encryption Standard, CAST-64, and CAST-40 Encryption Methods

The DES standard of encryption is considered to be the best available at this time. It can use keys up to 128 characters in length, but for export, only 40-character keys can be used. For legal reasons, you cannot export products that use more than 40-bit key lengths, except to the United States and Canada.

When using the 64-bit version of DES, only 56 of the bits are used as the key, with the remaining 8 bits being used as a checksum for the key. The data to be encrypted is divided into 64-bit sections, and each of these sections is encrypted using a 16-step process. This repetitive encryption is sometimes referred to as an iterated cryptosystem.

To show you how safe this method of encryption is, consider the process used for DES encryption:

- Each 64-bit block has data bits moved around according to an algorithm. This is called permutation of the block.
- Each of these permuted blocks is then divided into halves.

- Now comes the 16-step iteration:
  1. If this is not the first iteration, the left and right sides of the block are swapped. This is not done during the first iteration.
  2. Some bits are duplicated, others are switched around, according to an algorithm, expanding the 32 bits in the right half of the block to 48 bits.
  3. A key-scheduling algorithm is used to produce a 48-bit subkey.
  4. The subkey is XORed (the exclusive OR logical operator) with the expanded (48-bit) right side of the data block.
  5. The results of the previous XOR operation are manipulated so that they can be re-stored into 32 bits, using 8-bit S-boxes.
  6. The P-permutation is used on each of the 8-bit sections.
  7. The left and what has become of the right side of the original 64-bit data are XORed, further encrypting the right half of the data.
  8. Finally, back to step 1, where the left and right halves are switched, and all these steps are performed 16 times.
- After the 16 iterations, the remaining message is put through another permutation, just like on the original 64-bit data section.

Now does that sound like something you can decipher easily? Probably not! When the keys are larger (128 bits, for example), it gets even more difficult.

If you want to get down to the bits and bytes with an in-depth discussion of S-boxes and the manner in which the DES algorithm uses matrices to generate subkeys and permute blocks of text, see an excellent discussion of this at the following location:

```
http://www.math.ncu.edu.tw/~solomon/ComputerScience/Cryptography/
howto.html
```

The CAST method of encryption uses a different algorithm, but can use any variable length key from 40 to 128 bits. Again, only the 40-bit version is allowed on versions of NT products sold outside of North America. Microsoft Exchange supports only 40-bit and 64-bit keys using this method.

The name CAST comes from the initials of its developers: Carlisle Adams and Stafford Tavares (of Northern Telcom Research).

Now, after all that discussion about these two types of encryption, let's discuss the methods used by Microsoft NT for encrypting large amounts of data. These are called secret key–cryptographic methods, because there is only one key, which must be known to both sides of the communication.

Using what is called public-key cryptography, there is a private key and a public key, the latter of which can be common knowledge. If user A wants to send an encrypted message to user B, user A uses user B's *public* key to encrypt the message. User B, upon receipt of the message, uses his private key to unlock the message. In effect, you could compare this to having a house with front and back doors, each with a different key to use for entry. Each person has only one key, but using either one allows you to get into the house.

Microsoft uses public key encryption to send the single key used in CAST and DES types of messages, and for use of what are called *digital signatures.* CAST or DES is quicker to encrypt and decrypt, so it is used for messages and other large amounts of data. Just the public-key method is used to send the actual DES or CAST key to the recipient.

To use public-key cryptography, you need to obtain a certificate that contains your public key from a known authority for your server. This Certification Authority (CA) also digitally signs your certificate, to further prevent tampering.

URL

Microsoft recommends the use of the Verisign company for obtaining digital certificates for use with Microsoft NT products. Their home page can be reached at

```
http://www.verisign.com/microsoft/
```

Encrypted Messaging Between Different Encryption Methods

Because many businesses are deploying Windows NT as their strategic server and desktop platform and because many businesses now perform operations in more than one country, it is necessary that Windows NT understands the type of system it is communicating with and negotiates the lowest-common protocol for encryption that can be used between the sites. The basic rules for clients are as follows:

● U.S. and Canadian clients communicating with other countries—Even though both American and Canadian clients can understand and use the 128 DES encryption method, the receiving client in another country cannot. Therefore, the lowest form of encryption is used, CAST-40. If you are sending to a mailing list or to more than one client, as long as one client is limited to the 40-bit key, all clients, even those in the United States and Canada, will have to settle for the 40-bit encryption.

● International clients sending messages to the United States or Canada—Because the sending client has only the 40-bit encryption method available, all communications will use the 40-bit version.

● U.S. and Canadian clients communications—The message will be sent with whatever is the preferred method on the sending server, which is usually CAST-64 (the default, if you didn't select another) or DES. If several users are receiving the message, and some support only CAST-64, the lowest-common-denominator encryption will be used for all recipients.

Microsoft Exchange Security Issues

Microsoft Exchange Server (and client) software is a messaging service in the BackOffice family of products. It is based not on a domain model as is Windows NT Server, but has two organizational units that provide similar functions: organizations and sites.

Put simply, an *organization* is the largest unit by which you can administer Microsoft Exchange. It covers one or more *sites*, which are individual administrative units under the organization that contain their own set of directory database information (security controls). A site can be more than one computer (such as a domain) that shares the site's security information, or it can consist of a single computer or computers from different domains.

> **TIP**
>
> Although sites may actually overlap different domains or contain servers in different domains that communicate with each other, trust relationships must exist between the domains that compromise the site(s) that need to exchange information.

If you have remote offices, setting up your Exchange Server as one (or more) organization and then subdividing it into sites can enable the system administrator to administer the whole organization, or to leave subordinates in charge of local sites with which they may be more familiar.

As previously discussed, the Exchange Server's service account must be authenticated by the domain in which it resides or by a trusted domain server. For more information on trust relationships between domains, see Volume 4, Chapter 1.

TIP

If you run more than one Exchange Server at a site, each message transfer agent (MTA) will have to use the same service account if the two servers are to communicate, because each site can have only one service account for communication among Exchange Servers.

The User Account Used to Install Microsoft Exchange

When performing a fresh install of the Exchange Server, the default account used by the service will be the same account as the person who is doing the installation. If you are installing the server as a secondary server in an existing site, the registry of the remote server (which has already been set up) is searched to get the account to use at this site for the service account.

Whichever way the account is determined, the rights Logon as a service and the Restore files and directories are both added to the account if they have not been granted to the account. When you attempt to install the Exchange Server, the installation process checks your account (the account being used for the installation) to see that you have the correct rights and access to directories and files before it allows you to continue the installation. This is all done, as discussed earlier, by consulting the domain's directory database to check the security information.

TIP

To alter a service's account (any service running under Windows NT) or to assign a new account to the service, use the Server Manager tool found on the Administrative Tools. Select the domain and/or computer whose database you wish to create the account under. From the Computer pull-down menu, select Services. You will get a list of services in that window. Most common Windows NT services run under what is called the System account. You won't find this account in the User Manager or User Manager for Domains. It is a default built-in account that is specifically used by the system for a variety of purposes, one of which is to run services.

To change the account under which a server runs, select the Startup button from the Services window and you will get the Startup window, which allows you not only to change the account the service uses, but also to define the type of startup for the service.

The Components of Exchange Server

The Exchange Server is composed of several different components; each performs specific functions and interacts with the others:

- The System Attendant—This component is a program that does the ordinary day-to-day management of the Exchange Server. For example, use the System Attendant to set up advanced security features for the Exchange Server. It stores digital signatures and information used for encryption. The System Attendant also builds routing tables for the Mail Transfer Agent (MTA) component.

- The Directory—This portion of the Exchange Server does just what it sounds like it does. It stores all directory information, such as addresses, folders, and mailboxes. Any application can use the Directory component to get the information it needs. It also is responsible for creating the Address Book used by mail clients and other applications.

- The Information Store—This component is basically seen by the client as mailboxes or folders provided by Microsoft Exchange. The message database is accessible through this component. Both public and private folders can be created, allowing some messages to be seen by all users and others to be seen only by the specified user(s).

- MTA—This component is responsible for keeping track of the routes needed to transfer messages through the network to other sites. It also can expand a distribution list (a single name you can use to send messages to more than one user). The MTA also uses other components: It resolves addresses using the Directory, creates log entries that can assist the System Attendant, and routes to and receives from other sites' messages. Incoming messages are delivered to the site's Information Store.

Optional components of the Exchange Server include the following:

- Internet Mail Connector—You can use this to further protect your site by setting up the mail connector to accept or reject messages based on IP addresses or mail message size, by disabling auto-replies to the Internet (so only your Internet company employees know you're out of the office!), and by choosing which users are allowed to send mail through the connector.

- Microsoft Mail Connector—You can use this product to allow the interchange of messages between the Exchange Server and systems using the older Microsoft Mail product.

- X.400 Connector—One feature included in the X.400 specification is that passwords are encrypted.

Of course, these optional components may not be necessary if you are merely using Microsoft Exchange to route messages within your organization. However, if you include other types of host machines in your network that are not Windows NT-compatible, you may want to investigate these components further.

One last optional component, Key Management, is used if you are using digital signatures or encrypting messages.

The important thing to remember is that all these components run under basic Windows NT security, for which a username and password are required. This is the first security check that is made. You cannot run a service of any kind with a user account or the built-in System account associated with it.

General Security Measures

Security can be thought of as having two different functions: preventive measures and auditing measures. Preventive measures can include securing user accounts with passwords and applying file and share permissions to sensitive data. Auditing measures can include reviewing the Windows NT Event Log and other log files that other BackOffice products produce. In addition, Exchange produces transaction log files that contain auditing information (such as who accessed what) in a circular file. The older events are overwritten as needed (because of space limitations) or they can be set up to continually log all activity. If you choose the latter method, it will become necessary at some time in the future to archive the log file so that you do not run out of disk space.

The Windows NT Backup utility can be used to back up Microsoft Exchange Server information. When you use this utility, the log file information is transferred to an archive file, and the current log file is reset to contain no data. Note that the log file contains data that can be used to restore a database after a restore has been performed or after a catastrophic disaster.

I do not recommend that you use the circular logging method unless your security needs are low at your site. The log file can be used for recovery purposes if your server should fail. For example, if events are overwritten when using the circular method and you need to restore a database, you will need the log files to do this, or you'll be stuck with the information as it was when the last backup was performed.

For this reason, you should probably consider turning off circular logging for the Exchange Server. To do so, follow these steps:

1. Using the Administrative window, select a server on which you wish to perform this action.

2. Select File | Properties. After that property sheet appears, select Advanced.

3. Clear the Directory and Information Store fields in the Database circular logging box.

Accessing Public and Private Folders

Public folders are meant to be used to store information that more than one user will be allowed to access. A private folder is a folder that holds a mailbox for a specific user and is intended to be accessed by that specific user only. For public folders, however, you can perform maintenance functions to decide which users will be allowed certain actions in the public folders.

You can grant access to public folders to selected users. The types of access you can grant are

- Create Items—This enables the user to create new items in the folder.

- Read Items—This, of course, enables the selected user to read only the information in the public folder.

- Create Subfolder—Because folders can contain subfolders (similar to a directory and subdirectory tree), you must have permission to do so first. If you have been granted permission to create subfolders, you become the owner of that subfolder and can then grant or deny access to other users. This control of access to a subfolder extends to the owner of the parent folder from which the subfolder was created.

- Edit Items and Delete Items—These access types can be broken down into three different types of editing access. The None option means you can do nothing to edit or delete anything in the folder. The Own option enables you to edit or delete only those items that you created and still own. The All option enables you to edit or delete any item in the folder. Access control allows only the editing or deletion of items within the folder. Only the folder owner can actually delete the folder itself.

- Folder Owner—This access type indicates that you are the owner of the folder and can do anything you want to with it.

- Folder Contact—This is an access type you grant to an individual user (usually the owner) who is to be notified when problems arise. For example, replication conflicts can arise as well as conflicts over notifications about quotas. The designated person who should handle events such as these needs this access type granted to him for the specific folder.

In the preceding list of access types, it was stated that the owner of a subfolder could control the types of access to the folder he creates. If the owner of a subfolder does not wish to change the access controls, they will be the same as the parent folder from which they were created.

> The owner of a folder can assign access controls only to the entire folder. It is not possible in a public folder to assign access controls to each individual message contained within the folder.

The Administrator program is used to grant permissions for users to set up or use public folders. For example, to allow a user the permission to set up a top-level public folder—or if you already are the owner of the folder and wish to transfer ownership or grant the Folder Contact permission for another user—you would use the Exchange Client software:

1. From the Exchange Client software, select File | Properties.
2. Choose the Permissions tab, then Add.
3. Double-click on the name of the user you wish to grant the permission, and then click OK.
4. In the next dialog box, select the user you have just added, and then from the Roles box, select the permission Folder Owner or Folder Contact.

Administrators and users can also assign other permissions. Users can assign permissions to the folders they own, and administrators can assign permissions to any public folder.

If you want to use the Administrator program to add or modify permissions, follow these steps:

1. In the Administrator program window, select Public Folders and then click on the folder you want to administer.
2. Using the File pull-down menu, select Properties | General.
3. Select Client Permissions | Add, and then double-click on the username to which you want to add a permission. Click OK.
4. From the list of users in the next dialog box, select the user you just added, and then select the Folder Owner or Folder Contact permission. Click OK.

To grant a user the permission to create a top-level public folder using the Administrator program, follow these steps:

1. In the Administrator window, select Configuration, and then double-click on Store Site Configuration.

2. Select the Top Level Folder Creation tab and then Modify.

3. Double-click on the new user to whom you want to grant this permission, then click OK.

To grant permissions to a user allowing him to create subfolders using the Exchange Client software, complete the following steps:

1. Select the appropriate folder.

2. From the File pull-down menu, select Properties and then the Permissions tab.

3. Choose Add, and then double-click on the user to whom you wish to grant the permission. Click OK.

Exchange User Accounts

When you install the Microsoft Exchange Server on Windows NT Server, you will find that using the User Manager for Domains, after it has prompted you for the normal user information, will pop up a dialog box asking you to enter the information necessary to establish an Exchange Mailbox (and designated server, and so on) along with other information. This is part of the integrated security features that BackOffice products can offer. You don't have to go to the Exchange Administration Tools to add users to Exchange. It can all be done at one time when you enter the user for the first time using the User Manager.

Additionally, if you have users already entered into your Windows NT security directory database, there is a tool in the Exchange Administrative Program to allow the creation of mailboxes for all those users also. It will assign them a mailbox and use the same name and password that they currently are using.

> **TIP**
>
> You can also, with a little more work, import users from a NetWare bindery by extracting the list of users into a text file and then importing it into the Exchange database, using its administrative tools. You must have access to the NetWare database (a valid username/password for the NetWare network), and you must know the location of the server that handles their mail.
>
> In addition, Exchange provides tools to import users and data from the following:
>
> ● Microsoft Mail for PC Networks (MS Mail, PC Mail)
> ● Microsoft Mail for AppleTalk networks (usually MacMail or StarNine Mail)
> ● IBM PFOFS OfficeVision

> ● DEC All-in-1 IOS
> ● cc:Mail
> ● Verimation Memo

You do not necessarily have to import NetWare users into your NT Exchange Server. Clients running on a NetWare network can have the Exchange client installed on them, and, if you have the Gateway Services for NetWare product enabled on your NT server, you can create accounts for these Novell users, and they will be able to access their mail from an Exchange Server running in the NT network.

The NetWare client uses Service Advertising Protocol (SAP) broadcasts to locate an Exchange Server and binds to it. It then is authenticated against the NT security directory database.

Permissions on Directories

In addition to the NTFS file and directory permissions you can set under the Windows NT operating system, you can also use the Exchange Administrator program to further apply a set of specific permissions on directories, by assigning users to what are called *roles*. Roles are simply groups of access rights that are predefined for easier assigning. You can also create custom roles for your users if you wish. The built-in roles are

● Admin
● Permissions Admin
● Service Account Admin
● View Only Admin
● User
● Send As

Along with these roles, the following permissions can be granted:

● Add Child—This permission enables the user to create objects underneath the current object. It is held by the Admin, Permissions Admin, and Service Account Admin roles.

● Modify User Attributes—This permission enables the user to modify other user-level attributes associated with an object. Using this permission, for example, gives the user the ability to add or remove members from a distribution list. Again, the Admin, Permissions Admin, and Service Account Admin roles are granted this permission as the User role.

● Modify Admin Attributes—This permission gives the user the right to modify only administrative-level attributes of an object, such as the names fields that are displayed in a mailbox. The Admin roles are the only roles who possess this permission.

● Modify Permission—Holders of this permission (only the Admins roles previously listed) can modify permissions on *existing* objects.

● Delete—The holder of this permission (again, just the Admin roles) can delete any object.

● Send As—This permission enables the sender of a message to send the message with his or her return address. This permission is held by the Service Account Admin, the User, and the Send As roles.

● Mailbox Owner—The holder of this permission is given the right to read and delete messages from a particular mailbox. This permission is granted the User and Service Account Admin roles.

● Logon Rights—This permission is used to grant access to the Administrator program itself. It is held by the Admin groups, including the View Only Admin group.

● Replication—Only the Service Account Admin holds this permission. It is used to replicate directory information with other servers.

Using NTFS File and Directory Permissions on Exchange Directories

Although the setup program for Microsoft Exchange applies the most appropriate permissions (or, Access Control Lists) on certain directories that are sufficient for most organizations, you should consider the following:

● The directory called Tracking.log should be limited to administrators. It contains sensitive information pertaining to messages.

● The directory Connect/Msmcon/Maildata, which is present only if the Microsoft Mail Connector is installed, should be restricted to the administrators.

Encrypted Remote Procedure Calls (RPCs)

Remote procedure calls are best defined as external routines, or software modules, that can be executed by one machine on another machine. RPCs are used for sending control information about the transfer of messages, among other administrative functions.

Under Microsoft Exchange, these RPCs are encrypted to prevent being tampered with during transmission. This is another method that makes Microsoft Exchange a secure product.

The method used for RPC encryption is called RC4, which is a 40-bit RSA algorithm.

You must enable the encryption for RPCs. To do so, follow these steps:

1. Use the Tools menu in the Exchange Client software.
2. Select Services | Microsoft Exchange Server.
3. Select the Advanced tab. Choose Encrypt Information, and then choose to encrypt all or some of your communications.

Internet Information Server Security

This Internet Information Server (IIS) product is now included as a set of services under the Windows NT 4.0 Server operating system. You can install them just like you install other services in the Network applet found in the Control Panel.

Some products run as more than one service. In the case of IIS, you get three Internet services: the WWW server, the Gopher server, and the FTP server. Each can run under a different account as a service if you wish to choose the account. For example, by default, the account IUSER_computername is created when you install IIS and is used, unless you change it, to run the services and to allow anonymous logins.

You can just as easily configure each server to run under a different account (and thus restrict, using rights and permissions, the files to which each service has access), or you can use the simple generic account.

Administrative Functions

The Administrative Tool for the IIS product is called the Internet Service Manager. Using this tool, you can access the different services IIS offers and perform administrative duties, such as changing passwords for selected services before you change them in the domain security database.

For each service that runs under IIS, you can bring up a property sheet to change everything from the password and account used to run the service, restrict IP addresses from accessing your service, and even configure logging operations for the service. For more information on property sheets for these services, see Volume 2, *Windows NT Internet and Intranet Administration*, Chapter 23, "Local and Remote Administration of Your Internet Information Server" for a shorter discussion of the same.

The IIS Manager utility also allows you to stop and start services and make other administrative changes.

IIS and Encryption Methods

Secure Sockets Layer (SSL) is a form of encryption that the IIS server can use to send data across the Internet. If you are going to be doing business on the Internet and will be receiving or transmitting sensitive information (such as credit card data), you would be best off to consider using SSL. It can use the various forms of encryption discussed earlier in this chapter.

SSL requires that you first obtain a digital signature certificate from an authority that issues them. You enable SSL only on specific directories, so you can use your server for regular anonymous users and for those business customers from whom you will dispense or receive sensitive data.

SSL can also be used for encrypting user authentication. The user sends in his or her credentials (username/password) in the encrypted format, and it is processed through the directory security database. If authentication succeeds, the user can access other data on your server, be it unprotected or SSL-encrypted.

SSL involves the two-part key concept, as discussed earlier. There is a public key that can be given to anyone who needs it. These keys are usually available from the authorities who issue them. The private key is known only to your server and is used to decrypt messages encrypted with the public key.

> The public key is used to encrypt the data. The private key, which should be known only to its original holder, is used to decrypt the information. That is why having the public key is fine; it won't do you any good in trying to decrypt a message.

How Users Are Authenticated by IIS

User authentication, depending on the particular IIS service, can occur in several ways.

When you install the IIS services, an account is created in your domain security directory database. The format of the username is IUSER_*computername*, where *computername* is the name of your workstation or server. This account is used if you allow anonymous users to access your WWW, FTP, or Gopher services without a password. Of course, you can change the name of the IUSER_*computername* if you want to, as well as the password, but if you do so, you will also need to change it on the property sheets for each service that uses it.

The Log On Locally right is granted to this IUSER_*computername* account. If you change the account or create a new one to use, make sure it has this right granted to the account. The IUSE_*computername* account is an anonymous account that accesses selected information for users of your Internet services. You can force users to use a valid username/password contained in the directory database, but this type of access should be restricted to confidential files or information.

If you find you are having trouble using the anonymous account for your Web services, be sure the password has not expired in the domain security database (using User Manager for Domains tool). If so, update a new password both there and in the property sheets used by the IIS services you are running. Both passwords must be kept in sync. Also, check the Administrative Tools Event Viewer security log to determine if a login failure is due to an unknown account or a bad password.

If, on the property sheet for the IIS service(s), you decide to disable the anonymous logon capability, users will be prompted for a username and password each time they attempt to access the service. For some businesses, this may be the preferred method to validate every single user.

Securing Your SQL Server

The Microsoft SQL server is an important component of the BackOffice series. It is a client/server type of system where the client (the desktop PC) performs the user interaction and some of the application logic for the inquiry being made. The host, which can be anything from another PC to a mainframe computer, performs the actual storage and manipulation of the data and enforces security and data integrity.

You would think that this client/server approach would make the system(s) run faster. This is not necessarily the case, although it is the goal. If the application written for the client is not written using an efficient structure or algorithm, performance can be slower. For example, a client program needs only one row of data, but the programmer finds it easier to get several hundreds of rows, wasted network bandwidth, and much less processing speed on both the client (which has to read through the extraneous data) and the server (which has to locate and transmit the data) to occur. This is usually caused by a lazy programmer using the "cut-and-paste" method to use canned routines from one program to another rather than writing efficient code for the particular user application.

The SQL server can be fully integrated into the Windows NT security directory database. If it is, you can log into the Windows NT Server, and you should be able to access SQL server with no problems, provided you have been granted access to the data in the particular database you need to obtain. The next section discusses other types of user access.

Even though you can set up the server to allow users who are not in the NT directory database to access the database, the server software itself runs as a service on

Windows NT, and it must run under a valid account. By default, the account Local System is used. This is not a good idea if your server is to use network communications. If that is the case, you need to create a new user account, grant it the rights Log on as a service and Log on via the network, and put the account into the Administrators local group on the Windows NT server.

In a domain setup, you should use a domain account, not a local server database account, and let all the SQL servers in the domain use the same account. From a security point of view, it is much easier to maintain a single domain account rather than grant a separate account to each SQL service. Refer to the beginning of this chapter to learn how to change the username and password that a service runs under when using Windows NT.

General Security Issues

An SQL database, as defined by ANSII standards, consists of several different databases, of which some are optional and some are mandatory. Although most system managers or administrators already know the value of keeping accurate, timely backups of their data, it is important that at least one specific database, the master database, be kept offline or stored somewhere on another disk. Failure of this database can render the remaining databases useless. Protect the master database! This is where user accounts, configuration parameters, and stored procedures, among other things, are stored.

The SQL Security Manager is a tool that is responsible for setting the type of user validation to be used. There are three possible types of security mechanisms:

● Standard Security—In this mode, the user does not have to have an account in the Windows NT security directory database. Instead, the SQL server validates the username and password. I do not recommend using this method.

● Integrated Security—Using this method, both Windows NT security (the user must have an NT account) and the SQL database security are used. The user can have the same user ID and password for both of these mechanisms, or you can set up different passwords to create a more secure environment.

● Mixed security—This is a hybrid that allows either the Windows NT security directory database or the SQL user's database to be used to validate the user.

Another important point to remember is that a systems administrator account, called simply sa, is set up with no password during the installation process. As soon as you have finished the setup, one of the first things you should do is secure this user account with a password. The sa account can do just about anything on the SQL server! To change the sa password, follow these steps:

1. Using the SQL Enterprise Manager tool, select the server whose sa account you want to modify.
2. From the Manage menu, select the Logins option.
3. The Login Name box (a pull-down listing) is used to display users; select sa.
4. Enter the new password you have chosen, then click the Modify button to make the change. A confirmation box will appear. Click the OK button.

Disk Mirroring

Security involves protecting your data from not only unauthorized access, but also it provides fault-tolerant mechanisms to protect the data in the case of hardware failure—the most common being disk failure.

Using Microsoft SQL Server, you have three choices for mirroring data so that it resides in more than one place, should a disk experience downtime:

● Hardware-based mirroring—There are controllers that support Redundant Array of Inexpensive Disks (RAID) at the controller level. Data sent to the controller by the operating system is written to both disks, and the processing overhead is absorbed by the disk controller, not the Windows NT computer's CPU. The main disadvantage to this is that hardware RAID solutions are usually not cheap.

● Windows NT operating system disk mirroring—If you are running your SQL Server on an NT Server, the operating system provides several fault-tolerance mechanisms, such as host-based disk mirroring and parity disk striping. The only two disadvantages with this choice are that the CPU of the machine has to perform the extra steps to put the data on the different disks and if you are running Windows NT Workstation as your server, it does not support these fault-tolerant mechanisms. Only the NT Server product does.

Dumping Your Data

You can back up your SQL data by using a *dump device*. This simply means you use the SQL server command sp_adddumpdevice to create the dump device, which can be either another disk, a tape device, or even a floppy disk. You use the dump device to store the contents of a database. You cannot use a database device as a dump device; it must be created using the preceding command.

TIP

You can create a dump device, not just on the same computer on which your server resides, but also on networked drives that you have attached to your system.

Security Management from Within the SQL Server

In addition to the security measures you can implement on the Windows NT Server to restrict and audit access, the SQL Server also has several mechanisms that can be used for security purposes:

● Server level management consists of validating the username and password. The user will be authenticated based on the type of authentication discussed in the "General Security Measures" section.

● Users must be assigned by the sa to a database before they can access it. You must first create an NT or SQL Server account for the user before you begin to assign the user to one or more databases.

● Similar to the local and global groups used to assign rights and permissions to groups of users at the Windows NT level, you can also group users in the SQL database. However, a user grouped in a SQL group can be a member of only one SQL group, whereas a user in the Windows NT security directory database can be assigned to multiple local and global Window NT user groups.

After you create a group within the SQL database (using the command sp_addgroup "group name") and add users to the group (using the command sp_adduser user_name, [name_in_database], [group_name]), you can assign or revoke permissions on objects by the SQL group, rather than by the user.

Securing Objects

There are three privilege levels you can assign to a user account according to the type of access you want the user to have to objects in the database. The first privilege level is that of System Administrator, of which the only member is the sa username. Using this account, you can do practically anything to the SQL Server and its databases. There are even commands (such as DISK INIT and DISK MIRROR) that can be used *only* by this account.

The Database Owner (DBO) is another special type of login. This user owns a particular database and can do everything possible to that database. As with the sa account, there are several commands that the DBO can run exclusively, such as LOAD DATABASE and DROP DATABASE. The DBO is the user who can grant permissions (or revoke them) to the other users, allowing them to create tables, procedures, and so on for the database(s) that the DBO owns.

The Other Users category is used for normal users who log into the database to accomplish their jobs. The privilege levels each user acquires are granted by the DBO.

If an Other User type of user creates an object, he has all permissions granted to him for that object. Even the DBO and sa accounts must first be granted permissions to access these objects. However, the DBO can impersonate the user with the SETUSER command and grant himself privileges.

Using Views for Enhanced Security

Views are no more than a method of grouping data from one or more databases and presenting it to the user in a table format. The user does not have to know where each piece of data originated. You can place permissions on Views and use them for a lot of your users, while restricting their access to the databases themselves.

System Management Services

SMS is a major player in the BackOffice suite of products. It allows an administrator to examine specific information and processes running on other machines in the network. It also can be used to inventory software and hardware on the network and even for deployment and installation of software. It is, for all practical purposes, simply a tool that makes the system's network administration a lot easier, especially by monitoring this system on a continual basis, using the alert features. With SMS, you can also accomplish functions other than monitoring, such as automatically loading software on remote computers and creating inventory reports to determine which programs are installed on specific computers.

The actual features supported by SMS are

- Hardware inventorying
- Software inventorying
- Distribution (installation) of software packages
- Managing network applications
- Performing network monitoring and analysis
- Gathering network configuration information
- Troubleshooting remote clients to provide remote support for their problems

SMS Sites and Windows NT Domains

In the Windows NT networking scheme, the domain is considered to be the top-level logical grouping of computers that can be managed centrally by the PDC. You can have your domains interact by using trust relationships, but if you have many domains, this can be a cumbersome method to use for enterprise-level centralized systems management.

Sites are a logical grouping that SMS uses to group Windows NT domains into a manageable unit. An SMS site can consist of one or more domains. You can perform the functions listed in the previous section on any computer contained in the domains covered by the site.

There are several types of sites available:

- Central site—This site stores information about all other sites that are beneath it and can be used to manage any other site beneath it. The central site is the top level of SMS administration. One other important difference between the central site and other sites is that the central site must have available an SQL database for containing the information it manages. For performance reasons, it is recommended that the SQL Server runs on a different server than the SMS software, which itself can consume significant system resources, such as memory.

- Primary site—This type of site is just beneath the central site in the hierarchy. It also has a SQL database that it uses to track and manage other sites that fall under it.

- Secondary site—This type of site does not have a SQL database and is the bottom of the hierarchy. All requests for SMS services, such as inventorying software or loading new software packages, are passed to a primary site above the secondary site, or to the central site if there are no primary sites.

The organization of sites that SMS allows you to create gives you the flexibility of centralizing systems management at the top of the enterprise or distributing certain administrative capabilities to primary sites further down in the chain of servers.

Of course, this means that you need to consider what your security needs are depending on the way you choose to set up and manage sites.

Because SMS is designed to be an enterprise solution, it allows clients from not just the Windows NT network, but also from LAN Manager, AppleTalk, and NetWare. The last two networks require optional gateway software to be installed for communications to those networks, but you can still perform most of the same SMS administrative functions on those networks as you can on an NT network.

The transport agent for SMS communications, including downloading software and performing other system management functions, is called a *sender*. Senders can be of one of the following types: LAN sender, RAS sender, and SNA sender. The nodes that use a particular sender must have the appropriate software installed. For example, if you are connected to a local area network (LAN), the LAN sender can be used for your communications.

However, if you have employees who dial in from home or are connected across an SNA link, you can use SMS to manage those computers also, using the RAS or SNA senders.

Each sender type has a particular directory assigned to it. The sender directory contains the files and instructions for the types of management that will be performed. You can run more than one sender type on a single server. For example, if you have dial-up users (RAS sender) and clients connected locally to your LAN, you can use both types of senders, and, depending on the address of the particular machine, SMS will use the correct type of sender.

All this may sound complicated, and it can be, so the precautions you take for security will be well worth the effort. In some ways, centralizing management can make security easier, but you must fully understand how SMS is set up on your network to be sure you do not leave anything overlooked.

If you want to totally control all aspects of SMS management from a central site, you should place only secondary site servers under this site because they cannot perform any SMS management tasks locally, but are controlled by either the central site or any primary site above it. If you want to distribute responsibilities for management to different sites, you would design your SMS configuration to include primary sites at which you can grant the ability to perform management tasks with secondary sites, if needed, set up beneath the primary sites.

If you are using a SQL Server at a primary site, you should be familiar with the security measures enforced by the DBO for the database and machine you are using. The NTFS disk structure should be used on all sites if you want to be sure to enable file and directory security (and auditing), which cannot be done under the FAT system.

WARNING

Even though SMS provides the services necessary to download and install software packages on client machines, you must not overlook the licensing requirements of the software package you are downloading. It can make software packages available by loading them directly on the target machine, or it can set up the target machine to run the package from another network server. Any way you decide to set it up, be sure you have purchased the correct number of licenses for the users who will have access to the software.

SMS provides a software-inventory capability. This is not a software-metering utility. You can use the inventory capability to see where copies of software packages reside, but you cannot tell from the inventory how many users actually are using the package at a particular time.

SMS Security Mechanisms

After considering your enterprise SMS layout and after taking appropriate Windows NT security measures at each site (such as NTFS permissions and user rights), you can further increase and monitor security by using the SMS Service Account.

Because many SMS functions are run as services on the site machines, you must create an account (the Service Account) at each site and grant it the necessary access rights. For example, the account must be a member of the local machine's Administrators group (or a global group that is a member of the local Administrators group). It should also be granted the right Log on as a service.

If your site contains more than one domain, you will have to set up a trust relationship between the domains and grant the site's Service Account the appropriate rights in the trusting domain. This is easy to accomplish if you just created the account in your Domain Admins group and imported that global group into the trusting domain's Administrator group on the machine you are communicating with.

> You must use the User Manager for Domains to set up the SMS Service Account and assign it a password before you begin the installation of SMS. During the installation, the setup program will prompt you for the name and password of the account you have created for this purpose.

The point is that SMS does not allow you to bypass normal Windows NT security mechanisms. You must set up the Service Account in a particular domain to act like the domain administrator's users. This gives the account the ability to perform functions on other computers in the local or trusting domain(s).

The SMS Network Monitor

You are probably already aware of the network monitoring tool and agent that comes with the Windows NT Server software. Using that monitor, you can perform analysis of all network traffic bound to or from your computer. You cannot, however, due to security reasons, use this monitor to view network traffic destined to or from other computers.

The version of the Microsoft Network Monitor that is included with the SMS installation enables the administrator to view, capture, and analyze *all* network traffic on the local LAN. From a security point of view, this program can have bad implications if you grant the right to use it to the wrong user. One of the first security measures you should consider when using the administrative functions of any SMS site is the reliability of the users that you delegate SMS administrative functions to.

This Network Monitor uses the same agent program on target machines as the Windows NT version of the Network Monitor installed on that machine. If you have a particular computer that you do not want your SMS version of the Network Monitor to access, you can set a password on the agent by selecting its icon in the Control Panel and entering the password.

One other consideration is that when you are capturing packets from a remote computer, you use buffer space in physical memory on that remote machine to capture the packets. Thus, you can monitor several machines without downgrading performance on the SMS server on which you are working.

Client Services

The functions that a central or primary site can perform on other computers depend on some kind of local authorization using the normal Windows NT security mechanisms. As discussed earlier in "The SMS Network Monitor" section, the local user can set up a password on the monitoring agent program to prevent a central authority from monitoring traffic on that machine.

When using the software installation functions of SMS, the administrator can set up the package for an automatic installation, or can have the installation process prompt the user to get permission to install the package. This method provides some control over changes made in a large network where the central authority may not be familiar with all the users and their software needs.

Granting Access to Administrative Services

You can use the SMS Service Account to log into the SMS management software to perform all functions needed. If this is at a central or primary site that is using an SQL database, you must use the SMS Security Manager to add this service account to the SQL user database.

If you want, you can also add other usernames to both the Windows NT security directory database and the SQL database. By using the Security Manager program, you can grant access by modifying the following settings for a user:

- Security Object—This is the name of the object managed by SMS to which you are granting the user rights. An object can be an Alert, an Event (for the event log), jobs, and other functions SMS can perform.

- Proposed Rights—These are the rights you wish to grant to the user for the selected object. There are only four rights you can grant: No Access, which is self-explanatory; View Access (sort of like a Read access in NTFS), which allows the user to only look at information pertaining to the specific object;

Full Access, which allows the user to do anything to the selected object; and, finally, Current Rights, which are the rights already granted to the object for the user.

This is called Proposed Rights because they do not take effect until you use the Save User option to update the user database. When you save the user's record, the proposed rights become part of the current rights.

The objects to which you can grant access are

- Alerts—Alerts can be specified to occur when specific actions take place on the machine (such as a disk exceeding a free-space limitation you set).

- Architectures—This is the database component that contains the inventory tables for your site and the sites beneath it.

- Diagnostics—This gives the ability to use all the SMS diagnostic utilities.

- Events—This object enables the user to view events in the event window and change event properties, depending on the rights assigned to the object for this user.

- Helpdesk—This object enables the user to perform remote functions on another user's computer that is contained in the site.

- Jobs—The user can, according to the rights granted, view, modify, or execute jobs on other machines.

- Machine groups—This object enables the user to view members of machine groups and to modify properties for that group.

- Network Monitor—This object is discussed earlier in this chapter. Because sensitive information can be contained in network packets (such as clear-text passwords), you should be careful about to whom you grant access to this object and what rights you grant that user.

- Packages—This object enables the user to view or use packages, depending on the rights granted for this object.

- Program groups—This offers viewing or control over the window and groups on a remote machine.

- Queries—These are requests you can send to the inventory database stored in the SQL database. A query contains the criteria needed to identify the objects you want to find in the database.

- Site groups—This object allows the user to view or modify the groups created within the site.

- Sites—This object enables the user to view or modify the Sites window of SMS.

TIP

Some of the preceding objects will not give access to the user by granting access to the object. In some cases, there are prerequisites (other objects to which rights must be granted) that must be assigned in combination with the particular object you select.

For example, if you want to grant access to the Site Groups object, you must also grant the user View or Full access rights to the Sites object and the Architectures objects. The View or Full access for these objects depends on the type of access you are granting to the Site Groups object.

SNA Gateway

The SNA Server and Gateway products are designed to allow communications to take place between LANs running a variety of protocols, and between IBM mainframe and other minicomputers that use the SNA networking architecture.

The SNA architecture can use a variety of protocols to send and receive responses over a variety of protocols, depending on whether the communications are on a LAN or are passing through a public network (using the X.25 interface protocol, for example). However, whichever protocol is used is transparent to the user using the Windows NT SNA Gateway product.

When a user wants to run an application that interacts with a computer reachable by the SNA server, it creates what is called a *session*. A session is simply a channel through which the user's computer communicates with a network-addressable unit on the mainframe computer. There are two types of units the user can connect to:

- Physical Units (PU)—These are node-specific units that control the communications between different types of devices. For example, a Type 2 PU is resident on IBM cluster controllers. Type 4 is used by front-end processors and resides on them. PU Type 5 resides on a host mainframe to control the sessions that connect to it.

- Logical Units (LU)—These are the normal connections the user makes to establish a session on a mainframe. The types include Type 1, which provides for batch transfers of files in an interactive mode. Type 2 LUs support the IBM 3270 display terminal sessions. Type 3 is used by the IBM 3270 printers. Type 6.2 is used for program-to-program communication. Finally, Type 7 is used by IBM midrange-computer sessions (such as the AS/400 computer).

The SNA Gateway Server component of Windows NT enables connections to LU types 1, 2, and 3 to establish terminal and printing service, which includes terminal emulators and printers residing on the PC LAN. The gateway server connects to an

SNA network by acting like a PU 2 (a cluster controller). The server then manages all LU-emulated devices running on the LAN.

If you are connecting to an AS/400 computer, as opposed to an IBM mainframe, some of the functions performed by the gateway server are incorporated into the AS/400 version of SNA.

The Server Admin Utility for Managing the SNA Gateway

The day-to-day management of the SNA gateway can be done from an NT Server or Workstation. Control over Logical Units (LUs) and users are performed using the Admin utility. Using this tool, you can assign users and user groups to sessions that the SNA Server can access.

When considering security issues, it is a good idea that the SNA Gateway Server software is closely integrated into the Windows NT operating system. For example, the event log can be set up to provide after-the-fact information about troubleshooting connections or to determine when users are abusing the service.

It is also important to restrict the users allowed to run the Server Admin tool. From within the Admin tool, select Permissions from the Security menu. First, remove the group Everyone, which is present by default. Then click the Add button. You will get another dialog box that allows you to add users and grant permissions to the users. Select the user or group(s) to grant permission, and then select the permission (or access control) Full Control from the Type of Access list. Finally, click OK. When you return to the previous window, click OK again and you are finished.

> You can further ensure security by grouping other users into a different group or groups and then using the No Access type of access (using the same procedure just described).

Adding and Managing Users to the SNA Gateway

Once you have completed the setup of your SNA Gateway, including establishing connections and creating logical units, you need to grant users the ability to use these LUs. The steps for this include the following:

- Create a new group for the users who will have access using the User Manager for Domains Administrative Tool. You can use local or global groups, depending on where the users reside versus where the SNA server is installed.

- If you have new users, use the User Manager to create them and grant them membership in the group or groups created in the first step.

● After you have established a group or groups of users under Windows NT, you need to use the SNA Server Administrator program to assign users or groups (which are easier to manage than individual users) to the LUs you have created.

To use the SNA Server Administrator program to add users to LUs, select the administrative program, and then select the Users and Groups option. Select New User from the User menu. You will get a dialog box that enables you to add users or groups.

In this dialog box, you can specify the current Windows NT domain or any other domain with which you have a trust relationship. Then, select the users or groups displayed in the Names field and click the Add button. Finally, click OK.

To associate the user/group with LUs, under the Users menu, select the user(s) or group(s) and then click on Assign LUs. This will bring up the Assign User LU/Pool Sessions dialog box.

Finally, simply select from the display of LUs the units to which you want the user or group to have access.

LU Pool User Security

Logical Unit Pools can be created to provide redundant paths to one or more servers. Additionally, LUs from other SNA Servers in a domain can be added to a pool so that if the SNA server you are using goes down, your session can be re-established on another SNA gateway in the domain.

Data Encryption Using the SNA Gateway

Although basic encryption techniques are discussed in the "Encryption" section, it important to note here that SNA traffic can use the RSA RD4 data-encryption standard. You can enable or disable the encryption on a user-by-user basis.

The Windows NT File System

Unless you have a site where security is minimal, you may still be using the File Allocation Table (FAT) disk structure. Once again, you can establish permissions to shares using the FAT system, whereas you can discretely control access to directories and individual files if you use the Windows NT file system (NTFS).

The configuration files used by the SNA Server need to be protected from unauthorized access. For this, you must use NTFS and grant access only to those users who need to access configuration-management applications for the server. The configuration file is stored in

```
<SNA root>\SYSTEM\CONFIG
```

<SNA root> is the directory you chose during the setup of the server software. For security purposes, you should regularly back up the files in this directory and protect them with NTFS permissions.

To produce a backup copy, use the SNA Admin application, select File | Backup. All backup configuration files will have the .SNA file extension to distinguish them from the regular configuration files.

The Trace Utility

Unless you are a true networking guru, the information provided by the SNA Trace Utility can provide a wealth of information about specific services or sessions. If you are calling Microsoft for support purposes, the events logged by the Trace Utility will be important.

To invoke tracing, select the SNA Tracing Utility located in the SNA group. In a simple dialog box, you can select the service name you want to trace. Then, in the Message Traces fields, you can select:

● Admin messages

● 3270 messages

● Data link control messages

● SNA formats (data link control messages in the SNA Server format)

● LU 6.2 messages

● Level 2 messages

If the service you select is the SNA Applications service, you can trace the Application Programming Interface (API) messages to help debug applications using this form of program-to-program LU.

Summary

This chapter touches lightly on the built-in security mechanisms that the Windows NT Server operating system uses to validate users and grant and restrict access to resources. The other BackOffice products have their own methods of setting permissions on the objects they manipulate, but they can also be integrated into the NT Server security. Depending on your site's security needs, you may end up using one or the other, or all the BackOffice security mechanisms.

It is important to understand that when you use the Windows NT Server security directory database, you are only securing access to the system and its objects. The other BackOffice products may need further security.

Encryption can be used to authenticate users when using products that adhere to the Microsoft standards or to encrypt data for transmission across a network.

CHAPTER 15

Auditing

Auditing is a function required on any operating system that is used in today's production environments. Microsoft has designed the auditing features of Windows NT to meet the most stringent requirements of C2-level security, defined by the federal government. Although very few Information Systems departments require C2-level security, auditing can be used for other purposes. System activity can be tracked with auditing, which can be used for, among other purposes, troubleshooting problems with applications, file systems, and other system components. For the purpose of this discussion, auditing does have an impact on system security and file system resources, both of which need to be part of any production system's plan.

File system resources affect many areas of the Windows NT operating system. Auditing, although it does not have a huge impact from a performance or capacity planning standpoint, does require some planning for file system usage requirements. For example, some of the settings for the Event Log utility, which is the primary component of auditing, may require disk space on the NT system partition. This can affect the operation of the system. Should an event log grow to the point that all the disk space is absorbed on the system partition, the system may actually halt, depending on the other services requiring space on the system partition. Procedures for event log management are important to the overall system health and support of the Windows NT operating system.

Enabling Auditing

Auditing is enabled within User Manager of the Windows NT system. The procedure is quite simple and can be accomplished with no disruption to system operation. Simply launch User Manager by either selecting it from the Administrators Tools folder or typing usrmgr in the Run dialog box from the Start bar. Auditing is activated under the Policies menu (see Figure 15.1).

Figure 15.1.
Audit from the Policies menu in User Manager. This provides access to the different audit settings.

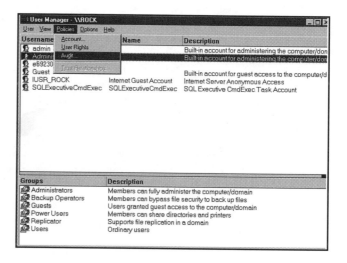

When auditing has been enabled, it has the capability to audit the success or failure of seven different types of system activities (see Figure 15.2). The next section reviews each type of event that can be audited.

Figure 15.2.
Auditing is turned on or off, and you can indicate which components will be audited.

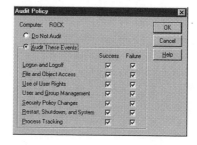

Types of Events Audited

Logon and Logoff records each time a user logs on to or off of the computer. These events are recorded differently, depending on the role of the NT Server. For domain controllers, logons and logoffs are recorded for the domain. For standalone and member servers, this activity is recorded for the local machine.

The File and Object Access event records each time a file, directory, or printer is accessed by a user. However, in order to audit the object, auditing must be turned on in User Manager at the Object security setting, which is discussed later in this chapter.

The Use of User Rights event records each time a user right is used. A list of user rights is in the Policy menu in User Manager. If the system time keeps getting changed, this level of auditing would indicate who was changing the system time.

With User and Group Management, each time a user or group is added to or deleted from the system, an audit event is written to the security log. Additionally, each time a user is put into or removed from a group, an audit event is written to the security log.

Making audit changes to the Security Policy generates an audit event in the security log. For example, removing auditing for "Process Tracking" generates an event.

Each time NT Server is started, a Restart event is written to the security log, in addition to numerous other related events that have to do with system starts, such as Shutdown and System.

The Process Tracking events provide detailed information regarding indirect object access, handle duplication, and program activation. This type of auditing is useful for programmers.

From Explorer, right-click the folder or files that need to be audited (see Figure 15.3).

Select the Security tab and then Auditing (see Figure 15.4).

The Directory Auditing dialog box offers the capability to select who to audit and what file activities to audit (see Figure 15.5).

This second step only applies to auditing File and Object Access: events. Furthermore, the more events that are selected for auditing, the more disk space is required to log those events. The events that are selected are recorded in the security event log, which remains inactive, or blank, until auditing is enabled. Configuring the logging process is required to control the event logging functions.

Figure 15.3.
*The pull-down
menu on Explorer
is activated by
clicking the right-
mouse button.
Once the menu is
active, select
Properties to get
access to the
Security tab.*

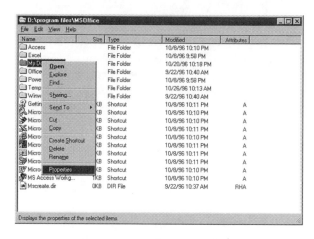

Figure 15.4.
*The properties
display for a
folder. Select the
Security tab to
gain access to the
audit setting for
this folder.*

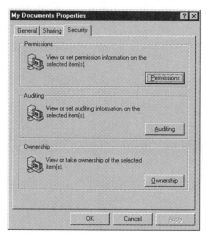

Figure 15.5.
*Select the desired
level of auditing in
this folder.*

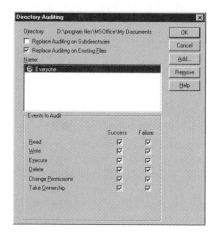

Audit settings on domain controllers affect all domain controllers in that domain.

Configuring Event Logging

The security event log is where all the audited events are tracked. A security management policy usually governs how the event logs are configured. The focus of this section is to understand the relationship between auditing and event log configuration settings, and how they affect file system resources.

The Event Log Viewer program is located in the same folder as User Manager, and it can be accessed by typing eventvwr in the Run dialog box on the Start bar. The configuration for the security log is under Log Settings in the Log menu (see Figure 15.6).

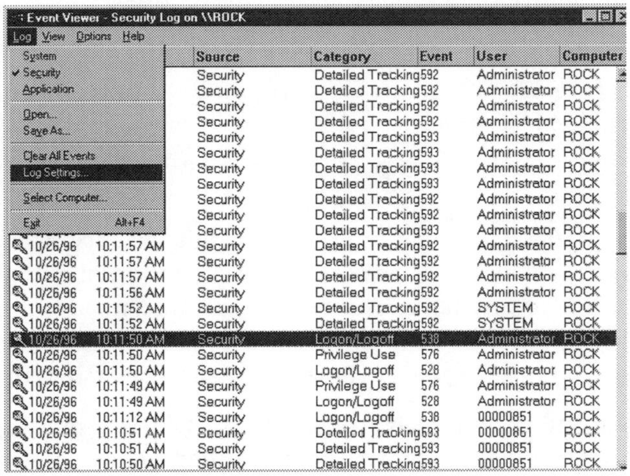

Figure 15.6.
Options for event logs can be changed in Log Settings.

These settings will dictate the disk storage requirements for the security log. The default settings have very little impact, but extensive security tracking will require larger disk space requirements. As previously mentioned, the security management policy determines the settings for the security log file (see Figure 15.7).

Figure 15.7.
Each event log setting has a different affect on system security tracking and file system resources.

For example, if all events must be captured, the last setting, Do Not Overwrite Events (Clear Log Manually), should be selected. This setting requires that the administrator manually clear the logs periodically. This is not necessary unless there is a need to track every event for an extended period. For systems that require high security, where no event can be lost or unrecorded, Windows NT can be set up to halt the system when the security log becomes full. This forces the administrator to log on to the system locally and clear the log before any system processing can continue. This feature has to be set in the Registry, in the following key:

`HKEY_LOCAL_MACHINE\SYSTEM\CurrentControlSet\Control\Lsa\`

Add the entry:

> Key: `CrashOnAuditFail`
> Type: `REG_DWORD`
> Value: `1`

This setting is intended for systems that require very high security. Most Windows NT installations will not require this setting.

NOTE

> Incorrectly making changes to the Registry can cause serious, system-wide problems that may require the system to be reinstalled in order to correct them.

For systems that do not require stringent security, select the first option, Overwrite Events as Needed. This setting simply overwrites the oldest events when the log gets full. No further interaction by the system administrator is required with this setting enabled. Administrators who need a low maintenance solution, with the option to review recent events, can use this setting for event log management.

The second selection, Overwrite Events Older than x Days, is designed for scheduled archiving. Weekly archiving would need to have seven days selected, and the log would need to be archived manually every seven days. The schedule is variable, up to 365 days; however, the proper size needs to be selected in the Maximum Log Size field to support the length of time selected. The settings should support the security management policy.

Interpreting the Event Log

Each event has up to 10 entries that are logged (see Figure 15.8). The event information is logged and displayed chronologically, with an option for oldest or newest event display order, which is selected from the View menu. Each type of event log entry is described in Table 15.1. The Description field is the primary source for interpreting the events. Other fields can be used to yield the desired information, depending on what information is needed. The filtering option on the View menu can be used to quickly isolate specific events for interpretation.

Figure 15.8.
A Logoff event is recorded in the Event Detail dialog box because the Logon/Logoff audit event was selected.

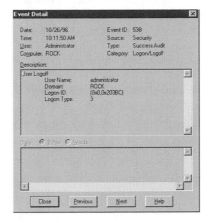

Table 15.1. Event log components.

Component	Description
Date	Date the event occurred.
Time	Time the event occurred; be sure the computer date/time is set correctly.
Source	Typically logged as security, but other sources include LSA, NetDDE Object, SC Manager, Security Account Manager, and Spooler.
Category	The category is how each source identifies each type of event.
Event	Logs a unique event ID assigned to the event.
User	User associated with the event.
Computer	The NetBIOS name of the machine that caused the event to be logged.
Type	Success or Failure are the types for security events.
Description	A brief description of the event.
Data	Any associated data, usually binary, associated with the event.

Filtering the event log is a technique used to quickly get the information needed. Filtering can be done on any of the major components of the event. For example, if an event needs to be located to determine if user FredF logged into the computer between the hours of 8:30 a.m. and 10 a.m. on Friday, filtering based on time, category, and user will yield all events matching the criteria. The filtering feature does not allow for detailed filtering on description or data; it only supplies the major components listed in the Filter dialog box (see Figure 15.9). Once the desired information is known, there are several ways the security event log can be used to interpret security-related events.

Figure 15.9.
In the Filter dialog box, each parameter can be used to narrow the search criteria.

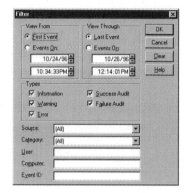

Summary

The file system requirements for auditing are somewhat limited, but still require some planning and consideration. An event log that has been allowed to grow beyond what a system can support can have negative effects on the Windows NT operating system. The settings for the event log should coincide with the security management policy. Monitoring log sizes and system partition space requirements will help avoid any problems associated with the event log and auditing.

Auditing is used in most production-computing environments today. Windows NT has included the necessary tools to monitor security and general access to the operating system. Each type of environment has different needs for deploying some sort of auditing. The federal government has security needs that require detailed auditing of the system. Others may also need this level of security auditing, but will most likely use auditing for troubleshooting and informational purposes. Regardless of the purpose, auditing is easily set up and configured to provide a wide range of functionality.

Part VI

Appendix

A   Internet Information
     Server

Internet Information Server

Internet Information Server (IIS) is a Windows NT Server–based application designed to facilitate information exchange for a company's internal and external communications. The Internet is quickly becoming the preferred method of communication, whether it's the World Wide Web or electronic mail. Additionally, sharing information and applications has gained a great deal of interest, because the same tools that are used on the Internet can now be used on an *intranet*. An intranet is used in the same fashion as the Internet except that access to intranet servers is limited to an isolated network. This isolated network separates access to the Internet with a network firewall. This can drastically change current systems' architectures and the ways system administration is done today.

Furthermore, most aspects of information dissemination can easily be incorporated into an IIS platform that can simplify the tasks of information management and increase the flow of information. This discussion of installation and configuration makes no distinction as to whether IIS will be used as an intranet or Internet server.

Installing Internet Information Server

The installation of Internet Information Server is one of the choices presented during the Windows NT Server installation process. By following the prompted installation, IIS is installed automatically; however, there is the option to bypass installation and install it at a later time. Both methods offer the same choices; therefore, only one of these methods is reviewed in detail in this appendix. The method reviewed in this appendix is installation from the distribution, which is typically the Windows NT 4.0 CD-ROM (where the IIS installation software is located). Distribution can also include a shared network drive where the media is stored for installation purposes. Typical networks can transfer data more quickly than most CD-ROMs, and therefore is the preferred method of installation in most circumstances.

Installing from the Distribution

This section reviews each step of the installation process. The steps for installation are similar to installing IIS during the Windows NT Server installation, but the dialog boxes are slightly different. Because the steps are nearly identical, this section only reviews the installation process of IIS with Windows NT Server already installed.

To begin the installation process, open the Network applet within Control Panel from the Settings selection of the Start menu. From here, select the Services tab (see Figure A.1). Windows NT will generate a list of services that can be added to the system. From this list, select Microsoft Internet Information Server 2.0 (see Figure A.2).

The next box is the File Location dialog box. The file location is the i386 directory from either the CD-ROM drive or a copy of the CD-ROM located on a network share point (see Figure A.3). Windows NT cautions at this point that other applications should be closed during the installation, because files may be open that Windows NT will need access to during the installation (see Figure A.4). It is always advisable to save and close all your work before proceeding with the installation of any new software. IIS has several components that can be installed.

Figure A.1.
*Starting the
installation
process with the
Network window.*

Figure A.2.
*Selecting from a
list of available
network services
for installation.*

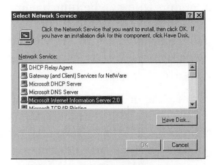

Figure A.3.
*Designating where
files are installed
from.*

Figure A.4.
*Closing all
running applica-
tions.*

The next dialog box, Microsoft Internet Information Server 2.0 Setup, presents the different components that can be selected or deselected (see Figure A.5). Directory locations default to the c: drive, but this can be changed by selecting the Change Directory button, shown in Figure A.5, and typing in a new path (see Figure A.6). If the directories do not already exist, the installation process prompts for their creation (see Figure A.7).

There are two versions of the Internet Information Service Manager available for installation at this point. The first one listed is run in a normal Windows NT format, while the second is used with a browser. This allows some flexibility in managing IIS services, because both a browser version and a regular version are available. Because most testing of IIS functionality and connectivity is done with a browser, having a browser version of the Internet Service Manager makes troubleshooting and testing convenient for the IIS administrator.

Open Database Connectivity (ODBC) is used in conjunction with database enabling applications that run on the IIS.

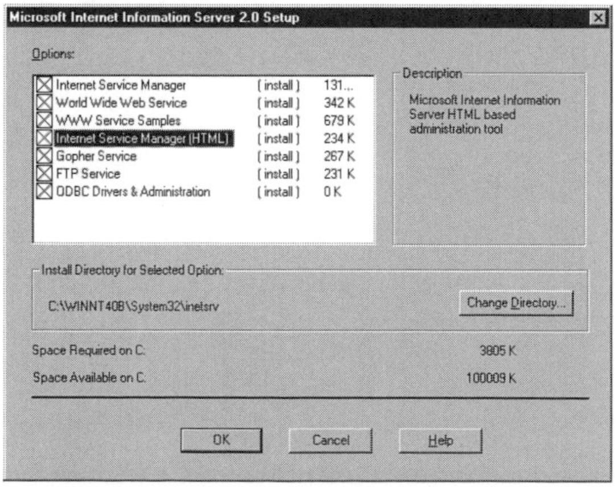

Figure A.5.
*The list of IIS
components
available for
installation.*

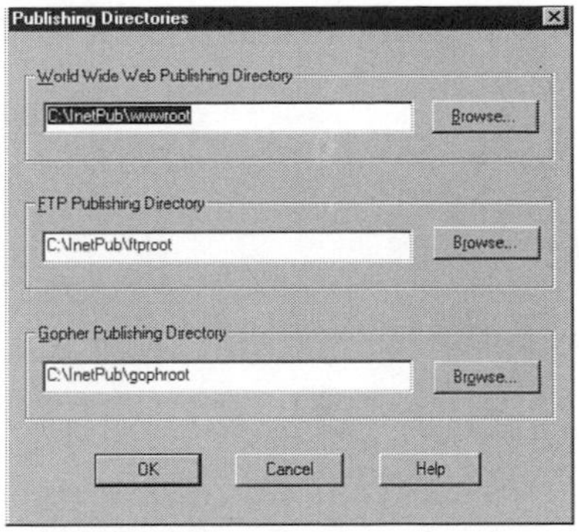

Figure A.6.
Directory locations
default to the C:
drive.

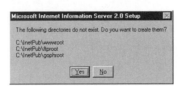

Figure A.7.
The prompt for
directory creation. If
you have mistakenly
entered the wrong
directories, simply
select No in this
dialog box, and
return to the
Publishing Directo-
ries dialog box to
reselect the installa-
tion directories.

While IIS is being installed, the status window indicates the progress, as well as what files are being copied and their destinations (see Figure A.8). If ODBC Drivers & Administration was selected for installation, Windows NT will need to close the Control Panel at this point in order to install the ODBC drivers (see Figure A.9). The ODBC drivers available are displayed in the Install Drivers dialog box (see Figure A.10).

Figure A.8.
The installation
progress status
window.

Figure A.9.
*Closing the Control
Panel for ODBC
installation.*

Figure A.10.
*The Install Drivers
dialog box.*

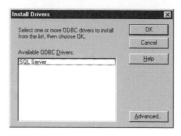

Microsoft's SQL Server is the only driver included with the distribution software. However, other ODBC drivers are available from other vendors, such as Oracle. ODBC drivers are required in order to integrate Web applications with existing databases. An example would be submitting a package-tracking number via a Web application form, which would then query a database and return the tracking information associated with that tracking number. The complexity of all the different configuration and administrative options associated with ODBC-enabled Web applications is beyond the scope of this section.

After you select SQL Server, click OK. Windows NT presents a successful installation message once the installation is complete (see Figure A.11).

Figure A.11.
*The IIS installation
is complete.*

Internet Services Manager

Internet Services Manager (ISM) is the interface provided to manage and configure the different IIS services. There are two separate interfaces shipped with IIS: HTML, which can be used with any browser, and the Internet Services Manager, which is presented in the traditional Windows or Explorer style of interface. Both have the same options available for administering and configuring IIS services.

ISM can be used to manage all IIS servers on the network. The only requirement is that the administrator use either NT Workstation or NT Server, version 4.0 or later. The three IIS services—WWW, FTP, and Gopher—can be configured from this interface. Additionally, ISM has several views that display IIS components in different ways. These views can be sorted based on service, server, or state of the service, or by the comments field.

Features and Functions

Changing the view only facilitates a different presentation of the same data, which is IIS services installed on different IIS servers. Configuration and management of the different services are still available regardless of the view selected. The different views work well with multiple IIS servers being managed from a single interface. Only Report View allows for sorting as seen on the View menu. When any other view is chosen, the sorting options are dimmed (see Figure A.12). Sorting will call an IIS administrator to quickly view the different IIS services either by server, service, comments, or by state of the server. Comments refers to the Comments field, which is variable; an administrator could put the subnet or building location in the Comments field to assist with sorting in the view. State of the server refers to whether the server is running, paused, or stopped.

Figure A.12.
*Selecting Report
View from the
View menu.*

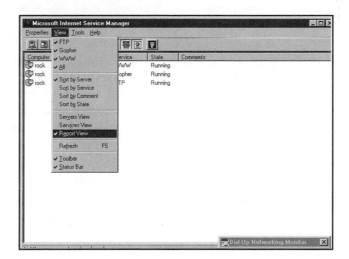

The key function of ISM is to manage and configure the different IIS services. Management of these services consists of stopping, starting, and pausing. Access to these functions can be either through the menu commands from the main menu or by right-clicking on the desired server/service combination (see Figure A.13). From here, the selected service can be stopped, started, or paused. In order for different types of changes in configuration parameters to take effect, the associated service may need to be stopped and started. These types of configuration changes are discussed later in this appendix. Access to key functions is an important part of managing IIS services.

Figure A.13.
Right-clicking on the drop-down menu allows the administrator to control the state of the services quickly and easily with the mouse.

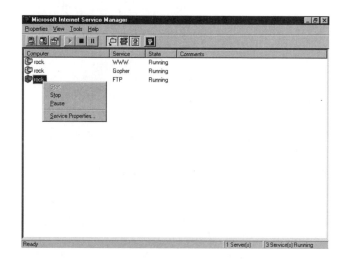

Configuration of IIS

The rate of Internet access growth has raised concerns about security and the risks associated with information exchange via the Internet. There are a number of different configuration parameters associated with each IIS service. The configuration governs access and security, as well as support of the different WWW, FTP, and Gopher services. The configuration parameters for all the services are easily accessed via ISM. The configuration parameters are displayed under the Properties window, which is accessed by right-clicking the desired service (refer to Figure A.13). The level of security needed for each service should be reviewed and managed via the different configuration options.

Configuring the WWW Service

Managing the WWW service incorporates security, file/alias locations and setup, auditing, and basic functions of the WWW service. These areas are accessed from the four different tabs of the Service Properties information screen (see Figure A.14).

The Service tab reveals the basic parameters that the WWW service will use. The defaults are displayed in Figure A.14, but they can be changed, based on the desired configuration.

Figure A.14.
Properties
windows for the
WWW service.

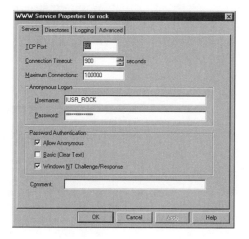

The TCP Port is the port used to access the WWW service. It can be changed to another port number; however, it must be unique. The Connection Timeout clears any "inactive" connections. This parameter keeps connections from adding up and keeps connections available. The Maximum Connections setting is useful when the maximum number of connections needs to be limited in order to prevent server performance degradation. Anonymous Logon governs security for everyone who accesses the WWW, FTP, and Gopher services. The security associated with this account is applied to everyone accessing the different services. This account must be granted the Log on Locally access right, which is done within User Manager. Additional NTFS directory and file-access privileges can be set to grant or restrict access (see the Windows NT Administration Guide for more information regarding NTFS file security).

Basic authentication can be used when clients are having difficulty accessing the WWW service, because most browsers support clear-text operations. Windows NT Challenge and Response (NTLM) supports only browsers that also support NTLM. As of this writing, only Microsoft's Internet Explorer (IE) supports NTLM. NTLM is ideal for secure transactions over the Internet, such as credit card orders and other types of confidential information exchange.

The Directories tab is used to manage aliases and directory structures used with the WWW (see Figure A.15). An alias can reference any directory path on the server or on other network servers. This section is helpful with troubleshooting access problems, because the Error field indicates such problems and gives a brief description. The default document setting is what a browser will be served when it does not designate a specific file. It needs to be in each directory in order to be effective. The Directory Browsing Allowed option presents the browser with a directory listing of files if one is not specified.

Figure A.15.
IIS administrators can manage directories and their associated properties from the Directories tab for WWW services.

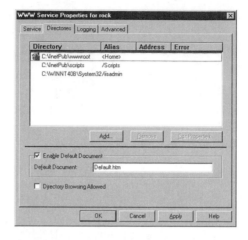

The Logging tab tracks activity of all IIS services (see Figure A.16). A number of options are available, including logging to a Data Source Name (DSN), which can be any SQL- or ODBC-qualified resource. The log files can generate reports and/or graphs with third-party tools to track IIS activities.

Figure A.16.
Tracking activity of IIS services, using the Logging tab.

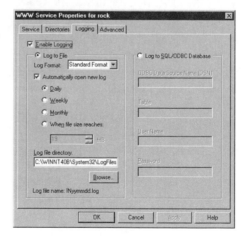

In order to enable the logging feature, simple check the Enable Logging box in the upper left. The log file format can be Standard, which is raw, comma-delimited format, or National Center for Supercomputing Applications (NCSA) format. NCSA is a research organization that is focused on creating a national strategy for communication tools and information technologies.

The next section of options allows the administrator to select how often a new log will be generated: Daily, Weekly, Monthly, or based on log size. The log file name will change according to this selection. For example, if you select Daily, the log file name becomes Inyymmdd.log, and if you select Monthly, the log file name becomes Inyymm.log. Also, be sure that the location has enough disk space to accommodate the logging option selected. Monthly will be much larger than Daily. Each environment will have different requirements for archiving and maintaining Web activities.

Logging to a SQL/ODBC database is a separate option in that you can log to either a file or a SQL/ODBC database, not both. Simply set the datasource name, table name, and valid user account credentials in order to access the database. Additionally, the ODBC driver setup needs to be completed within the Control Panel applet in order to use this option. The type of ODBC database dictates this option.

The Advanced tab allows for special access parameters to be set (see Figure A.17). These settings are particularly helpful in intranet environments. For example, a development team may need to publish information regarding a confidential project. By using the advanced settings, access to the IIS services (not just WWW) can be restricted, based on a browser's IP address and/or subnet. In this example, only browsers from particular IP addresses and/or subnets would be able to access IIS services.

Limiting network throughput on the server is also available with the Advanced tab. This is useful for controlling how much of the available bandwidth the IIS server will absorb. For example, if the IIS server is attached to an Ethernet LAN segment that is used by other network devices, limiting how much network throughput is allowed on the IIS server is one way to keep it from saturating all the available bandwidth and from affecting communications on that LAN segment. The Advanced tab should be used with caution and only when the environment requires these types of special settings.

Figure A.17.
Setting access parameters, using the Advanced tab.

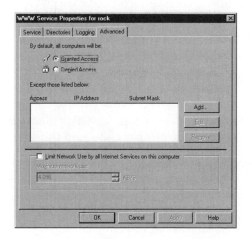

Configuring the FTP Service

There are a total of five tabs associated with FTP Service setup, two of which are identical to the Logging and Advanced tabs in the WWW configuration (see Figure A.18). For that reason, this section reviews only the unique Configuration/Property tabs associated with the FTP service.

Figure A.18.
Properties window for the FTP service.

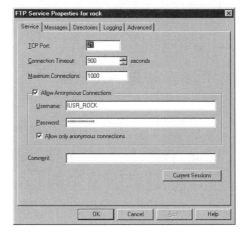

The Service tab is almost identical to the WWW Service tab discussed in the previous section. Some of the differences are specific to FTP services. Like the TCP port for WWW services, the FTP port can be changed from the default to a unique port address. The Connection Timeout and Maximum Connections options have the same purpose in that inactive users will be disconnected from the FTP service after the timeout period has expired, and Maximum Connections limits the number of simultaneous connections to the service.

The Username and Password fields are shared between all the services. Although there is a username and password entered here, it is only used to control access; users accessing the FTP service are able to do so anonymously and do not have to put in the username and password indicated here. The Allow only anonymous connections check box prevents others that might have user accounts on the IIS server from gaining access to the FTP service with their username and password. This feature basically forces everyone to use the security associated with the IUSER account instead of other accounts, which allows an administrator to grant or restrict access to everyone by simply changing the security associated with IUSER.

The Messages tab is unique to the FTP service in that it does not appear under the WWW or Gopher properties. The welcome message is echoed to the FTP session connected to the server. The exit message is presented when the session is closed.

As seen in Figure A.19, the welcome message is Welcome one and all, and the exit message is Come again soon!. In Figure A.20, these messages are present when the user logs in and when the session is closed. The Maximum connections message is presented to users who attempt to access after the maximum connection number set in the Service tab is reached.

Figure A.19.
*Message configu-
ration window for
the FTP service.*

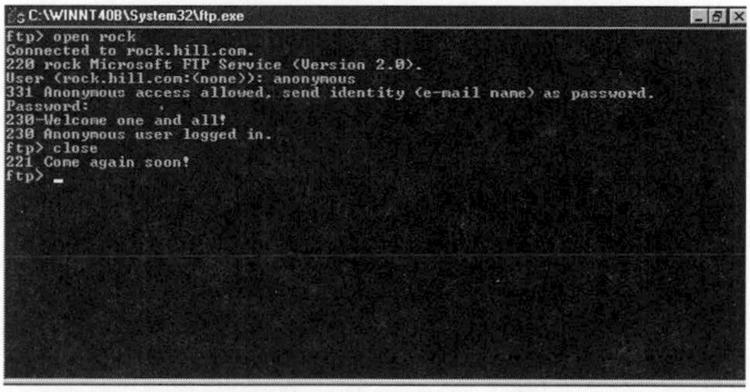

Figure A.20.
*Sample messages
presented to FTP
users.*

The Directories tab for FTP services is quite similar to the Directories tab for WWW services (see Figure A.21). It is used to manage aliases or virtual directories that can be accessed via the FTP service. As with WWW services, these directories can be either local or on remote network servers. Additionally, the Error field is also available for troubleshooting access to the directories set up in this window. The FTP directory listing style can be designated as either UNIX's LS (list style) or DOS's Dir (directory style) format.

Figure A.21.
Managing aliases or virtual directories with the Directories tab.

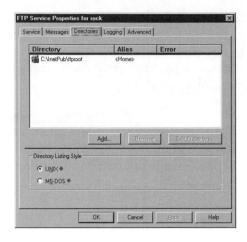

Configuring Gopher Service

Gopher service has only two unique tabs to configure: the Service tab and the Directories tab (see Figure A.22). The other two tabs are common with both FTP and WWW services. Please refer to the WWW services section for a configuration discussion on Logging and Advanced settings.

Figure A.22.
Properties window for Gopher services.

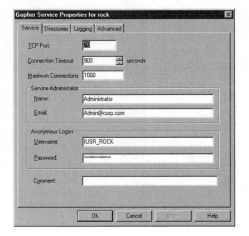

Gopher services configuration options are similar to the setting for both WWW and FTP services. The TCP port can be changed, but it must be a unique port number. Connection Timeout and Maximum Connections control Gopher connections in the same fashion as FTP connections. After the period indicated for Connection Timeout expires, Gopher connections will be disconnected. Once the Maximum Connections limit is reached, subsequent requests will be refused. The Service Administrator section includes information reported back to the Gopher clients that indicates the owner of the Gopher data. The Anonymous Logon fields are the same as the other IIS services. They are not required to access the Gopher service, but they do govern access to Gopher data. The Comment section appears in the Internet Services Manager interface, referenced earlier in this section.

The Directories tab functions in the same fashion as the WWW and FTP Directories configuration (see Figure A.23). Directories can be set up with specific aliases that reference either local paths or valid network paths. The Home directory specifies the root directory for the Gopher service. Virtual directories are set up here and can be accessed only by using the alias. When using network paths, the appropriate security must be in place for the anonymous account to access the referenced directory. If not, a Universal Naming Convention (UNC) reference in the Directory reference box will allow another set of credentials to be added in the Account Information section of the Directory Properties dialog box (see Figure A.24).

Figure A.23.
Any changes to the directories can be made at the Gopher services Directories tab.

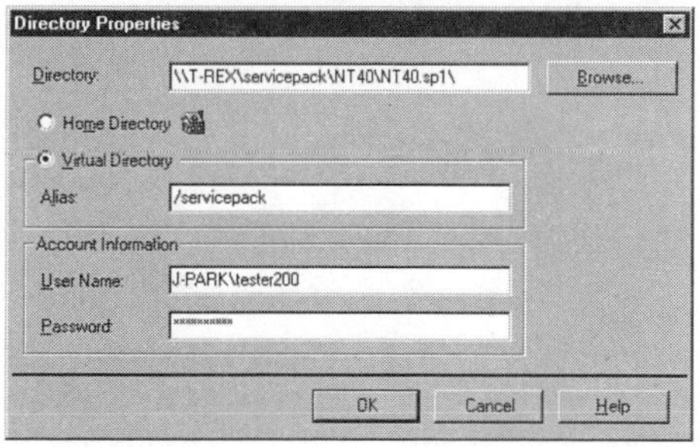

Figure A.24.
Gopher services Directory Properties dialog box.

Using Internet Explorer

Internet Explorer (IE) is Microsoft's client browser. A browser is required to access all the different services provided by IIS. Client browsers are far less complex than IIS. In fact, as of this writing, Microsoft includes a Web browser with every copy of both the Windows 95 and the Windows NT 4.0 platforms. Additionally, a new version is continually updated and distributed from Microsoft's Web site at `http://www.microsoft.com`. Although most of this appendix covers the configuration of the IIS platform, there are some configuration options included with the Internet Explorer client browser.

Internet Explorer Configuration

Very little configuration of the IE is needed. Once the operating system is installed, IE will function with or without a valid connection to the Internet. This section reviews some of the configuration options available with version 3.0, which is the current version. A good source of information regarding support and new additions to IE is located on Microsoft's Web site, which is updated regularly.

The configuration of IE primarily deals with the appearance and operation on the Internet or intranet. All the configuration options are located on the View menu, under Options (see Figure A.25).

Figure A.25.
Options for
Internet Explorer
are accessed from
the View menu.

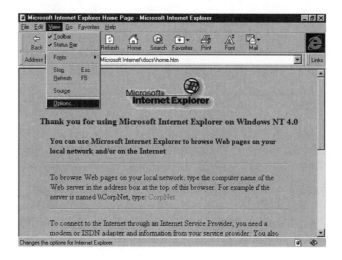

Each tab covers a different aspect of the IE configuration. The first tab, General, deals with the appearance of IE. However, some of these settings also affect performance, as described in the Multimedia box (see Figure A.26). The display colors can be changed to any desired color for both text and background, or the Windows colors can be used as the default. Links, which are references to other sites, can be underlined or not, and sites that have already been explored will be highlighted in the color of choice. Additionally, the navigation bar across the top of the browser has several options. The button display is optional, as are Address bar, Links, Text labels, and Background bitmap. Simply select or deselect these options to view the desired results.

Figure A.26.
As can be seen in the Multimedia box, performance can be increased by deselecting pictures, sounds, and videos.

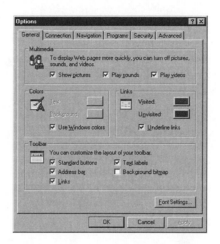

The Connection tab deals with site-specific connection information (see Figure A.27). Some corporate networks require a proxy to be used in order to access the Internet. This information would be available from an internal Network Support organization or from the Internet service provider (ISP) providing the Internet connection.

Figure A.27.
Choosing site-specific connection information.

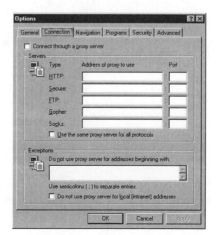

The Navigation tab is where the Start Page and History settings are located (see Figure A.28). The Start Page is what is displayed when the Home button is clicked on the toolbar, or when IE is first launched. It can be a local HTML file or any WWW Web page on the Internet.

History is used to keep a record of what sites have been visited. For example, if you cannot remember a previous site's name, it can be accessed from the history file, depending on the number of days that was selected in the History configuration box. If the site was visited over a month ago, the default setting of 20 days would not have that site in it.

Figure A.28.
The Navigation options tab allows your favorite site to be set as the Start Page.

The Programs tab is used for file associations, default browser setting, and mail and news server locations (see Figure A.29). File associations allow IE to be launched whenever an associate file is launched, which allows for smoother communications because IE does not have to be launched as a separate step.

Figure A.29.
Choosing mail and news services with the Programs tab.

The Security tab deals with some advanced security settings (see Figure A.30). In an effort to provide some censorship of the different sites available on the Internet, the Content advisor can restrict sites that do not meet the security requirements.

Figure A.30.
Restricting sites with the Security tab.

The final tab deals with some advanced settings (see Figure A.31). IE will frequently stop and warn users that "unsecured" communications are about to take place on the Internet. The Advanced tab is where those settings are controlled.

The first option deals with opening an unsecured connection. This means that the data that is exchanged between Internet Explorer and the unsecured site can be intercepted and read. There are two options: Always or Only when I'm sending more than one line of text. Most information exchanged on the Internet is unsecured. IE can also warn when changing from a secured to an unsecured site. The invalid certificate option will warn IE users if the certificate has come from an invalid site. When using certificates, this option should be selected. Cookies are created when a Web site has the ability to store and retrieve information from your PC. This security option will warn when a site is attempting to retrieve or download files to IE.

Temporary Internet files allow for temporary storage of Internet files. Under the Settings button is where the size of the storage can be set. You can also change the file locations and delete these files. This allows IE to quickly view previously viewed Internet files, because they are already on the hard drive of your PC.

Show friendly URLs changes the display of the Web address to be a full path, for example http://www.microsoft.com. Highlight links when clicked simply changes the appearance of a link once it has been selected. Use smooth scrolling changes the scrolling functionality.

Use style sheets allows viewing of Hypertext Markup Language style used on Web sites that have HTML. Enable Java JIT compiler creates or compiles all Java programs found on Web sites the IE visits. Enable Java logging logs all Java program activity.

Cryptography Settings has four different options. The first is SSL2 or Secure Sockets Layer level 2, which is a standard protocol used by all secured Web sites. The second is SSL3 or Secure Sockets Layer level 3, which is more secure than SSL2, but not used by all secured Web sites. The third is a protocol developed by Microsoft that also is more secure than SSL2; it's called Private Communications Technology (PCT). Not all secure Web sites support PCT. The last option specifies whether a copy of the certificate is stored locally on your computer, which is not recommended if your computer is shared with others.

Figure A.31.
In the Advanced options tab, the default setting works for most IE functions.

Although the default settings function properly for most installations, customization of the appearance and the configuration is available for the Internet Explorer.

Summary

IIS has been designed to be easily installed and to make information available on the IIS platform. With the recent growth of the Internet, IIS is a tool that can be used to share information for Internet and intranet users alike. With the development tools available for creating Web applications, most current applications could be made available via a single Web browser interface. Additionally, this method of sharing information is just as easy to accomplish with internal communications as it is for external or Internet communications. As Web development becomes more mature, information management as we know it today will change dramatically. Ease of information access is quickly being moved into the hands of those who need it via the IIS platform.

Index

SQL Server, 286-287
  disk mirroring, 288
  dump device creation, 288-289
  Master database, 287
  privilege levels, 289-290
  SQL Security Manager, 287
  system administrator password, changing, 287-288
  views, 290
WWW service configuration, 319
security operators (Windows NT Server team organization), 52-53
Security tab (Internet Explorer configuration), 329
selecting remote systems for monitoring, 156
senior management, support for implementation team, 59
Server Admin utility (SNA Gateway), 297
server administrators (Windows NT Server team organization), 50-51
Server Message Blocks (SMBs), 250
Server object (Performance Monitor), 138-139
Server Sessions statistic (Performance Monitor), 139
servers
  distributed processing (planning BackOffice implementation), 47-48
  domains (planning BackOffice implementation), 49
  Exchange Server, *see* Exchange Server

IIS, *see* IIS (Internet Information Server)
licensing, 64-65
memory requirements, 109
network design, 44-45
shared information (planning BackOffice implementation), 48-49
SMS, *see* SMS (Systems Management Server)
SQL Server, *see* SQL Server
Service Account (SMS security), 293
service packs (bug fixes), centralization, 14
sessions (SNA Gateway), defined, 296
shared information (planning BackOffice implementation), 48-49
shared resources (BackOffice applications), 31-32
shared services (BackOffice applications), 33
SIMMs (Single Inline Memory Modules), 97
sites
  Exchange Server security, defined, 275
  SMS (Systems Management Server), relationship with domains, 290-292
SMBs (Server Message Blocks), 250
SMP (symmetric multiprocessing), 78-80
SMS (Systems Management Server), 204
  network issues, 253
  requirements, 204
    compressing packages, 207
    CPUs, 90
    databases with SQL Server, 205-206

    memory, 111
    packages, 204-205
  security, 290
    administrative services, granting access, 294-296
    client services, 294
    Network Monitor, 293-294
    Service Account, 293
    sites, relationship with domains, 290-292
  team organization, 57-58
SNA Gateway
  creating users, 297-298
  overview, 296-297
  security
    encryption, 298
    logical unit pools, 298
    NTFS (NT file system), 298-299
  Server Admin utility, 297
  team organization, 58
  Trace utility, 299
SNA Server
  CPU requirements, 90
  memory requirements, 111
software, user support, 61
source-route bridging, 238
Spanning Tree protocol (bridges), 238
specific files, restoring, 191
SQL Enterprise Manager, backups, 193-196
SQL Security Manager, 287
SQL Server
  backups, 192-193
  network issues, 251-252
  Performance Monitor objects, 144-148
  requirements
    CPUs, 89

A V I A C O M S E R V I C E

The Information SuperLibrary™

Bookstore

Search

What's New

Reference

Software

Newsletter

Company Overviews

Yellow Pages

Internet Starter Kit

HTML Workshop

Win a Free T-Shirt!

Macmillan Computer Publishing

Site Map

Talk to Us

CHECK OUT THE BOOKS IN THIS LIBRARY.

You'll find thousands of shareware files and over 1600 computer books designed for both technowizards and technophobes. You can browse through 700 sample chapters, get the latest news on the Net, and find just about anything using our massive search directories.

All Macmillan Computer Publishing books

We're open 24-hours a day, 365 days a year.

You don't need a card.

We don't charge fines.

And you can be as **LOUD** as you want.

The Information SuperLibrary

MACMILLAN COMPUTER PUBLISHING USA

A VIACOM COMPANY

Technical ---- Support:

If you cannot get the CD-ROMs to install properly, or you need assistance with a particular situation in the book, please feel free to check out the Knowledge Base on our Web site at **http://www.superlibrary.com/general/support**. We have answers to our most Frequently Asked Questions listed there. If you do not find your specific question answered, please contact Macmillan Technical Support at **(317) 581-3833**. We can also be reached by e-mail at **support@mcp.com**.

Microsoft BackOffice 2 Administrator's Survival Guide, Second Edition

Arthur Knowles

This all-in-one reference describes how to make the components of BackOffice version 2 work best together and with other networks. BackOffice is Microsoft's complete reference for networking, database, and system-management products. This book covers the fundamental concepts required for daily maintenance, troubleshooting, and problem solving. The CD-ROM that accompanies the book includes product demos, commercial and shareware utilities, and technical notes from Microsoft vendor technical support personnel.

Price: $59.99 USA/$84.95 CDN   *User Level: Accomplished*
ISBN: 0-672-30977-7   *1,200 pages*

Microsoft BackOffice 2 Unleashed

Joe Greene, et al.

Microsoft BackOffice 2 Unleashed is an instrumental tool for anyone in charge of developing or managing BackOffice. This book covers the individual pieces of BackOffice as well as key phases in the development, integration, and administration of the BackOffice environment. It contains coverage on using BackOffice as the infrastructure of an intranet or for the Internet, and instructs readers on integrating individual BackOffice products. The CD-ROM that accompanies the book includes source code, third-party products, and utilities.

Price: $59.99 USA/$84.95 CDN   *User Level: Accomplished–Expert*
ISBN: 0-672-30816-9   *1,200 pages*

Designing and Implementing Microsoft Internet Information Server 2

Arthur Knowles & Sanjaya Hettihewa

This book details the specific tasks of setting up and running a Microsoft Internet Information Server. Readers will learn troubleshooting, network design, security, and cross-platform integration procedures. This book covers security issues, and how to maintain an efficient, secure network. Readers learn everything from planning to implementation.

Price: $39.99 USA/$56.95 CDN   *User Level: Casual–Expert*
ISBN: 1-57521-168-8   *336 pages*

Microsoft Internet Information Server 2 Unleashed

Arthur Knowles, et al.

The power of the Microsoft Internet Information Server 2 is meticulously detailed in this 800-page volume. Readers will learn how to create and maintain a Web server, integrate IIS with BackOffice, and create interactive databases that can be used on the Internet or on a corporate intranet. This book also teaches advanced security techniques as well as how to configure the server. The CD-ROM that accompanies this book includes source code from the book and powerful utilities.

Price: $49.99 USA/$70.95 CDN   *User Level: Accomplished–Expert*
ISBN: 1-57521-109-2   *800 pages*

Microsoft Exchange Server Survival Guide

Greg Todd

Readers will learn the difference between Exchange and other groupware, such as Lotus Notes, as well as everything about the Exchange Server, including troubleshooting, development, and how to interact with other BackOffice components. This book covers everything operators need to run an Exchange server, and teaches readers how to prepare, plan, and install the Exchange server. This book also explores ways to migrate from other mail apps, such as Microsoft Mail and cc:Mail.

Price: $49.99 USA/$70.95 CDN   *User Level: New–Advanced*
ISBN: 0-672-30890-8   *800 pages*

Intranets Unleashed

Sams.net Development Group

Intranets, internal Web sites that can be accessed within a company's firewalls, are quickly becoming the status quo in business. This book shows IS managers and personnel how to effectively set up and run large or small Intranets. Everything from design to security is discussed. The CD-ROM that accompanies this book contains source code and valuable utilities.

Price: $59.99 USA/$84.95 CDN   *User Level: Accomplished–Expert*
ISBN: 1-57521-115-7   *900 pages*

Microsoft SQL Server 6.5 Unleashed, Second Edition

David Solomon & Daniel Woodbeck, et al.

This comprehensive reference details the steps needed to plan, design, install, administer, and tune large and small databases. In many cases, readers will use the techniques to create and manage their own complex environment. This book covers programming topics, including SQL, data structures, programming constructs, stored procedures, referential integrity, large table strategies, and more. It also includes updates to cover all new features of SQL Server 6.5, including the new transaction processing monitor and Internet/database connectivity through SQL Server's new Web wizard. The CD-ROM that accompanies this book includes source code, libraries, and administration tools.

Price: $59.99 USA/$84.95 CDN   *User Level: Accomplished–Expert*
ISBN: 0-672-30956-4   *1,100 pages*

Windows NT 4 Web Development

Sanjaya Hettihewa

Windows NT and Microsoft's newly developed Internet Information Server are making it easier and more cost-effective to set up, manage, and administer a good Web site. Because the Windows NT environment is relatively new, few books on the market adequately discuss its full potential. *Windows NT 4 Web Development* addresses that potential by providing information on all key aspects of server setup, maintenance, design, and implementation. The CD-ROM that accompanies this book contains valuable source code and powerful utilities.

Price: $59.99 USA/$84.95 CDN   *User Level: Accomplished–Expert*
ISBN: 1-57521-089-4   *744 pages*

Add to Your Sams Library Today with the Best Books for Programming, Operating Systems, and New Technologies

The easiest way to order is to pick up the phone and call

1-800-428-5331

between 9:00 a.m. and 5:00 p.m. EST.
For faster service please have your credit card available.

ISBN	Quantity	Description of Item	Unit Cost	Total Cost
0-672-30977-7		Microsoft BackOffice 2 Administrator's Survival Guide, Second Edition (Book/CD-ROM)	$59.99	
0-672-30816-9		Microsoft BackOffice 2 Unleashed (Book/CD-ROM)	$59.99	
1-57521-168-8		Designing & Implementing Microsoft Internet Information Server 2	$39.99	
1-57521-109-2		Microsoft Internet Information Server 2 Unleashed (Book/CD-ROM)	$49.99	
0-672-30890-8		Microsoft Exchange Server Survival Guide (Book/CD-ROM)	$49.99	
1-57521-115-7		Intranets Unleashed (Book/CD-ROM)	$59.99	
0-672-30956-4		Microsoft SQL Server 6.5 Unleashed, Second Edition (Book/CD-ROM)	$59.99	
1-57521-089-4		Windows NT 4 Web Development (Book/CD-ROM)	$59.99	
❏ 3 ½" Disk		Shipping and Handling: See information below.		
❏ 5 ¼" Disk		TOTAL		

Shipping and Handling: $4.00 for the first book, and $1.75 for each additional book. Floppy disk: add $1.75 for shipping and handling. If you need to have it NOW, we can ship product to you in 24 hours for an additional charge of approximately $18.00, and you will receive your item overnight or in two days. Overseas shipping and handling adds $2.00 per book and $8.00 for up to three disks. Prices subject to change. Call for availability and pricing information on latest editions.

201 W. 103rd Street, Indianapolis, Indiana 46290

1-800-428-5331 — Orders   1-800-835-3202 — FAX   1-800-858-7674 — Customer Service